D0555760

Colorado
1870-2000
Revisited

Colorado

1870 - 2000

THE HISTORY BEHIND THE IMAGES

BY THOMAS J. NOEL AND JOHN FIELDER

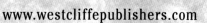

WESTCLIFFE PUBLISHERS

www.westcliffepublishers.com

International Standard Book Number: 1-56579-389-7

Text copyright: Thomas J. Noel and John Fielder, 2001. All rights reserved.
Photography copyright: John Fielder, 2001. All rights reserved.

Editor: Jenna Samelson
Assistant Editors: Martha Ripley and Kelly Clark
Designer: Mark Mulvany
Production Manager: Craig Keyzer

Published by:
Westcliffe Publishers, Inc.
P.O. Box 1261
Englewood, CO 80150
www.westcliffepublishers.com

Printed in China through C&C Offset Printing Co., Ltd.

Library of Congress Cataloging-in-Publication Data
Noel, Thomas J., 1945-
    Colorado, 1870-2000, revisited : the history behind the images / by Thomas J. Noel and
John Fielder.
        p. cm.
    Includes bibliographical references and index.
    ISBN 1-56579-389-7 (hardcover) -- ISBN 1-56579-418-4 (softcover)
        1. Jackson, William Henry, 1843-1942. Colorado, 1870-2000. 2.
Colorado--Description and travel. 3. Colorado--Environmental conditions. 4.
Colorado--Pictorial works. 5. Human ecology--Colorado. 6. Landscape
changes--Colorado. 7. Wilderness areas--Colorado. 8. Landscape
photography--Colorado. 9. Jackson, William Henry, 1843-1942. 10. Fielder, John, 1950-
I. Fielder, John, 1950- II. Title.

    F777 .N64 2001
    978.8--dc21

                                                                    2001033850

*For more information about other fine books and calendars from Westcliffe Publishers, please
contact your local bookstore, call us at 1-800-523-3692, write for our free color catalog, or
visit us on the Web at **www.westcliffepublishers.com**.*

Acknowledgments

I would like to thank John Fielder for this opportunity to collaborate with the crackerjack crew at Westcliffe Publishers: editor Jenna Samelson, ably assisted by Martha Ripley and Kelly Clark; associate publisher Linda Doyle and production manager Craig Keyzer; designers Mark Mulvany and Tim George; and proofreader Lori Kranz. Another tip of the hat to the Denver Public Library's heavenly Western History Department, especially Jim Kroll, Bruce Hansen, Phil Panum, Lori Swingle, Jennifer Tom, Barbara Walton, and Kay Wisnia. Thanks also to the angels at the Colorado Historical Society—particularly Dale Heckendorn, Becky Lintz, Debbie Neiswonger, and Eric Paddock—as well as additional contributors to this book, Mark Pearson and Jack Reed. For editorial assistance, I gratefully thank several history students at the University of Colorado at Denver: Gail Beaton, Eileen Sullivan Brozna, Karen Bryant, Jamie Field, and Pam Holtman.

—Thomas J. Noel

Many companies and institutions have embraced and supported the Jackson/Fielder rephotography project. Please refer to page 224 of *Colorado 1870–2000* to learn who some of them are. Particularly, I must again thank the Colorado Historical Society for becoming my partner and facilitating access to the Jackson archives. Similarly, the U.S. Geological Survey in Lakewood, Colorado, and the Denver Public Library's Western History Department provided access to their own Jackson archives. (See page 224 of the big book to discover which of these three sources provided each of the Jackson images and granted permission to print them in both books.) The support of what was formerly Public Service Company of Colorado (now Xcel Energy), KCNC-TV, *Rocky Mountain News*, Berger Funds, what was formerly Norwest Banks, Wiesner Publishing, Woodley's Fine Furniture, and the Cherry Creek Shopping Center helped me to share the project with many people.

This time, however, it is the people of Colorado whom I wish to thank for the part they have played in the project's success. The look in your eyes as you stepped forward after a long wait in line to have your book autographed largely formed my belief that together we can and will protect this most beautiful of states for future generations of people, plants, and creatures.

—John Fielder

Preface

William Henry Jackson, the pioneer photographer of the Rocky Mountains, remains the most influential artist ever to place Colorado images before the eyes of the world. Hundreds of articles and books celebrate this creative giant of the late 19th and early 20th centuries. His photographs, reproduced prolifically as postcards, books, booklets, stereographs, and prized prints, educated many Americans about the natural and manmade wonders of Colorado, once known as the Highest State.

Jackson lived a long and productive life — 99 years — leaving for future generations thousands of photographic prints, as well as hundreds of sketches and paintings. Thomas H. Harrell's book *William Henry Jackson: An Annotated Bibliography, 1862–1995*, a compilation of work by and about Jackson, lists some 500 published and unpublished works. Jackson's photos still help to lure countless tourists to the Rockies. His photoscapes inspired the creation of some of America's national parks — Yellowstone, Mesa Verde, Rocky Mountain, Black Canyon of the Gunnison, and Great Sand Dunes.

While pursuing grand landscapes and broad visions, Jackson never lost his human touch. His signature twist of including people and perhaps his own rolling photo studio, drawn by his mule, Hypo, adds an endearing personal element to his photography. Following that tradition, contemporary Colorado photographer John Fielder often playfully matches Jackson's figures with today's people and vehicles.

Historians cherish Jackson's sharp, engaging records of mining towns, railroads, and cities like Denver in their infancy. These views of Colorado's early built environments have also inspired, since the 1960s, generations of historic preservationists. Their efforts, ably coordinated and administered by the Colorado Historical Society (CHS) and its Office of Archaeology and Historic Preservation, have endowed the state with more than 200 National Register Historic Districts and more than 1,100 individual National Register Historic sites. The CHS, with its flagship museum in Denver and branch museums around the state, is the best single resource for exploring Colorado's past. Of the society's more than 600,000 images, Jackson's glass-plate photographs reign as its greatest treasures.

Mirroring Jackson's work, John Fielder has made great strides in educating 20th- and 21st-century Coloradans about the Highest State's landscapes. However, its scenic vistas are vanishing, annually sacrificed for new homes, shopping centers, strip malls, and "big-box" stores.

The 2000 federal census revealed that Colorado's growth exceeded even booster projections. A growth rate of 30 percent during the 1990s swelled the state's population from 3.2 to 4.3 million. Such rapid growth came as no surprise to John Fielder, who has photographed nearly every nook and cranny of Colorado since 1973, documenting the disappearance of open space and picturesque rural settings. Since 2000, John has become the leading volunteer advocate for significant growth management. That year he and other supporters of growth-curbing measures saw their Amendment 24 crushed at the polls after builders and other parties opposing the amendment had spent more than $6 million to convince the public that growth management was "too extreme." Undeterred, John continues to argue that we can do better by our environment for our children and grandchildren.

Colorado boasts as its greatest attraction the easy escape to wildlands — if the joys of wilderness solitude are not drowned out by the roar of SUVs, ATVs, snowmobiles, and other contraptions designed to keep people on their fannies and off their feet. The hills are alive with the sound of combustion engines.

Colorado's soaring population is leading some of the more glinty-eyed developers to search the state high and low for building sites. One developer from Douglas County, America's fastest-growing county during the 1990s, posted a "property for sale" sign atop Red Mountain Pass and threatens to bulldoze the historic silver city there to make room for summer homes. Federal efforts to protect ancient American Indian sites with the designation of Canyon of the Ancients National Monument in southwestern Colorado are also threatened. In Colorado's central Rockies, ever-larger ski areas aim to brand more of our national forests with their slope scars and real estate developments.

The following pages record not only the alarming alterations to the landscape, but also heartening stories of conservation. Savor the little-changed panorama of Garden of the Gods City Park and remarkable continuities of National Register Historic District towns such as Creede, Georgetown, Lake City, Leadville, Ouray, and Silverton. Some of the dramatic growth portrayed here has been beautiful — like Interstate 70's graceful route through Glenwood Canyon. Among the most soothing comparisons is the Interlaken Hotel preserved on the south shore of Twin Lakes; among the most ominous is the invasion of Roxborough Park by golf carts and trophy homes.

This book is number 31 for John Fielder. Since he founded Westcliffe Publishers in 1981, the company has produced more than 200 books and, as of 2001, some 30 scenic calendars each year. His book *Colorado 1870–2000* — an enduring legacy of the state's millennium celebration — became a spectacular success, enlivening media coverage of the turn of the century, selling more than 95,000 copies, and setting a standard for what we hope Colorado's landscape will look like in the future.

When John invited me to collaborate with him on this book, I jumped at the opportunity to provide expansive, interpretive commentary on both the change and the continuity that his classic book captured. So here we present a new, in-depth look at the work of Colorado's most famous photographic pairing: Jackson and Fielder.

What will a 22nd-century photographer find when attempting to match these photos with Colorado's landscape in 2100? Will high-rises completely obliterate Denver's Brown Palace Hotel? Will monstrous casinos bury the 19th-century relics of Black Hawk, Central City, and Cripple Creek? Will Black Hawk's Lace House have escaped its imprisonment behind multistory parking garages?

While enjoying Colorado today, we may wonder what will be preserved for the next millennium. My grandmother, Isabelle Griffith Jacob, was a schoolteacher raised as part of a Western Slope clan of cattle ranchers in Mesa County. When her family, the Griffiths, gave up cattle ranching in Collbran for an orchard home in Palisade along the Colorado River, they refused to call themselves "farmers" or "orchard keepers." They were "peach ranchers." My grandmother always said Colorado's greatness rested in the "air that only the angels have breathed before."

Angelic air, historic landscapes, and unspoiled views. We invite you to take another look at how those endangered legacies are faring in the new millennium.

—Thomas J. Noel

Introduction

At the time of this book's publication in September 2001, about 95,000 copies of its parent book, *Colorado 1870–2000,* will have been printed since its debut in August 1999. Many people have enjoyed this project—which compares Colorado's landscape today with the one portrayed by 19th-century photographer William Henry Jackson—in many different ways. Thousands of people have seen the exhibit of then-and-now photographs from the project on display at various history museums, and thousands more have attended the slide show that I have been presenting since 1999. Others saw me on TV every week during 1999 tracking down Jackson's photographic locations, and still more read a weekly serialization of the project in the *Denver Rocky Mountain News.*

Many of the people entertained by the conspicuous changes evident in the 156 pairs of then-and-now photographs were also shocked by how much land had been lost to development in Colorado since Jackson lived here. From 300-million-year-old sandstone spires intertwined with golf course fairways near Denver, to once-bucolic landscapes paved over with tract homes in suburban Colorado Springs, the manifestations of poorly planned growth were often egregious.

Though I had been somewhat publicly visible through the years because of the 29 other picture- and guidebooks I had previously published, *Colorado 1870–2000* took that recognition to a higher level. When the opportunity arose to help head an effort to change the way Colorado, by law, manages growth, I knew that I couldn't say no, that I was the perfect person to lead the charge.

By 2000, Colorado's population had increased by 1 million people during the previous decade. The majority of Coloradans were clamoring for better ways to manage the settlement of the next 1 million people expected to move here. The failure of our Colorado General Assembly to enact any meaningful growth management legislation in 1999 opened the door to a citizen-led initiative campaign in 2000. Our group, Coloradans for Responsible Growth, acquired the appropriate number of authorizing signatures and placed Amendment 24, the Responsible Growth Initiative, on the November 2000 ballot. A $6 million developer-funded campaign subsequently defeated it. Nevertheless, a strong message had been sent to the general assembly that Coloradans wanted to stop the loss of open space and farm- and ranchland to sprawl. Unfortunately, our elected representatives failed to enact any new growth management legislation in 2001, opening the door for another initiative in 2002.

The "1870–2000 project" struck a chord with many Coloradans. I have probably autographed close to 20,000 copies of *Colorado 1870–2000,* most at author signings in bookstores and at slide show events. The cumulative joy in the faces of the people who claimed native status on these occasions would be enough to light up the planet for 24 hours. Person after person proudly asked me to inscribe not only my name, but their native status, often modified with the number of family generations that had lived in Colorado. Just how much the book had touched them and the rest of their family, especially the older members who recalled the Colorado lifestyle of the early 20th century, was usually the next topic of conversation.

W. H. Jackson   **John Fielder**

I can't begin to express how personally rewarding this interaction was, how clear it was that Coloradans love their state passionately, and how much all of this motivated me to do the right thing as we drove our growth campaign toward victory. Though victory was elusive, the 1870–2000 project doesn't seem to want to die, and for that reason I have confidence that we will rewrite the laws of growth management in due course—hopefully before it's too late.

Many people with whom I engaged found the stories that I told about the challenge of finding William Henry Jackson's photographic locations fascinating. Many more wanted to know about the historic change manifest in the then-and-now pairs of photographs, as *Colorado 1870–2000* contains only brief captions. These questions were the impetus to publish this book. I knew that it would be fun recalling and writing about the travels and travails experienced in that very busy year of 1998: I drove 25,000 miles and hiked another 500 in order to stand where Jackson did in 300 total locations. But who would write about the history of the places depicted in the photographs, and about the reasons behind the change, or lack thereof? Tom Noel immediately came to mind. He and I did not know each other well, having only crossed paths at various book signings through the years, but his reputation as historian, raconteur, public speaker, teacher, and author—he has many books to his name—was distinguished. Tom gladly and generously accepted my offer.

To illuminate other photographs, especially those in which there is no clear human impact, I employed additional writers who explore variously the natural history and geology of places. A few photo pairs lent themselves to no discussion about historic change, human or natural, only a story about tracking Jackson's footsteps. In each case, I hope that the words and images in this book will both educate and entertain you.

HOW TO USE THIS BOOK

This book is intended to be read in conjunction with the original tome, *Colorado 1870–2000*, which I fondly refer to as the "big book." In the photographs, much more detail in the buildings and their signage, as well as the people and their modes of transportation, can be seen in the big book's reproductions. The thumbnail photographs in this book serve as reminders of what we are currently discussing. Page numbers for the corresponding photographs in the big book are printed at the beginning of each essay for easy reference.

Tom Noel penned most of the human history text, and usually discusses historic change in relation to what is seen in the then-and-now pairs of photographs. Other authors address subjects of human and natural history, as well. Eric Paddock, curator of photography for the Colorado Historical Society and a contributor to the big book, writes on topics of human history and historic photography. Environmentalist and Westcliffe Publishers book author Mark Pearson contributes text about natural history and Colorado's land protection efforts. Jack Reed of the U.S. Geological Survey discusses geologic history for the photographs that primarily feature the natural environment. In addition to helping edit this book, Westcliffe's Martha Ripley shares some reflections on Rocky Mountain National Park. The authors' initials accompany the essays, including the ones that I have written about finding Jackson's locations. They are as follows:

 Eric Paddock   **JF** John Fielder   **JR** Jack Reed

 Mark Pearson   **MR** Martha Ripley   **TN** Tom Noel

Some of you might want to stand where William Henry Jackson, Eric Bellamy (my assistant for the rephotography project), and I stood; therefore, I have tried to provide adequate directions to many of the places from which our photographs were made. To that end, the maps included in this book identify the general locations of the 141 total places discussed. These locations are grouped geographically into the same seven Colorado regions as in the big book. The numbers on the maps are keyed to the number inside the black oval at the beginning of each essay. Bear in mind that some of these places exist on private property and you will need to seek permission (yes, I know I didn't set a very good example for this) from landowners. Also please consider that about 20 percent of the places had changed so significantly that I could not stand in Jackson's exact location and make his same photograph. Perhaps the hillside on which he placed his camera had since been excavated for a highway, or more often, a wall of trees had grown up in the way of Jackson's purview. In both of these cases I would have moved the camera until I could achieve the best possible substitute location from which to shoot. If my directions ultimately prove to be vague, just remember that the best part about the project for me was the joy of discovering each and every location as a "perspective detective"!

Go ahead and try to make the repeat photograph yourself. If you wish to learn more about this process, read my introduction in *Colorado 1870–2000*. It will help you to understand the perspective detective's methodology, in which the photographer studies how two or more landmarks relate to one another to discover Jackson's locations. And, also in the big book, Eric Paddock's foreword about William Henry Jackson will, among other things, acquaint you with Jackson's life and the equipment that he used.

Whatever you do, my hope is that you will come to realize that the landscape, like history, defines who we are. In his foreword in the big book, Eric Paddock quotes the geographer Pierce F. Lewis: "Landscape is our unwitting autobiography, reflecting our tastes, our values, our aspirations, and even our fears, in tangible, visible form." May you come away from this project with a renewed passion for this greatest, most beautiful, and most fragile of states, Colorado.

—John Fielder

Regional Map of Colorado

141 Jackson/Fielder Locations

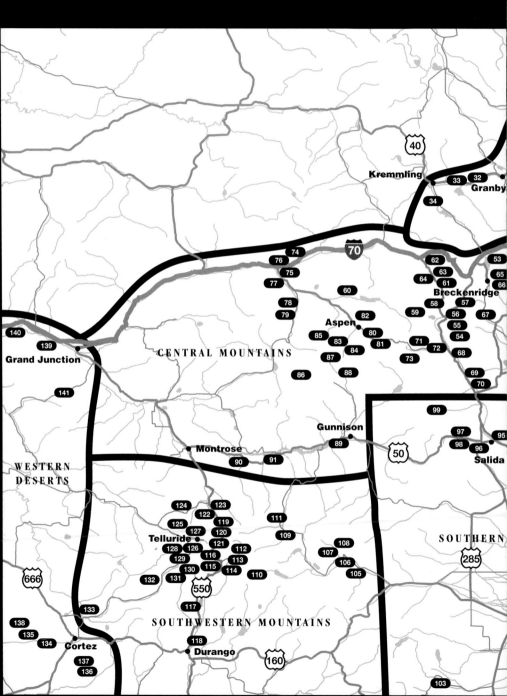

CONTENTS

Colorado 1870 - 2000 Revisited

Central Front Range Locations

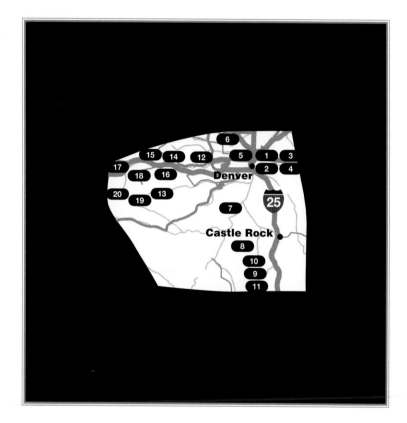

Central Front Range

1

DENVER

Central Area, 1892–1894

pp. 12–13
(Page numbers refer to
Colorado 1870–2000*)*

(Please see Colorado
1870–2000 *for the complete
series of photographs.)*

TN   Visitors to the State Capitol may savor this panorama from its observation deck. Although the Front Range mountain backdrop remains the same, an eruption of high-rises has transformed the cityscape. Most were constructed during the oil boom of the 1970s and early 1980s, when many of the downtown landmarks photographed by William Henry Jackson were demolished.

The photo pair at the far left reveals that Denver's Civic Center Park and City and County Building now dominate what was an 1890s residential area. Among the few surviving residences is the Byers-Evans House at the northeast corner of 13th Avenue and Bannock Street. Now a museum operated by the Colorado Historical Society, it is hidden behind the Denver Art Museum at the far left of the Fielder photo. The white, 10-story Metropolitan Building was converted to housing for the homeless in the booming 1990s. Even then, the city contained many people who found themselves without food and shelter, just as the 1890s city did after the 1893 Silver Crash robbed many Coloradans of jobs and homes.

The second Jackson panel from the left is dominated by the long-gone Denver Tramway Company office and car barn, and Fire Station No. 1 cattycorner across Colfax Avenue. In the center of the Jackson photo, the six-story red brick and sandstone Denver Athletic Club (1889) is now a designated Denver and National Register historic landmark. The DAC still thrives with additions at each end.

Behind the DAC in the Fielder photo, note the white frame of the roller coaster at Six Flags Elitch Gardens. Just to the left is the old Mile High Stadium, now the site of Invesco Field at Mile High. The white, circular McNichols Arena just to the left of Mile High was demolished in 2000 and replaced by the nearby Pepsi Center, illustrating Denver's continuing propensity for tearing down functional old buildings.

The old Arapahoe County Courthouse, shown above, complete with a traditional statue of Blind Justice and her scales atop the dome, commands Jackson's third panel. In the Fielder match, the Adams Mark Hotel has replaced the courthouse. On the other side of 16th Street, the six-story stone Kittredge Building is prominent behind one of the black-glass World Trade Center towers.

The Brown Place Hotel (1892) dominates Jackson's fourth panel, along with the stone spire of Trinity United Methodist Church. Now, the mountain view is obliterated by the pink, stepped Denver Post

Tower, the shiny former Amoco Tower with its rounded corners, and other high-rises. Central Presbyterian Church (1892) at 18th Avenue and Sherman Street takes center stage in both panels five. The once mansion-studded North Capitol Hill neighborhood housed many of Denver's movers and shakers. Nearly all of their fine homes have been torn down and replaced by apartments and office buildings, such as the rose-colored, 52-story Wells Fargo Bank.

A notable exception is the restored Fisher Mansion (1896) at far right in the Fielder photo and not yet present in Jackson's view. St. Paul's English Evangelical Lutheran Church in the center of the contemporary photo is a designated National Register Historic landmark, so it will be around for the future photographer who duplicates this marvelous six-panel view in the year 3000.

JF This six-part panorama of downtown Denver is one of Jackson's best-known images. Its view sweeps from southwest to northeast almost 180 degrees. His caption makes clear that he was standing in the Capitol dome, so I made a beeline for the tourist, or first, level of the gold-gilded landmark. This was one of the first sets of images that I tried to duplicate in the entire rephotography project, and I was still in the process of learning how to use "perspective" clues in order to find Jackson's original locations.

When I examined my processed film from the shoot, I noticed that something was wrong in the fifth photograph from the left, looking north up Sherman Street. In my shot, the horizon did not align with the same point on the Central Presbyterian Church steeple as in Jackson's photograph. The horizon was lower than it should have been, meaning I should have shot from higher up in the dome.

A week later, I went back to the Capitol and obtained permission to photograph from the dome's upper level (see Photo Pair 2). Sure enough, being 25 feet higher solved the problem. When I got there, I was surprised to see another photographer, Denver's Jim Havey, doing exactly the same thing. He was rephotographing Jackson's view for a project about the history of Colfax Avenue. That proved to be the only time during 1998 that I ran across someone else doing what I was doing.

2

DENVER

*Colorado State Capitol,
circa 1908*

p. 14

TN In the Jackson photo, note the dark, dull lead color of the dome. Although work on building the Capitol began in 1886, the final piece, the dome's gold leafing, was not in place until 1908. The small, flat top of the dome, as seen in the Jackson photo, was to have been the pedestal for a classical female figure with an uplifted torch. The legislature, however, after considerable study of models in various states of dress, could not agree on which feminine form was the most shapely. So a spherical glass lantern, as seen in the Fielder shot, now crowns the Capitol instead of the allegorical lady.

The Colorado State Capitol, a cruciform building of four stories, serves as the eastern terminus of the main axis of Civic Center Park. Like many domed state capitol buildings of its era, it was inspired by the national Capitol. The exterior walls are Colorado gray granite from the Aberdeen Quarry in Gunnison County. Lighter, cheaper, granite-colored cast iron was used for the three cylindrical stages of the dome. Colorado mining magnates donated the 24-carat gold leaf on the 272-foot-high dome, which was regilded in 1949, 1980, and 1991.

Elijah E. Myers, a Michigan architect, also designed state capitol buildings in Idaho, Michigan, Texas, and Utah. As in his other statehouses, Myers gave Colorado a building of classical design and Renaissance origins, but with unmistakably 19th-century proportions. Similar, symmetrical bays characterize all four sides, with a west entrance portico overlooking Civic Center Park. Triple-arched central entrances on each side are topped by triangular pediments with bas-relief allegorical sculptures.

The Capitol Board of Managers dismissed Myers in 1889 to save money. Board member Otto Mears explained, "The state has got his plans, and has paid for them. You see, we don't need him." Myers, who was then over 60, responded that "for a man of my age and experience, this is a most unpleasant occurrence," and returned to his home in Michigan. Denver architect Frank E. Edbrooke, who had placed second in the original architectural competition, completed the structure. He basically followed Myers' 1886 design, but suggested a gold rather than copper skin for the dome.

The Capitol's interior features Beulah red marble, Colorado-Yule marble wainscoting, and brass fixtures. Of the 160 rooms, the most noteworthy are the old Supreme Court chambers, the Senate and House chambers, and the first-floor rotunda, whose walls display murals (1938) by Colorado's premier muralist of the day, Allen Tupper True, depicting the state's history, as well as a poem by former Colorado Poet Laureate Thomas Hornsby Ferril. The spire behind the right side of the Capitol belongs to the First Baptist Church, which takes in the homeless but rarely sees legislators.

JF I don't know what long-gone building Jackson was standing on, but my only hope of achieving his elevation and location was to explore the City and County of Denver Annex building at Colfax Avenue and 14th Street. Using the "force"—my patented stare that allows me to forge past security guards without being questioned and has taken me years to perfect (bear in mind that I carry a conspicuous, 70-pound camera pack with my view camera mounted on a tripod over my shoulder)—I found my way to the outside deck on the fourth, and highest, floor. I used that location after making a few unsatisfactory Polaroids, with a view obscured by a tree, from the Board of Adjustment office on the second floor.

The location seemed almost perfect for elevation and latitude. Unfortunately, the tar-papered deck/roof was being checked for leaks and was flooded with 4 inches of water. With 300 locations to find and rephotograph in the coming months, Eric Bellamy, my assistant for the project, and I could not afford to let minor impasses like this one slow us down. In bare feet, we set up the camera and made a duplicate of Jackson's scene, including the same shadows on the north- and west-facing facades. Somehow we happened to be there the same season and time of day as had Jackson! This was one of many coincidences we experienced while rephotographing that reinforced, in my mind, that this challenging project was meant to happen.

DENVER

*The Denver Dry Goods
Company, 1908*

p. 15

TN "The Denver," as this block-long department store is labeled in the 1908 Jackson photograph, was one of the city's long-standing commercial anchors until its 1987 closure. In the 1990s, it was reborn as a retail, office, and residential complex. As both photos show, the Denver Dry Goods Company grew to incorporate several structures. The original 1889 store at 700 16th and California streets was designed by the premier architect of the day, Frank E. Edbrooke, who was almost single-handedly responsible for downtown Denver's architectural maturity in the late 1800s. Edbrooke's original three-story, red brick store for the McNamara Dry Goods Company had light limestone trim and almost solid plate-glass storefronts under the awnings.

In 1898, Edbrooke added a fourth story with arched windows, a wide, festooned frieze, and bracketed cornice suggestive of the Renaissance Revival mode. In 1907, Edbrooke's second addition extended the building the entire block along California to 15th Street. The 15th Street addition has six stories and wider windows, but similar broad-bracketed eaves and classical details. In 1924, a new story topped the original 16th Street structure; the addition was recessed to create a balustraded roof terrace for The Denver's famous Tea Room. This addition may have been done by in-house architects of the Frank E. Edbrooke Architect Company.

The Denver is legendary for its commercial and sentimental importance. The firm originated in 1886 with Michael J. McNamara's Dry Goods Company in the Clayton Building at 15th and Larimer streets. McNamara moved to 16th and California streets shortly before the Silver Crash of 1893, when the Colorado National Bank foreclosed and reorganized his business as the Denver Dry Goods Company. Between the 1950s and 1980s, this thriving store opened 11 branches in shopping centers from Fort Collins to Pueblo. The Denver's longtime rival, May D&F, bought the store in 1987 and closed it.

After being restored outside and remodeled inside with the help of the Denver Urban Renewal Authority, the building reopened in 1994 with retail space in the basement and offices on the first and

second floors. In 1997, floors three, four, and five reopened as 66 residential lofts, completing the $35 million renovation by a leading Denver architectural firm, Urban Design Group. Commercial entities continue to occupy the street-level floor of what is designated as both a Denver and a National Register Historic landmark.

Like Jackson, Fielder has a keen eye for street life. Note the street urchin at the lower left of the contemporary photo, dashing across California Street to beat the blurred Regional Transportation District (RTD) shuttle bus. Another figure is crossing in front of the waiting RTD Light Rail train, which the urchin is hoping to catch.

JF   Though I am not a Colorado native (I've lived here since the late 1960s), this photo was as nostalgic for me as it might be for older-timers. My first career was in the department store business, initially with the Denver Dry and then with May D&F. I spent the years of 1973 and 1974 working as an assistant buyer of men's clothing in the building shown here. In 1981, I turned what was then an avocation—nature photography—into a career.

On the corner of 16th and California streets, I set up my attention-getting, large-format camera. Jackson seems to have been a bit closer to the building than I was. Nevertheless, I remained on the sidewalk in order to avoid being run over by the Light Rail! What I like most about this pair of photographs is the mix of transportation modes in both scenes. See how many you can find in each.

4

DENVER

Brown Palace Hotel, 1911

pp. 16–17

TN The nine-story Brown Palace dominated Denver's skyline for several decades after its 1892 opening. Among its few rivals in the 1911 Jackson view are the nine-story Equitable Building four blocks down 17th Street and the 20-story Daniels & Fisher Building, whose tower was still under construction.

In the Jackson photo, note the old main entrance on Broadway where the central rooftop's extended cornice carried the name, carved in red sandstone, "The H. C. Brown Hotel." As the Fielder photo shows, that name and much more sandstone trim have disappeared during the past century. The now-closed Broadway arched entrance retains some original stone trim, including a bas-relief bust of Brown. Much of the rest of the reddish Arizona sandstone weathered and fell off; some was shaved off to prevent pedestrians from being bombarded by chunks of sandstone. Fielder had to wait patiently for direct sun and reflected sunbeams from surrounding glass towers to spotlight the hotel, now lost in the shadows of 50-story downtown high-rises. Although they overshadow the Brown, they have never outshone what is generally considered the finest work of Frank E. Edbrooke, Colorado's leading 19th-century architect.

The hotel, which has never been closed a single day, remains Denver's grand old place to stay, eat, drink, and, thanks to a 1997 cigar bar, smoke. Although remodeled in the 1950s in that era's distinctive style, the hotel was restored to a more original decor during the 1990s by former managing director Peter Aeby. The hotel offers tours showcasing the room where President and Mrs. Eisenhower stayed (one of many presidents to frequent the Brown), along with the rooms of other celebrities ranging from the Beatles to gold-mining tycoon Winfield Scott Stratton and the "Unsinkable" Molly Brown.

Henry C. Brown, who homesteaded Capitol Hill, commissioned this $2 million palace atop a Pikes Peak granite base. Architect Edbrooke wrapped the triangular structure with three graceful curves, arranging guest rooms around a skylighted atrium. The steel and iron frame, clad in terra-cotta, concrete, and stone, made this one of America's first fireproof buildings, according to an 1892 cover story in *Scientific American*.

Repetition of arcaded window patterns, cornices above multiple stories, and banding around corner curves add horizontal emphasis to what was the tallest building in town. Stone creatures once swarmed over the exterior, but nearly all were removed after deteriorated pieces began to pelt the sidewalk. Twenty-six carved stone medallions depicting native Colorado animals survive on the top-floor arcade.

The spacious 1890s interior retains many antique furnishings. Caramel and cream swirls flow through 12,000 square feet of onyx paneling from Mexico. The especially well-preserved Onyx Room bears a ceiling mural of cherubs hovering in a heavenly blue sky. Two 1930s murals by Allen Tupper True, depicting the stagecoach and airplane ages, adorn the Tremont Place entrance lobby. The Ship Tavern, a celebration of the repeal of Prohibition, was designed by Denver architect Alan B. Fisher. The tavern sports nautical artifacts, ranging from a crow's nest wrapped around the room's central beam to a collection of ships in bottles.

Although eclipsed on the outside, the Brown's magnificent skylighted atrium inside, complete with a harpist and high tea, remains a most special public gathering spot in the Mile High City.

JF You might remember me hauling my big camera and backpack up the elevator of the silvery Amoco Tower on the NEWS4 segment about this photo pair (Denver's KCNC-TV filmed 52 episodes about me rephotographing Jackson scenes). I was an unusual sight exploring the offices of the skyscraper at 1670 Broadway.

Jackson must have been standing on top of a building long gone. Nevertheless, the Amoco Tower (actually no longer called that—Amoco moved out in 1999) stands right where it did. My challenge was to find the floor that replicated the height of Jackson's rooftop, and hope that a window existed through which I could make the photograph. I obtained permission to rummage through the building. The fifth floor proved perfect, and, as luck would have it, there was a window right where I needed it to be— directly across Broadway from the Brown Palace. However, the skyscraper's glass was tinted almost black and the reflections on the inside of the window from the interior lighting made it difficult to see the hotel. In nature photography, polarizing filters help to eliminate glare and make reflections on water disappear. Presto! Using the polarizer, I was able to photograph the hotel clearly, albeit using a very slow shutter speed to override the light impedance from both the tinted window and the dark filter. Both images were made in broad daylight, but note the shadows cast by the surrounding buildings in my photograph.

5

DENVER

16th St. Viaduct, 1890

pp. 18–19

TN The 16th Street Viaduct opened November 1, 1889, for cable cars and general wagon and pedestrian traffic. The Denver City Cable Railway Company built it with financial assistance from the city not to exceed 15 percent of the cost, which was not to exceed $25,000. Following a century of replacements and repairs, the viaduct was torn down in the 1990s, leaving only the central span over the river in the Fielder photo. That central span is now also gone.

Commons Park was dedicated in 2000 by Denver mayor Wellington E. Webb along the South Platte riverbank on the northeast side of the vanished viaduct, shown on the left of the photo. The 16th Street Viaduct and its disappearance are a reminder of the also-vanished, once-vast street railway (light rail) system that provided Denver a fast, cheap transportation network between 1870 and 1950.

JF Thank goodness that a piece of the 16th Street Viaduct remained in 1998 so I could find Jackson's location. And how fortuitous it was that, for once, the same building from which Jackson pointed his camera still existed. On the roof of 1553 Platte St., I stood right where he did 108 years before me and photographed a significantly different downtown Denver to the northeast.

Actually, that piece of the viaduct was the last of a second version of the original viaduct depicted in Jackson's photo. Even it was razed as part of the Platte Valley redevelopment project by the time I returned in 1999 with NEWS4 to film the making of the photograph. (KCNC-TV began filming episodes halfway through the project, so I went back with them to 26 places to reenact the process of finding and rephotographing the scene. I became a pretty good actor, dramatizing the thrill of discovering Jackson's locations the second time!) Not only had the fragment of the viaduct over the South Platte River disappeared, the condos under construction in my photograph were almost complete, blocking the view of downtown Denver — proof that it doesn't require 100 years to witness change from growth, but sometimes only a few months.

WESTMINSTER

The Snowy Range from
Denver, 1892

pp. 20–21

The red sandstone tower of Westminster University had just opened when Jackson climbed to its top to take his photo. John Fielder used the same lofty perch 106 years later. Westminster, a Presbyterian university billed as "The Princeton of the West," was founded in 1892 with a magnificent stone "Old Main" designed by the famed New York architect, Stanford B. White.

That pioneer monument, which gave the town of Westminster its name, is superbly sited atop one of the most prominent hills in the metropolis. Construction on the 640-acre campus began in 1892, but the silver panic intervened in 1893. Finally completed and opened in 1907, "The Princeton of the West" struggled with economic and staffing difficulties, culminating in a fatal switch to an all-male enrollment on the eve of the draft for World War I.

The floundering university formed a real estate company that sold lots and residences around the campus, but the effort did not bring financial salvation. A local fundamentalist Christian sect, the Pillar of Fire Church, purchased the campus in 1920 for $40,000. The church still owns and operates a seminary and a radio station, KPOF 910 AM, the oldest religious broadcasting station in Colorado.

The school failed, but its towering Old Main became a focal point for the town that grew up in its shadows. Incorporated as Westminster in 1911, it remained a rural hamlet until after World War II. The few farms and vast sweep of open land in the Jackson photo have succumbed to the development captured in Fielder's view of what is now Colorado's eighth-largest city. In the far right center of Fielder's photo, note the Westminster City Hall bell tower, an architectural echo of Big Ben in London's Westminster district. Both photos share the foreground telegraph poles, those great tokens of 19th-century development, as well as the snow-capped Front Range crowned by flat-topped Longs Peak and the Indian Peaks, which Jackson mislabeled as "The Snowy Range."

JF If it had not been for my assistant, Eric Bellamy, I would not have easily found Jackson's photo location, the Pillar of Fire Ministry at Belleview Christian College. Eric grew up in Westminster and knew that the old church stood on a hill at 3455 W. 83rd Ave., and thought that it might be high enough to be the place from which Jackson photographed. Facilitated by the church's director, Dr. Robert B. Dallenbach, a quick trip to its highest floor confirmed that Eric was correct. Standing on the west-facing fire escape, we made the exact image that Jackson had, looking northwest toward Longs Peak and Boulder's Flatirons.

Another clue that we had found the right place hung on a wall in the main-floor hallway: a beautiful original Jackson panoramic print of the Rio Grande Southern Railroad near Telluride. Jackson must have given it as a gift to the college in 1892 after he photographed there. The image hangs in an old, ornate frame that most certainly dates to the 19th century. Once again, I followed Jackson's lead by leaving a gift of several of my nature photography books with Dr. Dallenbach.

7

DOUGLAS COUNTY

*Red Sandstone near
Platte Cañon, 1870*

pp. 22–23

TN | The Jackson photo shows the old County Road 5. Residents of upscale subdivisions on Roxborough State Park's east, north, and west sides closed public access to the park in 1981, hoping to create their own private enclave. In 1987, public protest finally reopened this 1,500-acre state park, now accessible for year-round use.

Roxborough State Park, established in 1975 at the south end of Roxborough Park Road, is popular for hiking and picnicking. The magical red rock planes and the relative shelter of the area also attracted prehistoric peoples, who left multiple archaeological sites within this park. The Long and Frémont expeditions exploring the South Platte River marveled at these formations, as did the Utes and Arapaho, who no doubt camped here. Pioneer settler Henry S. Persse, along with fellow investors, planned a large resort here that never developed, although Roxborough did become a favorite place for Denverites to enjoy an outing.

A single kiln near the park entrance is the last remnant of the Silica Brick and Clay Company operation of 1904–1913. Of the Persse homestead, a sandstone house (circa 1903) with a metal roof remains, as well as a barn constructed of old hewn and newer peeled logs with saddle notching. Two log sheds also survive. These ruins lent inspiration for the George T. O'Malley Visitors Center (1985, G. Cabell Childress Architects), a rustic textured and tinted concrete structure nestled into one of the rock formations and adorned with Fredrick Myers' sculpture, *Kokopelli*, the humpbacked Indian flute player whose figure also shapes the courtyard.

JF | The moment I saw this photograph in the Jackson archives, I knew instantly where it was and that I would enjoy finding the exact spot where he stood. Southwest of Denver, the South Platte River gushes from the Rocky Mountains onto the Great Plains at a place called Waterton Canyon. The canyon is also the eastern terminus for the Colorado Trail, which I have photographed for two books. Just south of the canyon is Roxborough State Park, one of my favorite places on Planet Earth. My excitement was further

fueled by the fact that this photograph was the oldest one used in the project, and among the oldest of all of Jackson's Colorado images.

These sandstone spires exist in the Lyons and Fountain geologic formations, and features of this type pepper Colorado's Front Range. Red Rocks Park and Amphitheatre in Morrison and Garden of the Gods City Park in Colorado Springs are both part of this 300-million-year-old upturn of rock. Given the prominence of the spires in the center of Jackson's photograph, it did not take long to find his location, albeit while driving a golf cart! This area is part of the Roxborough subdivision, through which courses the Arrowhead Golf Club. For me, the spires evoked a memory of having seen similar rock formations in a sketch made by the official artist of the 1820 Long Expedition into Colorado. A glance at my copy of Major Stephen H. Long's published journal revealed that the sketch was indeed of the same spires as in the Jackson scene.

The friendly staff at the club loaned me a golf cart (to the back of which was attached my golf bag — I enjoy swinging the clubs occasionally), and away Eric and I went. At the 15th fairway, I found what I was looking for. However, when I located the two spires in the foreground of Jackson's image, my view was completely obscured by scrub oak bushes that had grown tall and thick in the past 128 years. In order to make a photograph above the bushes, I had to move to the right and climb on top of a rock. As a result, Jackson's foreground rocks do not appear in my version. Nevertheless, the purview is essentially the same and shows the dramatic change as a function of human recreation, for better or worse (worse — I lost a lot of golf balls in the oaks that day).

The vehicle in Jackson's scene is a Civil War ambulance converted into a mobile darkroom. Notice that I have replaced his vehicle with my own: a golf cart. Also see Jackson's friends standing in the foreground in order to create a sense of scale.

8

DOUGLAS COUNTY

*Grand View—Perry
Park, 1882*

pp. 24–25

TN   Perry Park was named for John Dietz Perry, who bought the 4,000-acre, rock-rimmed park in 1871. Perry, the president of the Kansas Pacific Railroad, grew enamored of the scenic valley while conducting a railroad survey. He and his sons, Charles and Lewis, developed a ranch here for shorthorn cattle. The Perry clan amused themselves by naming the park's spectacular red sandstone formations: Walls of Jericho, Castle Rhein, and Washington Monument.

Before the Perrys branded this park as their own, it attracted the attention of the U.S. Geological Survey's Ferdinand V. Hayden, the first person to map Colorado thoroughly. Hayden mapped it as Pleasant Park, but by the time noted English world traveler and author Isabella Bird stayed with the Perrys in 1873, the name Perry Park prevailed. Bird reported in her classic book, *A Lady's Life in the Rocky Mountains*, "Perry's Park is one of the great cattle-raising ranches in Colorado.... Mr. Perry devotes himself mainly to the breeding of graded Shorthorn bulls, which he sells when young for six pounds per head. The cattle run at large upon the prairies, each animal being branded, they need no herding, and are usually only mustered, counted, and the increase branded in the summer. In the fall, when three or four years old, they are sold lean or in tolerable condition to dealers who take them by rail to Chicago."

After a horse fatally kicked Charles Perry in the head in 1876, his father sold Perry Park. Subsequent owners continued ranching the park, quarried some of the red sandstone and gypsum formations, tried gold mining and making stucco and plaster, and established a hotel, grocery store, and post office, for which the Denver & Rio Grande Larkspur Depot served as a railhead. A proposed Perry Park Railroad from Sedalia via the park to Palmer Lake never materialized, nor did various schemes to convert Perry Park to a fashionable resort area.

In more recent decades, Perry Park has become an upscale residential area centered on the Perry Park Country Club. The ongoing development of this spectacular natural setting of Perry Park with large

homes on large-acreage sites is well captured by the foundation Fielder photographed in 1998. As the name Perry Park suggests, this spectacular natural enclave might have been a public park for all to enjoy.

JF   Even in Jackson's day, Perry Park was a favorite scenic location to visit. Resplendent with red rock formations similar to, though not as tall as, those at Roxborough to the north, along with oak brush and stately ponderosa pines, this place represents the most beautiful aspect of the Rocky Mountain foothills ecosystem. Just west of the town of Larkspur, today's Perry Park is a residential community with a golf course, characterized by large homes nestled among the rocks, oaks, and pines.

This was a difficult Jackson location to find. Because of the suppression of forest fires, the pine forest has grown relatively dense and covers most of the rocky landmarks conspicuous in Jackson's photograph. The ridges in the distance served as the chief clues for me, the photo detective.

During this project, I developed a method of deciphering Jackson's locations that I call the "ridge trick." Aligning the ridges in the distance to match how they appear in the Jackson photograph usually got me close to his location. The alignment had to occur on both the lateral axis (latitude) and vertical axis (elevation), so I would walk or drive left to right, up and down, backward and forward, until I could recognize with the naked eye the accurate alignment of all ridges in relation to one another. Moving 50 feet away from the correct spot was enough to throw things off, even using landmarks miles away.

The ridge trick helped me find the correct line of sight, but I needed to locate at least a couple of the foreground rocks to zero in on the exact spot. Though you cannot see them, the same rocks exist in my photograph's purview as in Jackson's. However, one rock is gone: It was obliterated to make way for the foundation of a new home.

9

EL PASO COUNTY

Lake on the Colorado Divide Looking North, 1874

p. 26

Palmer Lake is just a lake, not a town, in Jackson's 1874 view. Arrival of the Denver & Rio Grande Railroad in the 1870s helped transform this foothills valley into the town captured in Fielder's photograph. General William J. Palmer, founder and president of the Denver & Rio Grande, gave his name to both the lake and the town. Planned as a resort town, it was soon eclipsed by nearby Colorado Springs when Palmer built his own home there and made Colorado Springs, not Palmer Lake, the center of his plans for a railroad tourist resort.

This Hayden Survey photograph had me fooled from the beginning. I recognized the buttes in the distance as those east of Interstate 25 and south of Castle Rock on the way to Monument Hill. I thought that this point on the Colorado Divide — the east-west ridge separating the waters of the South Platte River from those of the Arkansas River — must be where Interstate 25 crosses over Monument Hill. I also remembered a pond that might have been the body of water in the Jackson photograph. I was wrong. So I headed west toward the town of Palmer Lake, established in 1889, and what do you know — the ridges lined up almost correctly. However, I needed to be quite a bit higher than the town's elevation. There are plenty of foothills just west of Palmer Lake on which Jackson must have stood, but a quick scan revealed nothing but dense forest and no vantage point from which to photograph.

Eric and I spent at least an hour scrambling up the steep ridges until we found one small gap in the trees through which to point the camera. Again, 20th-century fire suppression and its resulting masses of trees had almost foiled us. Thinking back to my first viewing of the photograph, I suppose I could not imagine a Palmer Lake isolated on the plains with nary a subdivision or tree around it.

10

DOUGLAS COUNTY

*Tablelands near the
Colorado Divide, 1874*

p. 27

TN Both photographers captured the elevated tablelands in Douglas County that separate the South Platte River and Arkansas River drainages. As elevation gains mean precipitation gains, this divide is distinguished from the lower, drier surrounding prairie by the Black Forest. This sea of ponderosa pine was diminished by early lumbering and sawmill operations. Opened in the 1860s, these "pineries" provided much of the lumber used to build pioneer Denver, Colorado Springs, and other area settlements.

Both of these photos were taken just west of Greenland Ranch, the last large undeveloped tract between the fast-growing metropolitan areas of Denver and Colorado Springs. Frank Kirk put together this cattle ranch in the 1890s by persuading every cowboy in sight to homestead a claim and sell it to him. In this way, he acquired about 12,000 acres for Charles and Augustus Kountze, founders of Denver's Colorado National Bank.

Greenland was an overnight stop for stagecoaches traveling between Denver and Colorado Springs. The remains of a hotel, livery, and railroad stock-loading station endure on the site. The L-plan frame ranch house near the railroad tracks has corbelled brick chimneys, decorative shingle patterns in the gables, and bracketed porch posts. Antique outbuildings include the large frame barn and square-frame silo with hipped roof. The Higby family, who acquired the ranch in 1909, sold it to an investment group in 1981, which planned to develop it.

In 2000, a coalition of public and private agencies acquired the ranch and additional lands around it to conserve it. So the view captured by Jackson and Fielder should continue to provide welcome relief from shopping malls, residential subdivisions, factory outlet stores, and other developments that once threatened to form a solid conglutination between Colorado's two largest cities. Bordering both sides of Interstate 25 between Larkspur and Palmer Lake, Greenland Ranch still provides magnificent views of open country, backdropped by the Front Range stretching from Pikes Peak to Mount Evans.

 The proximity of the Greenland Ranch buttes in the distance to the bluff on which Jackson stood allowed fast identification of the location in this Hayden Survey photograph. These buttes are the same ones as in the Palmer Lake view (see Photo Pair 9), and I would bet that Jackson made the two photographs on the same day. Standing in the valley and extending the line of sight west from the properly aligned buttes led me straight to Eagle Mountain, conspicuous from Interstate 25 a few miles to the west.

I acquired permission from the Noe family to climb this snow-white bluff located on their ranch. A quick and steep hike through ponderosas led Dennis Johns, a friend who helped me occasionally during the project, and me to the exposed cliffs in the photograph and an easy discovery of Jackson's location. Notice Jackson's mule on the left. I asked Dennis to stand in the animal's place in order to create the same sense of scale. Look closely and you will observe that some of the rocks on the lower ledge have disappeared, probably from natural erosion during the past 124 years. In my photograph, you can see Interstate 25 and the old town of Greenland below the buttes.

11

EL PASO COUNTY

Natural Arch under the Citadel Rock
on the Colorado Divide, 1874

p. 28

JR　This small natural arch, identified as Elephant Rock on the modern U.S. Geological Survey map, is carved from soft, coarse-grained sandstone of the Dawson Formation. This part of the Dawson Formation was deposited between about 65 and 55 million years ago during the Paleocene epoch. The sandstone is composed largely of feldspar and quartz eroded from the great body of Precambrian granite that makes up Pikes Peak and much of the Rampart Range, a few miles to the west.

As the mountains were uplifted during the episode of geological upheaval known as the Laramide orogeny, streams flowed northeastward off the rising mountains, carrying great quantities of feldspar-rich sand into the subsiding Denver Basin. The sand visible in these photographs is made up of angular fragments of feldspar measuring a half-inch or more in diameter, as well as somewhat smaller grains of quartz loosely cemented by gray clay. Pebbles of white quartz several inches in diameter are scattered through the sandstone like plums in a pudding. Many of the beds, such as the one in the lower left of the

Jackson photo, are inclined layers formed when the sand was deposited in sandbars in the ancient streambeds. The rock's soft, crumbly consistency makes it easy to dig with a small pick or scratch with a knife, as the initials visible in the lower left part of the contemporary photo testify.

The arch probably formed when erosion isolated a thin fin of rock along two parallel weak zones or fractures. Wind, water, and frost action attacked the sides of the fin and eventually broke through it, creating a hole. Once this breakthrough was achieved, loose chunks fell from the ceiling. Eventually, the opening assumed the shape of an arch, which — as engineers and cathedral builders discovered long ago — is the strongest shape for supporting the load of the overlying rock.

Because the sandstone in the arch is so soft, the formation must have developed very recently, certainly within the last million years. It is surprising that so little change has taken place since the time of Jackson's photo. However, you have to wonder what happened to the large boulder in the left foreground of his picture.

With no real landmarks in the distance, this Hayden Survey photograph might have been difficult to find. Knowing that it was on the Colorado Divide certainly helped. I suppose that 30 years of nature photography develops an eye for detail, which I apparently employed as I drove over Monument Hill on Interstate 25 on my first pass at rephotographing this scene. Looking a few miles to the west, I spied an orange rock outcrop with what appeared to be a large hole through it. Exiting at the town of Monument, I began to explore a circuitous network of subdivision roads in my search for the rock. Driving a few miles to the northwest of Monument, I glanced up through my windshield and past a thick forest of pines to see this huge sandstone arch looming above me. Unfortunately, it stands on private property so you must seek permission from the landowners, who live on-site, in order to climb to the arch.

Notice Jackson's horse and canvas darkroom in the old photograph. Those transient elements obviously would not recur in my photograph, but what happened to the large rock in the foreground and the tall ponderosa pine?

12

GOLDEN

circa 1885

p. 29

TN   As Jackson's photo shows, Golden had become a substantial town by 1885. Squeezed into a narrow valley between North Table Mountain and South Table Mountain on the east and Lookout Mountain on the west, Golden was founded in 1859 and named for prospector Thomas L. Golden. The town began as a business venture of the Boston Company, one of the better-organized and better-capitalized early colony builders operating in Colorado. Despite the hilly terrain, the company imposed the usual grid pattern upon the townsite, which is bisected by Clear Creek.

Golden became an industrial center with clay, coal, copper, and iron mines, as well as smelters, brickyards, and railyards. As Denver's early-day rival, it even reigned as the territorial capital from 1862 to 1867. After losing both that designation and railroad dominance to Denver, Golden became famous for locally made, pressed, fired, and white-glazed bricks. Rich and varied local clay deposits also made it a center for the manufacture of drain pipes, pottery, and porcelain. Since World War I, the Coors Porcelain Company has emerged as the world's leading manufacturer of high-grade, heat-resistant porcelain for laboratory and scientific uses. Golden grew slowly after its initial 1860s-to-1880s boom, with a stable population of around 3,000 until the 1950s.

Much of Washington Avenue (Golden's main street) and the 12th Street residential district remain fairly intact. An old-fashioned welcome arch reading, "Howdy Folks! Welcome to Golden Where the West Lives," erected in 1949 by the Chamber of Commerce, spans Washington Avenue. In 1992, the city spent $2 million on a facade restoration and streetscaping for Washington Avenue. The grounds around Clear Creek, which flows through town, were converted into a park in 1994 and endowed with some relocated pioneer buildings including a blacksmith shop and several log cabins. During the 1990s, Goldenites successfully defeated a plan by the Nike Company to build a huge footwear plant atop South Table Mountain. Private owners, however, continue to thwart plans to convert these rimrock mesas into public parks.

Although both the Coors Brewery (founded in 1873) and the Colorado School of Mines (founded in 1869) were there in 1885, by the time Fielder duplicated Jackson's image they had grown into much larger operations. The mass of gray concrete structures in the center of the contemporary photo is home to

America's third-largest beer maker and the largest single brewery in the United States. In the far right of Fielder's photo, the red-roofed structures are part of the expanded campus of the Colorado School of Mines, which claims to be the "World's Foremost College of Mineral Engineering."

JF The general location of this photograph was simple to find, but reaching the exact spot required some steep hillside scrambling. Looking west from Golden, it was clear that Eric and I should drive up historic Lookout Mountain Road. A few miles up, we parked along one of the northernmost switchbacks and reconnoitered. We were at the right latitude, but North and South Table mountains did not align properly with the horizon. So we began what turned out to be a long hike down the hill until we spied a large, flat rock.

One of the rules we formulated in the process of tracking W. H. Jackson's footsteps around Colorado was to avoid setting up the tripod and camera on particularly precarious or sloped terrain. Jackson used larger cameras than I do, and needed a steady mount in order to photograph effectively. Whenever the tripod setup made me uneasy, I would look around a little while longer and often discover a large, flat rock nearby — most likely Jackson's exact location. This was the case on Lookout Mountain.

13

CLEAR CREEK COUNTY

Chicago Lakes, 1873

p. 30

MP   The pyramid summit of Mount Evans marks the highest point along the mountainous skyline west of Denver. Many are familiar with the paved road, the nation's highest, that takes innumerable tourists to the breathless 14,000-foot heights of this summit. Other than the paved road, the rugged alpine landscape surrounding Mount Evans still appears as it did in the 1800s, prior to European settlement.

The breathtaking beauty of the glacial-carved gorges, alpine lakes, and granite cliffs surrounding Mount Evans is permanently protected within the 74,401-acre Mount Evans Wilderness Area. The U.S. Congress designated this wilderness area under the 1980 Colorado Wilderness Act, a law that preserved 1.4 million acres of Colorado's mountains and forests — the largest wilderness designation in our state's history.

Wilderness is a land designation applied by Congress to preserve and perpetuate the natural ecosystems as they existed when Europeans first arrived on the scene. The Wilderness Act itself was passed into law in 1964, with the goal that "an increasing population, accompanied by expanding settlement and growing mechanization, does not occupy and modify all areas within the United States." As a means of preventing such occupation and modification, Congress defined wilderness this way: "In contrast with those areas where man and his own works dominate the landscape, [wilderness] is hereby recognized as an area where the earth and its community of life are untrammeled by man, where man himself is a visitor who does not remain." To achieve its goal of preventing the expanding settlement and mechanization from dominating the landscape, Congress took pains to prohibit logging, mining, and road-building, as well as the encroachment of permanent structures, commercial enterprises, and motorized vehicles, in these areas.

The 1964 Wilderness Act initially designated just five areas in Colorado, but it also directed the U.S. Forest Service to review its lands for potential wilderness designation. Citizens frustrated by the Forest Service's slow pace of identifying new wilderness areas later pressured the agency into conducting a nationwide evaluation of its roadless lands, the so-called Roadless Area Review and Evaluations (RARE) I and II, in the 1970s.

In Colorado, the Forest Service finished its review of 6.5 million acres of the state's most magnificent undeveloped landscapes in 1979 and, among its recommendations, proposed wilderness protection for the bulk of Mount Evans, nearby Mount Bierstadt, the Chicago Lakes, and surrounding alpine terrain. Colorado's congressional delegation responded promptly to these recommendations and enacted the 1980 Colorado Wilderness Act a year later.

JF W. H. Jackson photographed some of Colorado's wildest places during the Hayden Survey. On horseback and by foot, with mules carrying 350 pounds of cameras and darkroom equipment, Jackson and his assistants penetrated many places that today are federally designated wilderness. The well-known Chicago Lakes lie in the middle of the Mount Evans Wilderness. As a nature photographer and hard-core backpacker, I looked forward to finding Jackson's most remote photographic locations. Having never been to Chicago Lakes, I was especially excited to search for this and two other Jackson photo locales in the area.

Notice Jackson's oft-present darkroom and mule. Always searching for ways to duplicate not only the place but the moment in time, I thought it might be appropriate to take along my own pack animals. Not only would I get some relief from carrying the 70-pound pack, but I'd have a stand-in for the mule. However, when I use pack animals in my job, I use llamas, not mules! With Tensing, Kirwood, and Tommie in tow, Eric and I, along with Mary Brenneman and Dan Fox from KCNC-TV, made a one-night, 12-mile round-trip trek into the Mount Evans Wilderness.

Finding the lakes was easy, as was finding two of the three Jackson photographic locations. The apparent ones were around the lower of the two Chicago Lakes in the cirque, but the third was somewhere high on a ridge above the highest lake. After finding the lakeside locations after sunrise, Eric and I spent the balance of the morning scrambling as high as 13,000 feet in quest of the third. We managed to make a photograph similar to Jackson's, but never did find the exact foreground rocks as in his photograph. With more time, I am certain we could have found the right spot. But two out of three was not bad, and the project did have a deadline.

During the nine months of photographing in 1998, a handful of places eluded us. Perhaps someday (when I don't have anything better to do) I will ferret out those mysterious locations. In the photographic pair shown here, observe how the alpine willows in the foreground have filled in, and that the rocks around the lake are the same.

14

BLACK HAWK

circa 1885

p. 31

TN   The frame house surviving amid an asphalt sea of parking lots and garages in the center of the
Fielder photo is the Lace House. Since 1863, this fancy fronted miner's house has treated travelers to an
uplifting view on the downhill side of Black Hawk. As Fielder's photo shows, a casino parking lot now
engulfs it. Behind the house is a rocky remnant of its picturesque hillside site overlooking Clear Creek.
The small surviving clump of pines still shelters the Lace House's outhouse. Both buildings are exquisite
examples of Carpenter's Gothic construction. Although not visible in these photos, the house's front
features graceful window arches pointing heavenward past wooden trim that drips from the eaves like lace.

This lacy landmark is the premier residence and a cornerstone of the Central City–Black Hawk
National Historic Landmark District. Carefully restored, Lace House has been lovingly maintained by
volunteers and by city, state, and federal funding. As Colorado's nationally known example of how wooden
trim could enhance a miner's shack, it is one of the most photographed and postcarded examples of
Gothic Revival architecture in the Rockies. Along with its hillside outhouse and dry-stack stone retaining
walls, it was donated in 1974 to Black Hawk for use as a house museum.

Eagle Gaming, Inc., of Denver forever altered the site in the mid-1990s by cutting off easy access to
and surrounding it with its casino parking lot. Objections from the Colorado Historical Society, Colorado
Preservation, Inc., and other concerned groups did not prevent this travesty.

Lace House has long been the saving grace of this mill town named for its pioneer quartz mill, a gold-ore crusher built by the Black Hawk Company of Rock Island, Illinois. Strategically sited at the junction of Gregory Gulch and North Clear Creek, Black Hawk became Colorado's first great ore-processing hub.

In 1991, Colorado voters approved a change in the state constitution allowing limited-stakes gambling in Black Hawk, Central City, and Cripple Creek. Afterward, Black Hawk switched from gold mills to gaming mills. Because it's closer to most gamblers than either Central City or Cripple Creek, the smallest of the three gaming towns, Black Hawk, has come to dominate the industry. Having moved its mountains for casino slots and parking lots, Black Hawk is now jingling night and day. Its money mills are reminiscent of the smelters that once engulfed the town with thumping, ore-crushing stamp-mills and smoky, sulfurous furnaces that cooked gold ores. Jackson's 1885 photo well captures Black Hawk's previous life as a major gold-milling town.

JF Jackson was standing farther forward than I was when I reshot his photograph. As was the case with about 20 percent of the 300 project photographs, the landscape in this scene had been altered to the extent that I could not stand where he did. Legalized gambling has changed the character of this historic mining town in many ways, one of which was the advent of soaring land prices within a physically constrained valley. There was no room for casino parking lots, so mountainsides were leveled to make way for vehicles.

I perched on the edge of an 80-foot-high, manmade cliff. The historic Lace House was out of Jackson's view and the mountainside from which he photographed is gone. Nevertheless, in the upper left of both photographs stand the county courthouse and schoolhouse built in the 1860s. Isn't it ironic that the 65-million-year-old mountain is gone and part of the more fragile human landscape remains? Or does that evoke other reactions? I remember the Black Hawk and Central City of yesterday, when most buildings were deserted and the charm of what once existed was what made Colorado history fun. Gambling certainly has changed the flavor of these towns.

15

CENTRAL CITY

circa 1885

pp. 32–33

As these two views prove, Central City is a smaller town today than it was during the 19th century, when it hoped to become Colorado's "central" city and state capital. Founded in 1859, Central City sparkled as the first hub of the Rocky Mountain gold rush and the Colorado Territory's most populous city during the 1860s. On May 6, 1859, John Gregory struck gold in what was afterward called Gregory Gulch, which runs from Central City to Black Hawk, where it joins Clear Creek. Within weeks of the strike, canvas, slab, and hewn-pine shacks climbed the rocky hillsides like stairs. Locals joked that "a fella can't spit tobaccy juice out his front door without putting out the fire in his neighbor's chimney."

Mountain City, the original settlement in Gregory Gulch, was soon overrun and annexed by Central City. Mines, homes, and businesses expanded into nearby American City, Apex, Black Hawk, Eureka, Gold Dirt, Missouri City, Mountain City, Nevadaville, Nugget, Perrigo, Rollinsville, Russell Gulch, Tip Top, and Wide-awake.

To build these towns, timber the mines, and stoke the smelters, hillsides of fir, pine, and spruce were sacrificed (the Fielder photo shows some greenery returning to the shorn hilltops of Jackson's era). In one of the nation's first environmental abuse suits, U.S. Secretary of the Interior Carl Schurz charged in 1877 that Nathaniel P. Hill had fueled his Black Hawk smelter with timber stripped from public lands. Not only was the natural setting ravaged, but much of the built environment was later ripped down. During the 1930s and 1940s, people demolished much of Central City's outlying residential area to avoid paying property taxes, maintenance, and liability, and to make a few dollars selling used lumber, bricks, firewood, and furnishings.

Central City, as *Rocky Mountain News* editor William N. Byers christened it, was the center of gold-mining activity during the 1860s and 1870s. The population, which peaked at 3,114 in 1900 and hit a rock bottom of 226 in 1970, bounced back slightly to 515 by 2000.

Perhaps the most impressive thing about this pair of photos, as close scrutiny reveals, is how many of the downtown commercial buildings survive in often near-original condition. After a fire devastated Central City in 1874, it rebuilt, in sturdy brick and stone, buildings that have held up well. On the upper left hillside in the Jackson view, St. Aloysius Academy, with its slender, silver-domed central bell tower, has been razed; a cross and stone overlook marks the site today. Just below this large Catholic school, St. Mary's Catholic Church is a one-story, pinnacled building that grew into the large brick church seen in Fielder's photo. The well-preserved Teller House Hotel at the center of both photos stands in front of the elegant stone St. James United Methodist Church. Despite alterations since 1991, when casinos began moving in, Central City remains one of Colorado's best-preserved mining towns.

The ridge trick got me close to Jackson's location on a hill southwest of Central City. To perfect the alignment, all I needed to do was to find the scalloped granite rocks prominent in the bottom of his photograph. It was a snap, given that he was standing on the edge of a cliff and that many of the same buildings could serve as perspective clues. It wasn't long before Eric and I were standing in our predecessor's footprints.

How different Central City is today from Black Hawk! Many of Black Hawk's historic buildings have disappeared, and others have been moved to make way for casinos. Most of Central City's buildings in the Jackson photograph still exist. Why? The town is second in line after Black Hawk on the drive up State Highway 119 along North Clear Creek. Not as many people gamble there. Casinos have actually gone out of business. So what's on the horizon for Central City? In 2002, Gilpin County will build a $40 million highway to connect Central City directly with Interstate 70. What do you think Central City will look like after that? Does Black Hawk ring a bell?

16

IDAHO SPRINGS

circa 1885

pp. 34–35

TN This duo is undeniable evidence of how an interstate highway can disrupt a community. Interstate 70's cement barrier and high-speed, 24-hour-a-day roar of traffic have severed the south side of Idaho Springs from the heart of town. In the right edge of both photos, note how little the built environment has changed at the base of Virginia Canyon Road ("Oh My God Road"). The stone, castle-like house at the mouth of Virginia Canyon is prominent in Jackson's work, and survives, although obscured by vegetation, in the sequel. This is Castle Eyrie, built in 1878–1881, at 1828 Illinois St. The two-story, random-coursed "country rock" house perches on a promontory overlooking the town. Posing as a medieval castle, it has round towers on the south corners, and the smaller tower on the west sports a conical stone cap. A crenelated parapet and two corbelled brick chimneys rise above the flat roofline.

Outside the frames of both photos to the left are the hot springs that gave the town its name. George A. Jackson camped near the hot springs in January 1859 and struck placer gold in Chicago Creek near its confluence with Clear Creek. A swarm of miners established mines, mills, and outlying camps for which Idaho Springs emerged as the core supply town.

Since 1900, Idaho Springs has stabilized at a population of about 1,900. Strung along the narrow stretch of Clear Creek Canyon, the town retains a well-preserved commercial main street (Miner Street), whose two-story, red brick commercial buildings appear in both photos. Most of the pioneer frame buildings along Clear Creek in the 1885 view are gone. Colorado Boulevard, a block north of Miner Street, is lined in the contemporary photo with many frame cottages, four-squares, and Queen Anne–style homes built after the 1885 photo was taken. Colorado Boulevard's impressive residences include the Cooper House (1905), 1122 Colorado Blvd., a Classical Revival frame house occupied until the late 1920s by novelist Courtney Riley Cooper. In the surrounding hills, the Argo Mine, Mill, and Tunnel; the Phoenix Mine; and the Edgar Mine still welcome tourists.

JF How many buildings can you find in Jackson's photograph that still exist today? Of course, this was not a difficult location to pinpoint. Thank goodness not more of the hill on which Jackson stood was excavated during Interstate 70's construction. That was not always the case along other highway corridors that I rephotographed. The only challenge to making this image was waiting for the right combination of vehicles on Interstate 70 before opening the shutter. That, and deciding which microbrew beer to have with lunch in Idaho Springs!

17

SILVER PLUME

circa 1885

p. 36

TN Like Idaho Springs, Silver Plume was cut in half by construction of Interstate 70 during the 1970s. Silver Plume, founded in 1870, is noted for its silver mines and granite quarries. While merchants and mine owners gravitated to Georgetown, Silver Plume housed most of the mines and miners. The town, named for ore so rich that silver flakes broke off in feathery plumes, runs the length of a narrow, steep-sided valley carved by Clear Creek. Some 1,500 people lived here in 1890, 10 times the present population.

Small, vernacular homes reflect the limited space in the narrow valley and the meager wages of miners. Most homes have fewer than four rooms, with ornamentation limited to pediments over doors and windows demonstrating a Greek Revival influence. Relatively stable property values and lack of development pressure have left much of Silver Plume's 19th-century architecture intact, making it one of Colorado's best-preserved mining towns. The miniature Main Street, rebuilt after an 1884 fire, is a dirt lane complete with a tiny post office and bandstand.

Among the surviving 1880s buildings in Silver Plume is the New Windsor Hotel/Collins Home (circa 1880) at 45 Woodward St. Narrow dormers extend from the hipped roof of this two-story clapboard hotel, with its full-width front porch and a balustraded balcony. Established as a hotel, it is now a private residence.

At Ma Buckley's House (1881), 54 Woodward St., a Doric-columned porch graces the frame cottage where Alice and Jeremiah Buckley raised 13 children. Alice was reportedly one of the first white children born in Gilpin County, to parents living in Nevadaville in 1862. She and her husband raised one of the best-known local families, with enough sons to keep the town's baseball team vigorous despite a population that dwindled to 86 at its low point in 1960.

The jailhouse (circa 1881) also survives at the northwest corner of Main and Garfield streets. Two-foot-thick walls enforce this small, square, one-story granite dungeon built into a hillside; the structure became a dog pound after humans were moved in 1915 to the county jail in Georgetown. Originally used by the security guards working for British mine investors, the jail became town property upon Silver Plume's incorporation in 1880. Facilities were spartan, and prisoners had to be taken to a nearby boardinghouse for meals.

In the foreground, on the south side of Interstate 70 and Clear Creek, note the surviving house and railyards; the latter is experiencing new life with the Colorado Historical Society's reincarnation of the Georgetown Loop Railroad that connected Silver Plume with Georgetown.

Just above Georgetown lies the mining town of Silver Plume. As was the case with the town of Idaho Springs, this location handily revealed itself, though I could not stand exactly where Jackson did. A grove of aspen trees has grown up during the intervening century in front of his spot, so I had to move 50 feet to the right. Look what that did to the angle of the buildings in the bottom of my photograph. Yes, those century-old wooden structures still exist. And it looks like a few trees have grown up around town since Jackson was there.

18

GEORGETOWN

Loop, Devil's Gate Bridge,
circa 1885

p. 37

TN This photographic pair captures one of the most breathtaking restorations in Colorado. For the state's centennial and national bicentennial in 1976, the Colorado Historical Society began a $2 million reconstruction of the Devil's Gate Bridge and reactivated the moribund Georgetown Loop Railroad. Eight years later, in 1984, the restored narrow-gauge railroad opened for summer tourist excursions.

The Georgetown Loop originally functioned as the final segment of the Colorado Central Railroad built from Golden up Clear Creek Canyon during the 1870s and early 1880s. That narrow-gauge steam train crawled up Clear Creek to service the mines, negotiating steep terrain via engineering wonders such as the famous Georgetown Loop.

Two miles — and a rise of 638 feet — separated Georgetown and Silver Plume. Robert Blickensderfer, a Union Pacific engineer, designed the original 4.47 miles of track, which includes two hairpin turns and loops over itself to cut a 6 percent grade to 3.5 percent. At the Devil's Gate Bridge, a 300-foot-long span crosses the track and Clear Creek, 95 feet below. Sightseers from all over the globe came to gawk, if not to "do the loop" on "that famous knot in a railroad."

Mining and tourism had both played out in 1939 when the Colorado & Southern Railway, the last operator of the Georgetown Loop, abandoned the line, scrapping the Devil's Gate Bridge for $450. In the 1970s, the Georgetown Loop became the railroad that moved a highway: Interstate 70 was blasted out of a mountainside in order to avoid ripping up the Clear Creek Valley, therefore protecting the ruins of the engineering marvel.

This now-popular summer excursion train stops at the 1870s Lebanon Mine for a tour of the underground mine and 1970s restorations of the 1870s Lebanon Mill, the office of mine manager Julius Pohle, a change room, and a blacksmith shop. The restored mine and railroad serve as the centerpieces of the Georgetown–Silver Plume National Historic Landmark District.

Jackson's photo site was obvious, but it posed difficult and dangerous challenges. A drive up to and past the Georgetown terminus of the Georgetown Loop Railroad took me to this vantage point. Unfortunately, since Jackson's day, the rocky hillside had been excavated to make way for a new road up to the Georgetown train station. Jackson had stood on a part of the hill to the left of what remains.

In order to reproduce his photograph as faithfully as possible, I had to set up my $5,000 view camera much too close for comfort to the edge of the 50-foot cliff above the road. I adjusted my camera tripod's legs to allow it to sit squarely on the brink of the cliff. However, the only way in which I could take the photograph with my head beneath the black cloth and make all of the adjustments necessary on a view camera—focus, tilt, and swing—was to lean out into space over the cliff. And that precarious positioning could only be achieved with my wrist and hand locked around Eric's wrist and hand, which left one hand free to work the camera. Not an easy thing to do. One slip on either of our parts and we'd lose the camera, and most likely our lives! The only good thing about this shoot was the fact that the train actually stopped on the trestle long enough for me to be deliberate in composing the photograph.

19

GEORGETOWN

1901

pp. 38–39

TN   Thanks partly to the Colorado Historical Society's efforts, Interstate 70 cuts into the mountainside northwest of town instead of through the vintage silver city of Georgetown. Consequently, Georgetown has been widely acclaimed as a model for historic preservation. You can still find approximately 200 of the buildings in Jackson's 1901 photo in Georgetown today.

Georgetown's genteel and stable ambiance began in 1860 with town founder George Griffith. He brought his wife and family to settle in "George's Town." Griffith also encouraged other families to settle, supposedly by offering free town lots to respectable women. Women, as Griffith reckoned, fancied a civilized community with painted houses, gardens, churches, schools, an opera house, and other refinements that distinguish Georgetown from the usual ramshackle mining town.

In 1860, Griffith discovered gold near where the Griffith Mine portal still stands at the east end of 11th Street. Georgetown boomed as Colorado's first silver city after the 1864 discovery of the Belmont Lode and became the supply town for many surrounding silver-mining districts. After the Silver Crash of 1893, Georgetown shrank and has seen little new construction since.

From a peak population of some 3,300 in the 1880s, Georgetown dwindled to an all-time low of 301 in 1950. Since then, the population has climbed back to 1,088. A private preservation group that formed in the 1970s, Historic Georgetown, Inc., enacted one of Colorado's first and toughest local preservation ordinances. To keep development from creeping up the surrounding mountainsides, in the 1980s the town bought out a developer angling to build condominiums along Guanella Pass Road. Since the 1970s, Georgetown has lost only two of 211 19th-century structures in its downtown historic district.

Another key to Georgetown's preservation has been its four fire stations (although the Catholic church at the lower right corner of Jackson's photo burned down). One of these, the Alpine Hose Station, a tall, white tower, stands in the center of both photos. Thanks to the vigilant "fire lads" therein, Georgetown has Colorado's highest percentage of surviving 19th-century frame structures.

Can you find the Georgetown Loop trestle in both photographs (see Photo Pair 18)? How many buildings can you find that are common to both? Jackson photographed from a little bit higher on the hill to the east of town than I did. Unfortunately (but not in the sense of biological integrity), many trees have grown up since Jackson visited Georgetown, and my view from his photo location was obscured. Still, the vantage point provides a great view of this historic town, looking west up Clear Creek.

Examine the hillsides in both photographs. Do you see how many more trees exist today? This disparity proved typical across Colorado. Why? One reason is that in Jackson's day, seemingly every tree in sight was cut for building material, firewood, and other purposes, especially close to towns. Another is the fact that no one suppressed forest fires in the 19th century. Then Smoky the Bear came along in the 20th century and encouraged fire prevention, and old-growth forests have never been the same. That's right, fire actually improves the health of a forest and promotes old-growth ecosystems, which differ biologically in many ways from the ecosystems of secondary-growth forests.

20

CLEAR CREEK COUNTY

Grays and Torreys Peaks, circa 1883

pp. 40–41

Grays (14,270') and Torreys (14,267') peaks both bear the names of distinguished 19th-century botanists who visited Colorado. They were originally named Twin Peaks until another botanist, Charles C. Parry, went on a peak-naming rampage. Dr. John Torrey did not even make his first trip to Colorado until 1872 at the ripe old age of 86, several years after Parry had honored him with the naming. In the 1860s, Torrey's friends and admirers founded the Torrey Botanical Society, the country's oldest society dedicated to botanical study still in operation today.

Asa Gray is known as the father of American botany. He is said to have dominated American taxonomy more than any other botanist, and for a time Gray worked closely with Torrey on various flora projects. Gray also paid his first visit to Colorado in 1872, in his case at the age of 62. Along with Parry and friends, Gray and his wife climbed the peak named after him and celebrated by singing the national anthem when they reached the top. Gray was a close friend of Charles Darwin and a major supporter of his views. Charles Parry also named two Colorado peaks after himself (why not enjoy some of the spoils?), a peak after his wife, Eva, and another after botanist George Engelmann.

Grays and Torreys peaks' proximity to Denver and Interstate 70, along with their status as "Fourteeners," make them popular hikes. Many people attempt to climb all 54 of Colorado's 14,000-foot-high mountains, and these two offer a quick and relatively easy trip. Straddling the Continental Divide, the peaks offer views extending as far as other Fourteeners, including Mount of the Holy Cross, Mount Lincoln, and Longs Peak.

 Eric and I parked at the Bakerville trailhead, from which most folks begin their ascent of these two well-known Fourteeners. One-and-a-half miles up the trail, the ridges in the mid-ground began to line up with those in the background as they do in the Jackson photograph. I was able to find this relatively obscure place in less than five minutes once I was in the general vicinity. However, I goofed while making this photograph. I should have stepped back another 10 feet in order to duplicate exactly Jackson's image area. Nevertheless, notice that many of the rocks in the creek have remained in the same position since Jackson was there. Imagine that. After 115 years, neither weather nor earthquake has dislodged these alpine rocks.

Obviously, Jackson photographed Grays and Torreys a bit earlier in the summer than I did — there's more snow on the peaks. Though I usually came close to capturing Jackson's scenes at the correct time of year, finding and rephotographing 300 places in less than nine months precluded perfection.

Colorado 1870 - 2000 Revisited

Northern Front Range Locations

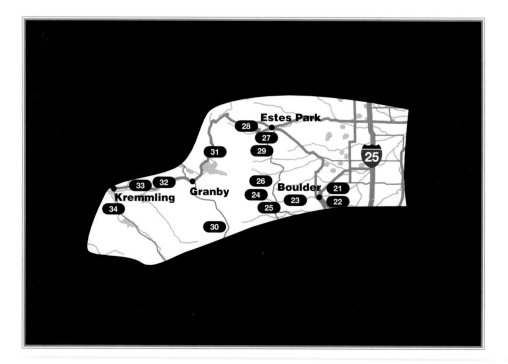

Northern
Front
Range

21

BOULDER

1900

pp. 46–47

(Please see Colorado 1870–2000 *for the complete series of photographs.)*

TN   As these views show, Boulder has protected its foothills from development. As early as the 1890s, the town began acquiring outlying open space to build a mountain park system. By a 35-to-1 margin, voters approved a bond issue to set aside 171 acres for a Chautauqua complex surrounded by Boulder's first mountain park. Chautauqua Park's open meadow lies between the town and the foothills, as seen in both panels. Today, the town enjoys more than 7,500 acres of mountain parks, allowing Boulderites to walk, bike, or cross-country ski from their homes to mountain recreation.

The domed 1883 Boulder County Courthouse in Jackson's photo above burned down in 1932 and a lower, modern building replaced it. Fielder's photo captures some of the town's landmarks, such as the First Congregational Church with its distinctive square crenelated corner tower, and the Hotel Boulderado, featuring four corner towers. Trinity English Lutheran Church stretches from Fielder's panel two into panel three on the far left, where the square towers of St. John's Episcopal Church are also prominent. Thanks to Boulder's downtown historic districts and height ordinance, churches dominate the city skyline rather than the usual high-rise offices and penthouses.

Boulder's only downtown high-rise (in Fielder's left and central panels) is the nine-story Colorado Building at 14th and Walnut streets. It inspired a 1971 citizens' initiative establishing a 55-foot height limit for downtown buildings. Boulder further strove to preserve its small-town scale by converting Pearl Street to a pedestrian mall in the 1970s. The mall district focuses on preserving historic architecture, public spaces, and mountain views.

Boulder Canyon cuts through the foothills in the left-hand panels. This scenic route of Boulder Creek is protected by several Boulder mountain parks, including Eben G. Fine Park and Boulder Falls Park. Boulder's prized and protected foothills setting also gave the town its logo, the Flatirons, the vertically tilted stone slabs seen in the panel above.

Eric knew Boulder better than I, so he took the driver's seat to find this panorama looking south toward the Flatirons. There exists an escarpment in the vicinity of 19th and Alpine streets just northeast of the downtown area. The high point of this ridge delivered us to a nursing home, the Terrace Heights Care Center. Using the "stealth" search technique (during which, in the interest of saving time, we would explore first and ask questions, such as seeking permission, later), we quickly climbed onto the roof and set up the camera. After making a couple of Polaroids, it was clear that we were too high up and too far to the east of Jackson's location. It was also evident that this ridge was undeveloped in 1900 and that Jackson had unobstructed views with which to work.

We descended one street to High. Driving very slowly and peering in between each home toward landmarks in the distance, eventually we found the correct latitude. I knocked on the door of the home at that point, and the owner greeted us cordially. I explained who I was and what I was doing, and that I wanted to climb onto his roof to make a photograph. He answered back that he already knew who I was and owned several of my nature photography books. This proved not to be the last time during 1998 that my reputation preceded me and facilitated fast work — and for that I was grateful.

22

BOULDER

*Chautauqua
Auditorium, 1900*

p. 48

TN The 1898 Chautauqua Auditorium dominates both photographs, but in Fielder's view, trees obscure the Chautauqua cottages, which still exist although the tent residences are gone. Chautauqua was a national program originating in Chautauqua, New York, where the first of these educational halls opened in 1874. The Seneca Indian word "chautauqua" ("moccasins tied together") came from the peculiar shape of Lake Chautauqua. Chautauqua halls and residences sprang up across the country to provide lectures and courses for adults hungry for education and culture. By 1898, more than 150 Chautauquas dotted the country. Boulder capitalized on its cool, sunny climate to entice schoolteachers to its Chautauqua summer school.

To lure the long-skirted schoolmarms, Boulder donated land, constructed permanent buildings, and laid a streetcar line out to Chautauqua. In exchange, the teachers promised summers of entertainment and education to Boulder's citizens at no charge.

The Chautauqua Auditorium and Dining Hall were built in 45 days, opening on July 4, 1898. Four thousand celebrants heard seven hours of speeches from 17 orators, including Colorado Governor Alva B. Adams and Boulder Mayor Crockett Ricketts. Subsequent programs featured William Jennings Bryan, the Reverend Billy Sunday, and Senator Robert LaFollette, as well as John Philip Sousa's band. Silent movies first screened at Chautauqua in 1918. To this day, programs include a Silent Film Series with live musical accompaniment, lectures on current issues, as well as the Colorado Music Festival, which has made the Boulder Chautauqua its home since 1978. This June-to-August program attracts nationally prominent classical musicians who offer a popular concert series in the antique wooden hall. Chautauqua also hosts its own Summer Festival, with an eclectic group of international, gospel, and acoustic artists, special family-oriented entertainment, and even big bands. The Dining Hall, noted for fine views and fine food, is now open year-round.

In 1990, the National Trust for Historic Preservation honored the Colorado Chautauqua Association and the City of Boulder for restoring one of the few surviving Chautauqua facilities and for offering, as in Chautauqua's glory days, edifying public programs.

Eric led the way to Chautauqua Park on the south end of town. A brisk hike up the Boulder Open Space trail south of the auditorium, followed by a scramble through ponderosa pines to the top of the ridge, got us to the place where Jackson must have been standing. Unfortunately, we could barely see the auditorium through the trees. The bare ridge of Jackson's day was later planted with trees and has grown into forest. Because we had to descend back to the trail and make the photograph there, the perspective is different in my scene.

In the process of finding the real location, an interesting thing happened. Jackson's image actually formed half of a two-part panorama. The left-hand panel (not pictured in *Colorado 1870–2000*) contained an old and uniquely shaped ponderosa that we had looked for but did not find while searching for Jackson's location. At least not until I spied on the ground a dismembered tree that had died perhaps 10 years before, fallen over, and begun to rot and break apart. I looked at the tree in Jackson's photograph one more time, then reassembled in my mind what remained of the tree on the ground. It was Jackson's tree! Once alone on that ridge, today it lies at the feet of generations of trees.

Take a look at the previous Boulder panorama (see Photo Pair 21). In the middle image, on the far left below two hills that look like a camel's humps, you can see the auditorium and the bare ridge from which Jackson photographed.

23

BOULDER COUNTY

Boulder Falls, 1902

p. 49

TN Astonishingly, Fielder almost exactly duplicated Jackson's photo taken 98 years earlier. Even some of the ponderosa pine and spruce trees are the same, as well as the rocks in the stream. The area has been well preserved since 1919, when Boulder banker Charles Buckingham donated Boulder Falls and its environs to Boulder City as a park.

Buckingham was one of many inspired by the falls and jubilant Boulder Creek. After an 1878 horseback ride through Boulder Canyon, Helen Hunt Jackson compared it in her book *Bits of Travel at Home* to "a joyous outburst of the soul of Beethoven or Mozart." Of her 16-mile ride from "Nederland Meadows" to "Bowlder City," she wrote, "Bowlder people [are] lucky not in that gold and silver are brought down to their streets every day, but that they can walk of an afternoon up into Bowlder Canyon."

Among the marvels of Boulder Canyon was a shapely specimen spruce that for decades attracted tourist pilgrims who congregated worshipfully at the base of the "perfect" tree. Critics blasting modern-day Boulder environmentalists as tree huggers forget that earlier generations also loved trees, coming to picnic and play and photograph at the spruce until it toppled into the creek in 1998.

JF The drive to Nederland from Boulder on State Highway 119 up Middle Boulder Creek is spectacular. Along the way, a parking lot serves as a jump-off point for the short hike to the falls, a cinch to find. The joy of rephotographing this scene derived from just how little change had occurred during the intervening 96 years. Nevertheless, establishing solid footing for the tripod proved a challenge, as the hillside on which Jackson stood above the creek has eroded.

So many perspective clues with which to pinpoint Jackson's spot still existed! Notice the two large ponderosa pines on the left, and the standing dead one in my photograph that still thrives in his. How about the rocks in the creek that are still there despite the fact that numerous flash floods must have violently rushed through the canyon since 1902? Still, a perceptive eye can discern that Jackson actually stood a couple of feet to the right of where I did. Can you find the clues that prove this?

24

BOULDER COUNTY

Caribou, 1885

pp. 50–51

TN   Traces of the old street grid and two stone shells of the Potosi Mine Boarding House complex linger at the site of Caribou, about 6 miles northwest of Nederland. Most Caribou buildings had to be braced against the wind, but not the town's only three-story structure, the Sherman House, the large white frame structure dominating Jackson's work. This sturdy hotel and an instant silver town sprang up soon after *Caribou Post* editor Amos Bixby reported in 1870, "In a few weeks after the snow had disappeared there were from 300 to 400 hardy prospectors on the ground."

After a brief mid-1870s boom, Caribou shriveled and began to blow away, even though buildings were braced on their east sides against the 100-mile-an-hour gusts roaring down from the Great Divide. Caribou residents joked that summer lasted two days and winter three years. In winter, residents climbed through second-story windows over the snowdrifts that buried one-story buildings.

The Sherman House, erected in 1875, became the town's social center, offering lyceum lectures and Caribou Silver Coronet Band performances. Townsfolk opened a school and a Methodist church and, in 1881, persuaded the city fathers to close the notorious Shoo Fly Saloon and run its prostitutes out of town. These enterprising ladies set up shop a few miles down Middle Boulder Creek at Cardinal, where red lights and scarlet women were welcome.

Caribou's church, school, and moral ways could not save it from the Silver Crash of 1893. Major fires in 1879, 1899, and 1905, as well as a 1903 earthquake, finished the town. After peaking with an 1880 population of 549, Caribou declined to 44 by 1900 and became a ghost town in the 1920s. Survivors moved down Coon Track Creek into Nederland. Nowadays, only a few tourists prowl the dead silver camp, scrutinizing the stone ruins of the Potosi Mine Boarding House and the cemetery where former residents slumber, free at last from Caribou's chilly winds.

JF I knew that Jim Guercio, ex-drummer of the defunct rock band Chicago, owned a place called Caribou Ranch, but did not know that an old mining town named Caribou existed in the 19th century. County Road 128 ascends to treeline about 6 miles from Nederland's northern edge. By looking at my photograph, except for the two stone ruins, you would never guess that a town once existed there. Yet, when silver was king, it boomed.

Looking back to the east from the valley floor, Eric and I determined that we must climb a steep, rocky hill covered with trees. Once on top, we found Jackson's approximate location, though we had to shift about 10 feet to the side, thanks to the obligatory new tree blocking the view. Can you find clues that prove we missed our mark?

Notice how nature has reclaimed this valley with an alpine willow wetland. Do you rejoice in that as I do? As photo editor of the project, I could pick and choose which of the 300 pairs made it into the book. I did not always want the images to manifest significant change, but also no change, and change for the better, between centuries.

25

NEDERLAND

Nederland Park, 1885

pp. 52–53

TN   Barker Reservoir now replaces Jackson's view of Middle Boulder Creek and the pioneer valley ranches of Nederland. The town hugs the western shore of the reservoir, with Lake Eldora Ski Area visible on a hill beyond the lake.

Nederland was initially known as Dayton, then Brownsville or Brown's Crossing for pioneer innkeeper Nathan Brown. It was christened Middle Boulder when the post office opened in 1871. After the Nederland Mining Company purchased the town and its mill in 1873, it incorporated and renamed the town Nederland.

During the early 1900s, tungsten mining triggered Nederland's greatest boom. Nederland's old silver mill was retooled as the Wolf Tongue Mill, named for a combination of two names for the same ore, "wolframite" and "tungsten." It and several other tungsten mills hummed night and day during World War I, when the demand skyrocketed for this mineral used to harden steel armaments. With the end of the war in 1918, the tungsten market collapsed. Nederland's wartime population of more than 1,000 fell to 291 by 1920.

Construction of Barker Dam in 1909 created Barker Reservoir, to the delight of fishermen, boaters, and sightseers. The Nederland Fish and Game Club stocked the lake with 50,000 trout and the nearby woods with elk relocated from Wyoming. A rail line, the Switzerland Trail, brought in tourists by the trainload. Sightseers flocked to the town — which puffed itself as "cloudland" — not only by rail but in a fleet of Stanley Steamer Mountain Wagons. After a 1919 flood again washed out much of the trackage, the Switzerland Trail was never rebuilt. To smooth the way for automobile tourists, Boulder Canyon Road was widened and straightened by laborers from the Colorado State Penitentiary.

Unlike most mountain mining towns that boomed in the 1800s and busted in the 1900s, Nederland got a second wind when its tungsten-mining era began in 1900. Nederland's population, just 182 in 1900, has climbed to more than 1,394 residents a century later.

Not knowing Boulder and its environs well (until this project, most of my Colorado explorations took me to remote places, away from the Front Range), I had no idea that I would find Barker Reservoir covering the valley that Jackson had photographed. The joy of discovery! The reservoir stores water for Boulder and makes electricity for what was once called Public Service Company of Colorado (now Xcel Energy).

Because the valley and Middle Boulder Creek have disappeared here, the only perspective clues remaining were the ridge intersection points in the background. The peaks in the distance were overexposed in Jackson's photograph and unavailable as points of reference (his film emulsions inherently had more contrast than ours, so clouds and snow-capped peaks often disappeared in his photographs); therefore, determining where to stand could have been problematic. However, above the valley there exists a certain narrow rock outcrop with only one small area appropriate for placing a tripod. It was clearly Jackson's location. His habit of finding flat rocks on which to set up his camera again saved the day!

26

BOULDER COUNTY

Long Lake and Snowy Range, 1901

pp. 54–55

MP Tucked high against the Continental Divide, Isabelle Glacier remains one of Colorado's few true glaciers. Isabelle hugs the shady north slopes in the core of the Indian Peaks (which Jackson called the Snowy Range) above Long Lake. Only a few of the hardier fragments of such once-mighty glaciers cling tenuously to these high basins. They are the survivors of our most recent "mini" Ice Age, the so-called Little Ice Age, which ended about 200 years ago.

The sweeping, U-shaped valleys of the Indian Peaks are the characteristic signatures of glaciers. Just 10,000 years ago, rivers of ice thousands of feet deep filled these mountain valleys. Only rugged points of gneiss and schist — arêtes, horns, and nunataks, in the parlance of geologists — rose above these shimmering ice sheets.

The rock itself is unimaginably ancient. The geologic strata comprising the Front Range and the Indian Peaks formed from molten rock buried deep within the Earth's crust more than 1.5 billion years ago. For eons the rocks remained unrevealed until the initial uplifted folding of the Rocky Mountains between 65 and 50 million years ago. But these high peaks didn't reach their present lofty elevations until 28 to 10 million years ago, when a region-wide uplift raised them 5,000 feet higher. The immense pressures and temperatures of these mountain-building events reshaped the rock into the banded gneiss and layered schist we see today.

At the end of the glacial retreat 10,000 years ago, high-elevation Engelmann spruce and subalpine fir forests slowly took hold on the barren landscape of ice-scoured rock. Fires burn rarely in these cool, damp forests, and natural events that replace vast stands of timber are uncommon for spruce and fir — unlike the hotter and drier lodgepole pine forests at lower elevations susceptible to vast conflagrations. Historically, the spruce-fir forests likely succumbed only to Mother Nature's least-noticed creatures, the insect world. Infrequent epidemics of spruce beetles might have occasionally stripped the forests, resetting the ecological clock with new generations of shade-tolerant spruce trees sprouting in the midst of insect-denuded trunks.

While these subalpine forests appear little changed in structure in the past century-and-a-half, drastic change overtook their native inhabitants. The howl of the wolf reverberates through the Indian Peaks no more, and grizzly bears no longer search out summer berries or dig for marmots high on the tundra. European settlement meant extermination of species that vied for dominance in these wilderness ecosystems, especially those that preyed on valued domestic livestock.

JF The rephotography project was the catalyst for my first visit to Long Lake during my 30 years of living in Colorado. As I explained before, I did not photograph in the Front Range until the last few years. Since then, I've scoured Rocky Mountain National Park, the James Peak area, and portions of the Indian Peaks Wilderness in the effort to produce books about the park and the Continental Divide National Scenic Trail, which straddles part of the Front Range.

What a beautiful place! The quarter-mile hike from the parking lot led us to the east side of the lake from which Jackson photographed. Though nothing in the mid-ground or foreground provided perspective clues as to where he stood, the many ridges and unique rock landmarks in the background helped us reach lateral exactness. The final goal was to include enough land in front of the lake to achieve the proper earth-to-water proportion.

Notice that the snow patterns are nearly identical in both photographs. Throughout the project, I attempted to duplicate not only place, but also season and time of day. Sometimes I got lucky and other qualities fell into place, too.

27

ESTES PARK

St. Mary's Lake, 1901

pp. 56–57

TN St. Mary's Lake, a small natural lake 3 miles southwest of Estes Park, has become a much larger artificial reservoir. Tourists now arrive in SUVs instead of by horse-drawn carriages.

Now known as the uncanonized Marys Lake, it was transformed by the Colorado–Big Thompson Water Project, which diverts water from Grand Lake and the Colorado River headwaters under Rocky Mountain National Park to Estes Park and the Front Range. Water flows through the Alva B. Adams Tunnel under the park and emerges at an eastern portal. From there it is channeled into Marys Lake Power Plant. Completed on the western edge of Marys Lake in 1948, the plant generates electricity for Estes Park and the environs. Above the pines in the left of the Fielder photo, some of the hydroelectric powerlines are visible.

Started in 1938 and finished in 1959, the Colorado–Big Thompson Water Project did not lack critics. The Wilderness Society, in a May 1, 1937, bulletin, urged "all lovers of wilderness, defenders of primeval national parks, the President and government of the United States, Congress, and the people to resist to the utmost…misuse of Rocky Mountain National Park in the interest of beet growing in the South Platte Valley of Colorado. To drive a tunnel through Rocky Mountain National Park for conveyance of irrigating water from west to east of the Continental Divide will not only rob the park of primeval character, but will by the Congressional precedent, open every American National Park to commercial use."

The Sierra Club, the American Society of Landscape Architects, and others fought the project in Washington, D.C. Frederick Law Olmsted, Jr., the nation's leading park planner and landscape architect, scoffed at the engineers of the U.S. Bureau of Reclamation who claimed that the tunnel would be "totally innocuous to National Park values." Olmsted argued that parks were sacred places whose primeval nature should extend "downward to the center of the earth and indefinitely upward to the sky."

Such objections did not stop what became the fourth-largest New Deal U.S. Bureau of Reclamation project, surpassed only by California's Central Valley Project, Arizona's Hoover Dam, and Washington's Grand Coulee Project.

Marys Lake is next to State Highway 7, southwest of Estes Park. We found this location easily, and I was able to duplicate Jackson's photograph almost exactly. Plenty of the same rocks remained in the foreground, and lines and ridges added to the wealth of clues. I even convinced Eric to stand where Jackson's friend had stood. (Eric is an accomplished rock climber, a talent that served this project well on many occasions.) I often tried to reenact the "moment" captured in Jackson's photographs, so where he placed a vehicle or person, I added one, too.

Notice that a lot more water fills the lake today than in Jackson's day, a result of the damming by the Colorado–Big Thompson Water Project.

28

ROCKY MOUNTAIN
NATIONAL PARK

*Ypsilon Peak from
Sprague's Ranch, Estes
Park, 1901*

pp. 58–59

MR The glaciated peaks, gorges, alpine lakes, high meadows, and expansive valleys now preserved as Rocky Mountain National Park have made for a grand and stunning wilderness since the retreat of the glaciers that formed them some 15,000 years ago. With the arrival of Western poineers in the mid-1800s, this wilderness finally ran up against civilization and its attendant hazards.

The wilderness amazed and delighted early Euro-American settlers, and in time, they built resorts and guest ranches to cater to vacationers. Estes Park settler Abner Sprague arrived in 1864 from the Midwest; finally, in 1875, he claimed his homestead at what is now Moraine Park. He discovered over time that tourism was a better use of the land than cattle ranching, and more profitable than prospecting. Sprague became a successful resort developer at Moraine Park and later at Glacier Basin. (After the National Park Service acquired the Sprague ranches, the buildings were all removed and the land reverted to its former wild state.)

Concerned settlers in the young town of Estes Park saw firsthand both the unique and precious quality of their neighboring wilderness and its lure to tourists and commercial interests alike. One hundred years ago, this wilderness was being considered for a forest reserve or national forest but had already been harnessed into commercial development. Dams and scarring water-diversion projects small and large, like the Grand Ditch at Never Summer Range, were common; cattle ranching was popular; logging interests weren't far behind.

Enos Abijah Mills loved Longs Peak and the surrounding wilderness with the zeal of a convert. Born in eastern Kansas in 1870, Mills was a sickly child who decided at age 14 to "take the cure" in the Western mountains he'd heard of in gold-rush tales but never seen. Homesteading at the foot of Longs Peak in 1885, young Mills came to adore the natural beauty and wildlife in his midst. In winter, he traveled the West, working as a plains cowboy and Montana miner, and chanced to meet Yosemite conservationist John Muir in a visit to California. Muir strongly impressed the young homesteader and urged him to work to save the Western forests.

His health restored, Mills took up as his life's work the cause of preserving the area around Longs Peak. He introduced many visitors to the splendors of the land during climbs up Longs Peak and other mountains. A naturalist, mountain guide, and innkeeper at first, he became an author, photographer, lecturer, and wilderness conservation proponent. Despite commercial opposition, Rocky Mountain National Park was established, aided greatly by the ceaseless campaigns of Enos Mills, in 1915. Many had become convinced that "from the wilderness the traveler returns a man, almost a superman," as Mills wrote in *Your National Parks*.

Rocky Mountain National Park exists because of the efforts of Enos Mills and others to extol the virtues of a great public preserve. Thanks to the work of later park supporters in the 1930s, the Colorado–Big Thompson Water Diversion Project that traverses the park and irrigates the state's arid Front Range and Eastern Plains operates underground with hardly a trace. Today, numerous ski resorts and other backcountry development across the rest of Colorado's mountains only amplify the pristine glory of the park. No wonder, then, it remains a premier tourist destination. This long-lived popularity creates many challenges: Sustainable use, funding, education, transportation, and the effects of population growth are among the many concerns of today's national park supporters in light of an ever-increasing number of visitors.

JF Today, Sprague's Ranch in Rocky Mountain National Park is called Moraine Park, a well-known and much-visited destination. With spectacular views of the Front and Mummy ranges, one can achieve inner peace quite naturally while savoring the beauty of this place where both Jackson and I stood. I was lucky to have made the photograph at all, given my state of mind at the time!

Find my perspective clues. Several of the same rocks still rest in the creekbed, and one tree along the banks is still there. I'll give you a hint: Not much of it remains. And I've replaced Jackson's four-horse-power stagecoach with my own 250-horsepower Chevrolet Suburban. Yuck!

29

ROCKY MOUNTAIN NATIONAL PARK

The Climb to the Top of Longs Peak, 1901

pp. 60–61

(Please see Colorado 1870–2000 *for the complete series of photographs.)*

THE BOULDER FIELD AND LONGS PEAK.

MR   For those heading west over the plains, the stately eastern face of 14,255-foot Longs Peak near the Front Range has always beckoned. Major Stephen H. Long, the peak's namesake, led the first official expedition down the South Platte River to the foothills of the Rockies in 1820. A stunning valley and entry-point into what is now Rocky Mountain National Park, Estes Park has been a spectacular showcase for Longs Peak, which in turn has held a special allure for mountaineers.

An ascent up the mountain's austere and fearful east face, with its 2,500-foot sheer vertical wall called The Diamond, was seldom attempted and even prohibited for decades. The long, meandering, and walkable western route to the summit, commonly followed during the last 130 years, has had its own perils, however. William H. Jackson's early images show the traditional summit route as it passes across an expanse called the Boulderfield and through a unique rock formation known as the Keyhole at more than 13,000 feet in elevation.

Early mountain guide Carlyle Lamb, Enos Mills' mentor, led many visitors to the summit of Longs Peak. In September 1884, one such vacationer, Carrie J. Welton, was descending from the summit with Lamb when she collapsed near the Keyhole. Lamb returned with a rescue party, too late to save her life. In January 1925, Denver businesswoman Agnes Vaille and a Swiss mountaineering companion made a remarkable ascent up the east face of the mountain. Vaille's feat became a tragedy when she succumbed to cold and fatigue on the descent, her companion was disfigured by frostbite, and a member of her rescue team perished. A rock-walled storm shelter, visible in the left mid-ground of Fielder's repeat photograph, still stands near the Keyhole in her memory.

Still others have lost their lives in falls, lightning strikes, and accidents. Nevertheless, the national park's lone Fourteener continues to attract traditional and technical climbers. Of 3.4 million people who visited Rocky Mountain National Park in 2000, about 15,000 attempted and 8,000 succeeded in attaining the summit of Longs Peak.

 Our first attempt to rephotograph all five Jackson scenes from his 1901 climb of Longs Peak ended in frustration during the last week of August 1998. We had planned to do a backpacking trip, including one night out under the stars at the Boulderfield Campground, a primitive group of clearings for tents in a square-mile cirque of talus. We planned to make the first two photographs on day one, and the other three on the next day. We achieved the first goal, but not the second—that night 6 inches of snow fell. Clouds covered the peak for the most of the morning, so we gave up and went home. The climb is steep, and with 60 pounds of camera gear, I did not want to be skunked out of a photograph after making the effort to reach 14,255 feet in elevation.

Eric and I returned on a gorgeous, 70-degree day in late September, this time on a one-day trip. We departed the trailhead at 6:30 a.m. and quickly achieved the Boulderfield, somewhat of a halfway point for mileage (it's about 8 miles to the top of Longs), but nowhere near halfway for the time it takes to ascend the peak. I would guess that 1 billion rocks fill the Boulderfield, and our first job was to find any one of those in the foreground of Jackson's photograph. By walking around until the ridges on Longs aligned with one another correctly, we got within striking distance. Astonishingly, we succeeded in 10 minutes, thanks to the ridge trick. Soon we found the specific rocks and Jackson's exact location.

On the other hand, we never did find the exact foreground rocks in the photograph of the Keyhole. Perhaps a rockslide had changed the lay of the land. Soon after lunch, Eric exacerbated an injured toe, so I was left to climb Longs Peak by myself with every bit of the load of camera equipment we had planned to split between us on the way to the top. You don't see too many folks with large packs on top of Longs. It's pointless as no camping is allowed past the Boulderfield, and common sense dictates otherwise.

Nevertheless, at 2 p.m. I summited and proceeded to recruit a man from Chicago to stand on the promontory where Jackson's model stood. After enjoying one of the greatest 360-degree views on the planet, I headed down to meet Eric and return to the trailhead parking lot. We arrived at 6:30 p.m., 12 hours after our departure, and several pounds lighter from the "quick" jaunt up Longs.

30

BERTHOUD PASS

North from, 1874

p. 62

TN Edward L. Berthoud, an engineer and surveyor in Golden, blazed an 1861 toll road with mountain man Jim Bridger over this 11,315-foot pass. Their dirt road to Hot Sulphur Springs became a stage road in 1874 and the first paved road over the Continental Divide when U.S. Highway 40 was completed in 1938. The current two-lane highway offers beautiful views plus the excitement of hairpin curves and occasional avalanches and rockslides.

The Berthoud Pass Inn (1950) on U.S. Highway 40 atop Berthoud Pass was preceded by the first Berthoud Pass Inn, which L. D. C. Gaskill opened in 1876 as a stage stop. Berthoud Pass Ski Area, evidenced by the chairlift in the Fielder photo, boasted Colorado's first rope tow in 1937, followed by the first double-seat chairlift. During the 1940s, Berthoud attracted a third of Colorado's skiers; since then, newer and much larger ski resorts such as nearby Winter Park have dwarfed it.

As the rephotography project proceeded, witnessing the cumulative evidence of massive change in the character of Colorado's landscape since Jackson's day began to alter my consciousness. That fact, coupled with being away from my family for an average of 18 days a month, depressed me from time to time. Such a mind-set sometimes made me hope that the next landscape I sought would now be a nuclear waste dump. I began to want the then-and-now images to serve as a testament and warning to Coloradans that their state's sublime natural environment was being desecrated. At least, I felt that way on bad days.

On such days, when I knew that a place had the potential to manifest significant change, as I surmised might be the case at Berthoud Pass (I knew that a ski area exists there), I hoped that the conspicuous evidence would happen to appear in the middle of my scene. Often, I lucked out, as was the case with this photograph. I could find no rocks unturned by the grooming of the ski runs, but I did use the ridges of James Peak and the distant Front Range as clues to get me close to the correct location.

31

GRAND LAKE

Middle Park, before 1881

p. 63

GRAND LAKE, MIDDLE PARK.

TN   Picnic tables and boats have replaced the driftwood in the foreground of Jackson's photograph, but Grand Lake — the western gateway to Rocky Mountain National Park — remains a small, rustic town. It lies on the northwestern shore of Colorado's largest natural body of water, a 400-foot-deep, glacier-made bowl of sparkling water that reflects the surrounding mountains. The Utes, in awe of its white mists, called it Spirit Lake, or White Buffalo Lake. Its water was perfectly clear and drinkable before the U.S. Bureau of Reclamation built the adjacent Shadow Mountain Lake, a dirty, shallow reservoir. Water from Shadow Mountain Lake is pumped through Grand Lake and into the Alva B. Adams Tunnel, which runs under Rocky Mountain National Park (see Photo Pair 27).

Founded in 1879 as a mining settlement, the town of Grand Lake attracted hunters, fishermen, and prospectors. After Sir Thomas Lipton presented the Lipton Cup to the Grand Lake Yacht Club in 1912, it began hosting the world's highest yacht regatta. Now bypassed by the main highway, U.S. Highway 34, this end-of-the-road town retains rustic public buildings and private cabins. Most were constructed before 1929 of the straight, skinny lodgepole pines that still envelop this sleepy summer resort, with its sandy beach and a few new summer homes. Many of the finer structures cluster on the southwest edge of the town and along the lake, which is rimmed by picturesque boathouses of log and log-slab siding.

JT   Thank goodness it was April, a while before Grand Lake's busy summer season, when I initiated the search for this location. Jackson's photograph made it obvious that I should start looking on the west side of Grand Lake, a place now populated with summer homes. Once I had Mount Craig, the conspicuous mountain in the middle of the photograph, approximately in line, I began to hike through backyards near the lake's outlet to Shadow Mountain Lake. No one seemed to be home, so I ranged back and forth freely until one particular backyard allowed proper alignment of Mount Craig with the ridges to its left and right. I never did find the exact rocks in the foreground of Jackson's image, but was content to have a picnic table, dinghy, pleasure boat, and dock where there was once only a natural shoreline.

I was happy not to have been caught trespassing. During this project, I preferred to respect private property rights — for the most part. I would always try to locate the land- or homeowner before searching private property for a Jackson location. If no one was home, I'd sometimes take a quick peek at the lay of the land, just in case the location was obvious and close by, then make the photograph if I felt no one would be worse for wear. The Grand Lake location was such a place, so I decided to make the photograph and skedaddle.

A year-and-a-half later and a couple of months after the book was published, I visited the town of Granby, not far from Grand Lake, performing my *Colorado 1870–2000* slide show. There was a great turnout at the high school, and everyone seemed to enjoy my presentation that evening. After the show, a woman approached me with a compliment and the statement that she very much liked the photograph of her backyard. I asked her what she meant. She responded that she was glad to have provided the location from which I rephotographed Jackson's Grand Lake scene. I realized that I had just been caught trespassing! Nevertheless, there were no hard feelings, and she was delighted when I fulfilled her request for a complimentary autographed copy of the book.

32

HOT SULPHUR SPRINGS

Looking up the Grand River from the Hot Springs, Middle Park, 1874

pp. 64–65

TN Despite its large and proud American flag, the primitive bathhouse, inn, and hot springs plunge that Jackson found in 1874 are a virtually unrecognizable ancestor of today's far more developed resort. Explorer John C. Frémont camped here on his 1853 expedition. Frémont was followed by other Euro-Americans who took a dip in what the Utes called "The Big Medicine"—sulfur-scented water that comes out of the earth as hot as 120 degrees Fahrenheit. Ute legends credit the water's healing properties to an old chief who came here to die. With the Great Spirit's guidance, he built magic fires within the springs, then drank and bathed in what had become a fountain of rejuvenation.

Such magic attracted *Rocky Mountain News* founding editor William N. Byers, who built a log lodge here shortly after Jackson visited in 1874. Today's outdoor pool is supplemented by steam and soaking rooms built into the rocky hillside along U.S. Highway 40 and the Colorado River, both visible at the right of Fielder's photo.

JF I knew that this would be a fun and relatively easy photograph to remake. Hot Sulphur Springs was a popular place then and still is today. Next to U.S. Highway 40 between Granby and Kremmling, the town and accompanying resort are much different from the Hot Sulphur Springs of Jackson's day. A quick stop at the lodge produced the necessary permission to climb the hill to the west of the resort. It did not take long to get the ridges in the distance to align as they did in Jackson's vista. I made the photograph shown here, as well as two more that Jackson shot in other directions, from the top of the hill.

In Jackson's shot, the log structure and the American flag mark the old resort. However, another example of change — just as conspicuous as the new buildings — is the alteration in the stream ecology of the Grand River between 1874 and 1998. Not only has the name changed to the Colorado River, but the vegetation along the riverbanks has metamorphosed from willow bushes to the now-dominant cottonwoods. Why? After performing my slide show a few dozen times and expressing puzzlement about this botanical transformation, a couple of stream ecologists from the audience came to my rescue. Between the late 19th century and the present, farms and ranches claimed most of the water from Colorado's rivers and creeks. In Jackson's day, spring floods would uproot any tree saplings along the riverbanks, and in winter, sheets of ice floating downriver would sever them. River damming and water diversion for irrigation brought an end to the flooding, and an end to the inability of cottonwood trees to grow thick and tall.

33

GRAND COUNTY

Middle Park East from
Mt. Bross, 1874

p. 66

EP Jackson stood on the shoulder of 9,468-foot Mount Bross, a promontory just northwest of Hot Sulphur Springs not to be confused with the Fourteener of the same name in the Mosquito Range west of South Park. It appears that both summits bear the name of the same man, Illinois Lieutenant Governor William Bross, who owned land in Park County. Legend has it that Bross was so moved by the scenery and thin air atop the higher peak that he offered up a loud rendition of The Doxology so memorable that locals took to calling the place "Bross' Mountain."

Jackson climbed atop the lower Mount Bross less for inspiration than for work. Part of his job with the 1874 Hayden Survey was to photograph prominent landmarks and topographical features to illustrate the field notes and published accounts of other survey members. In this case, his aim was to record the view looking up the Grand (now Colorado) River, across rough pastures, through a broken hogback, to the misted peaks of the distant Front Range. The stone cairn in the foreground marked the earlier arrival of others who doubtless enjoyed the view — probably surveyors from Hayden's expedition and a handful of tourists who had made the long, slow wagon trip from Denver to relax in the pools of Hot Sulphur Springs.

The utility pole in Fielder's photograph commemorates another kind of visitor. Direct-current electricity reached Colorado in the 1880s, and by 1890 many towns featured small generators to light their streets and a few saloons. Early in the 1890s, a visionary German immigrant named L. L. Nunn, with advice and tactical support from George Westinghouse, installed the state's first alternating-current generator — a makeshift, water-powered affair — in a shack beside the San Miguel River at Ames. The stated purpose of the setup was to power motors at the Gold King Mine above Telluride. But it provided constant amusement for locals and visitors alike, who called the plant's operators "Pinheads" and rode out after church on Sundays to watch ferocious 6-foot sparks fly out when the generator was revved up for the week.

Alternating current was more practical than direct current for industrial and domestic use. Power companies extended the utility's reach across the state throughout the 20th century, consolidating local outfits to form giant corporations and replacing small generators with monumental power plants. But the pole in Fielder's photograph — with its tiny crossbar, guy lines to brace against wind or snow, and two lonesome wires — suggests how rural some parts of Colorado have remained.

JF　As much as hiking, skiing, and rafting are my preferred modes of travel, I've put in many hours behind the wheel driving around Colorado during the past 30 years. My highway skills are fine, but my four-wheeling skills are best. In the early days, when my photography was an avocation, I would spend short weekends and infrequent vacations learning how to pilot an SUV along the edges of cliffs and to the tops of mountains in order to see as much scenery as possible in relatively brief periods of time. Colorado's ubiquitous and intricate web of old mining roads allowed me to visit parts of the state that I wouldn't have seen on wilderness treks. Not as beautiful, but good nonetheless.

I recognized the valley in Jackson's photograph, as well as the gap through which the Colorado River flows, while driving U.S. Highway 40 to find the site of the Hot Sulphur Springs image (see Photo Pair 32). In fact, from the highway I spotted a large mountain directly north of the town, looming above the valley. I knew this mountain would be a good first place to investigate, if only I could find a way up other than climbing it. Don't get me wrong—I prefer hiking and climbing. However, Eric Bellamy and I had to find and rephotograph 300 places in less than nine months, and any opportunity we had to drive to a location would help increase our chances of achieving that goal. I extracted my trusty *DeLorme Colorado Atlas & Gazetteer* from between the seats of my Suburban, and, what do you know, there seemed to be a road to the top of Mount Bross. A quick ascension of County Road 20 led us to a host of unmarked, primitive roads. It took us a couple of wrong turns, but eventually we wound our way to the top of the mountain, where we parked just feet from the Jackson spot.

This view looks east. Not only was the rock cairn gone, but in the middle of the photograph stood a utility pole and related wires! In the distance, one can see U.S. Highway 40 and the Colorado River as it meanders through the valley. The cottonwood trees along the river must be the same ones as in the Hot Sulphur Springs photograph.

34

KREMMLING

*From the Mouth of the
Blue (River), Middle
Park, 1874*

p. 66

TN The town of Kremmling seems to magically appear in the distance of what was in 1874 a remote, unpeopled bend in the Colorado River. Kremmling did not materialize until 1885, originating as the general store of Kare Kremmling near the junction of the Blue and Colorado rivers. The 1905 arrival of the railroad stabilized Kremmling as a town. It remains the supply town for a large, sparsely settled area of hay and livestock ranches.

Notable buildings include the Dan Hoare Blacksmith Shop on the northeast corner of 2nd Street and Central Avenue, with shiplap siding and a false front. On 4th Street a half-block north of U.S. Highway 40, the 1904 McElroy Livery Stable, a well-maintained example of a log barn, faces the Kremmling Town Park. The two-story building has a gabled vent in the center of the roof ridge and a faded "LIVERY" sign on the front. The Grand County Historical Association acquired it in 1993 and converted it into a museum.

 As this northern view reveals, there was no town of Kremmling when Jackson passed through in 1874. In my version, it sits below the mesa in the distance. Wolford Mountain, the high point in the photographs, was the landmark clue for which to look, though Jackson's caption gave away his location. Unfortunately, the Blue River meets the Colorado River on private property. I drove south on State Highway 9 to County Road 1, which led to a private ranch road that I thought would provide access to the ridge on which Jackson stood. I proceeded down the road until I reached ranch headquarters.

I am a confirmed loner. Despite having a close family, a few good friends, and meeting thousands of people — with whom I share a biocentric appreciation for the miracle of 3.8 billion years of the evolution of life on Earth — I like being alone, doing things my way, and not asking for a whole lot of help. When people suggest places for me to photograph, I usually file the information away, preferring to discover new places spontaneously as I wander the planet. I found most of the Jackson locations without help by searching until I found the landscape features in his photographs.

Nevertheless, an element of community infuses this project. I met many wonderful Coloradans, often randomly, as I traced Jackson's footsteps. The drive down the ranch road near Kremmling led me to ranchowner Jim Yust, fresh off a tractor and looking at Eric and me as if we didn't belong in his driveway. I've always been quick to break a smile in such situations, especially when I need help. Jim smiled back and before long I learned that he had a passion for photography, knew of my work, and actually owned a few of my books. Small world. I took it as another sign that this project was meant to happen.

An hour later I was on the ridge where Jackson stood, now part of Jim's ranch, inspecting the change that occurred during the past 124 years. Notice that the river once made an oxbow to the north. Today, the river flows west, to the left and outside the range of my photograph. Another oxbow to the west of the area featured in Jackson's photograph probably converged with this one, severing the western oxbow and straightening the river's course.

Colorado 1870 - 2000 Revisited

Southern Front Range Locations

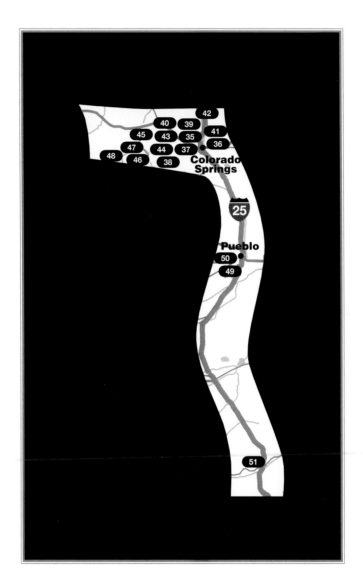

Southern
Front
Range

35

COLORADO SPRINGS

Colorado City and Cheyenne Mountain, 1873

p. 71

TN Colorado City is barely visible in both photos, under the eastern slope of Cheyenne Mountain. Established in 1859, Colorado City preceded its eastern neighbor, Colorado Springs. As El Paso County's first Anglo-American settlement, Colorado City rivaled Denver and briefly held the title of territorial capital. After the 1870s, it was eclipsed by Colorado Springs, which annexed it in 1917. Colorado City became a smelting center, processing most of the gold ore that poured out of Cripple Creek. Although the Golden Cycle Mill was dismantled in 1949, mountains of smelter waste at the base of the Golden Cycle smokestack, located on the south side of U.S. Highway 24 near 21st Street, remain Colorado City's most massive monument.

"None of the refined gold was left here," claimed William "Big Bill" Haywood, a labor organizer in Colorado during the early 1900s. Haywood described Colorado City as "a forlorn little industrial town of tents, tin houses, huts, and hovels, bordered by some of the grandest scenery in nature." Of some 6,500 remaining structures, about one-fourth are 19th-century working-class frame cottages. Many are protected by the Old Colorado City Historic District, roughly bounded by Colorado Avenue and Pikes Peak Avenue between 24th and 27th streets.

Cheyenne Mountain in the background is home to the Cheyenne Mountain Zoo. After a monkey from the Broadmoor Hotel menagerie bit a guest, the creature and its companions were moved to this nearby Cheyenne Mountain site. Founded in 1926, this zoo remains a first-rate small zoo, which takes special pride in its lively primate population.

On a northern promontory of Cheyenne Mountain stands the Will Rogers Shrine of the Sun, a five-story medieval tower of rough-faced granite, with buttressed corners and a crenelated parapet. Built in 1927, it brims with memorabilia honoring cowboy humorist Will Rogers. Neither the zoo nor the shrine is visible in these photos. Neither is the North American Air Defense Command, the U.S. military's nuclear bombing and missile launching center buried deep within Cheyenne Mountain.

JF Photographing other Jackson locations in Garden of the Gods City Park helped me find this one. The view east from the park reveals a long, north-south ridge along which I could see cars driving. When leaving the park to the east, Eric and I spied Mesa Road climbing up to the very place where we suspected we needed to begin the search. Unfortunately, when we arrived at what seemed to be a good longitude from which to start the search on foot, we found ourselves in the middle of the private Garden of the Gods Club parking lot. A quick reconnoiter to the club's backyard revealed that Jackson had in fact photographed from the ridge, but farther to the north in a place now hidden behind a high security fence.

I've never had much trouble getting the small things in life. Important things are more elusive — they require things like planning, hard work, and brains. However, a smile, a straight look deep into the eye sockets, and well-chosen words — part and parcel of the "force" I mentioned previously — always seems to get me past square one. In this case, the general manager of the club happily granted me access to the property in question, the club owners' beautiful estate. A week later, I found myself standing next to the swimming pool, in the middle of well-kept shrubbery, with my feet and tripod exactly where Jackson had placed his.

The only thing human-related in Jackson's scene is Colorado City and the precursor to North 30th Street. Note the Garden of the Gods Visitors Center and parking lot in the lower left of my photograph.

36

COLORADO SPRINGS

and Pikes Peak Range, 1894

pp. 72–73

(Please see Colorado 1870–2000 *for the complete series of photographs.)*

Pikes Peak Avenue in both photos leads the eye to its namesake mountain. Close comparison of the 1894 and 1998 photos reveals that little of 1894 Colorado Springs remains standing in this fast-growing town, Colorado's second-largest city. Not even the Denver & Rio Grande Railroad overpass survives. The D&RG, which created and nourished Colorado Springs, was the original main street. The larger buildings in the historic photos are clustered along or near the D&RG tracks.

Note the handsome three-story spire atop the old El Paso County Courthouse in the center of Fielder's left panel. When the county offices moved to the newer boxy buildings just to the north, the old courthouse was recycled as the Pioneers Museum, with extensive collections and exhibits on Colorado Springs.

Both photographers took these views from the Colorado School for the Deaf and Blind, with snow-capped Pikes Peak prevailing in the background. The school opened at 33 N. Institute St. in 1874. Jonathan R. Kennedy persuaded Colorado's territorial legislature to establish this school by showing them the abilities of his three deaf children. Colorado Springs founder General William J. Palmer donated this site, which boasts superb hilltop views.

JF Jackson's location proved especially hard to find, but only because I faked myself out! In the beginning, I failed to notice the church standing tall in the middle of the center photograph of Jackson's three-part panorama. It's still there today. But my worst mistake was yet to come. Notice the design of the wrought-iron fence in the foreground of the center and right-hand Jackson photographs. While initially cruising eastern Colorado Springs, Eric and I spied the same kind of fence in front of the Union Printers nursing home a little farther to the east and south of where we needed to be. The unique fence convinced us that this had to be the place, so we spent half a day making photographs and disturbing older folks (we took the first photographs from an occupied room on the fourth floor). Looking more closely, we discovered that the ridges of the foothills were slightly out of alignment with Pikes Peak. We had been seduced by a false lead.

A week later, we resumed exploring the eastern part of the city until we found a fence of the same design surrounding what was then and still is the Colorado School for the Deaf and Blind. Apparently, that fence was not unique to the Union Printers home. From the roof of the administration building, we remade Jackson's panorama. Notice the fence in the bottom right corner of my right-hand photograph. The building I stood atop replaced the one on which Jackson perched (it burned down in the early 1900s). As a result, I was closer to the scene and could not include the complete fence conspicuous in Jackson's photographs.

37

COLORADO SPRINGS

Broadmoor Casino, 1891

pp. 74–75

TN How the ever-resourceful William Henry Jackson elevated himself a hundred feet or so into the air for his 1891 bird's-eye view remains a mystery. A balloon? A now-gone tower of which no record remains? Levitation? After reviewing more than 100 historic photos of the Broadmoor complex, I have no clue how Jackson worked his magic. John Fielder, of course, could climb to the top of the International Convention Center added to the Broadmoor complex in 1961.

Jackson's photo captured the original resort opened in 1891 by Count James Pourtales, a wealthy German adventurer, at what had been the Broadmoor Dairy Farm. The main building, the count's Neoclassical Revival–style Broadmoor Casino, resembles a larger-than-life wedding cake sporting gobs of architectural frosting. Inside, the count offered European cuisine, fine wines, ballroom dancing, and Sunday afternoon concerts. Colorado Springs bluenoses blasted the Broadmoor as "a sunny place for shady people." Pourtales fired back with a letter to the *Colorado Springs Gazette* defending his Sunday "sacred music" concerts and pointing out that Christ himself changed water into wine.

Pourtales grew frustrated in his attempt to give Colorado Springs a fashionable resort and sold out to a wealthy Philadelphian, Spencer Penrose. Penrose, who made fortunes in both Cripple Creek gold and Utah copper, spent millions to make the Broadmoor Colorado's first world-class resort hotel.

As Fielder's photo shows, the 1918 Broadmoor Hotel now dominates the site with its various additions. Broadmoor South is the modern building in the center, with the rooftops of the spa and golf clubhouse peeking over the treetops. A steel skeleton ornately clad in terra-cotta and stucco with plaster trim constitutes the nine-story, 350-room main hotel. The Broadmoor originally boasted its own stock exchange, a doctor's office, Turkish baths, a squash court, and a little theater. To this day it remains Colorado's grande-dame hostelry, annually outclassing all rivals to capture a top honor, the Mobil Five-Star Award.

Close scrutiny of Cheyenne Mountain's foothills beyond the Broadmoor Golf Course reveals that the Broadmoor has sold off some of its once-vast holdings to make way for upscale luxury homes.

JF I've not been fortunate enough to have ever spent the night at the Broadmoor Hotel, but I have attended meetings there and have taken my family to its fabulous Easter brunch. So I knew about where I needed to be, but did not know if I could gain the elevation from which Jackson apparently made his image. As Tom Noel explains, maybe he rode in a balloon or climbed atop some sort of weather tower to get so high. A phone call to the hotel's general manager prompted his admonition that we had better bring climbing ropes! Eric Bellamy is a proficient rock climber, so I knew I had my man for this job.

The Broadmoor's convention center rises eight stories high, and our first visit revealed that its roof would be the spot from which to attempt to duplicate Jackson's purview. However, getting there was tricky. A necessary climb up a constricted, 60-foot-high iron ladder prevented me from carrying the camera gear on my back during the ascent. Therefore, Eric climbed up first, then lowered ropes for hauling up the gear. I trailed the gear. That first feat only got us into the ductwork and theatrical paraphernalia suspended high above the convention center stage. A crawl through dusty ventilation ducts and stage wires brought us to a 2-foot-square portal opening to the roof. Getting beyond the portal required squeezing our bodies between two large ducts, like cavers pushing through a tight passageway. This maneuver required as much strength and flexibility as any that Eric had used on cliff faces outdoors.

Our perch on the roof's southwest corner rewarded us with the opportunity to almost exactly duplicate Jackson's view. Notice that the ridges of Cheyenne Mountain in both photographs align nearly the same way. Our success was tempered only by the fact that before the project was completed, we would have to make the climb twice more to satisfy the needs of our Denver and Colorado Springs television partners.

38

COLORADO SPRINGS

Point Sublime, 1901

p. 76

(Please see Colorado 1870–2000 *for the complete series of photographs.)*

TN   Point Sublime was a photo opportunity on a rail line between Colorado Springs and Cripple Creek. Winfield Scott Stratton and other Cripple Creek gold kings built the Colorado Springs & Cripple Creek District Railway, popularly known as the "Short Line," in 1901. It brought Cripple Creek gold to Colorado Springs and Colorado Springs supplies and tourists to Cripple Creek. The railroad was taken out in 1923 and its roadbed became the Gold Camp Road, a scenic backroad to Cripple Creek. Winding, slow, and never entirely paved, it has remained the far-less-traveled alternative to the major automobile artery of U.S. Highway 24 and State Highway 67.

In Jackson's 1901 panel on the left, Colorado Springs is a small city of 22,000 occupying just the center of the scene. The right-hand panel shows cleared land and a few early structures of the Broadmoor Hotel complex. Fielder's follow-up shows that Colorado Springs has developed into a city — the second-largest city in Colorado — with 360,890 residents as of 2000. The Broadmoor complex, still crowned by the grand 1918 hotel and now boasting a championship golf course, appears in Fielder's right-hand panel.

It had been years since I traveled the famous Gold Camp Road from Colorado Springs into Cripple Creek mining country. A horizontal scar along the foothills, it remains conspicuous from just about anywhere in the city. Eric and I guessed that Jackson might have photographed his two-part panorama from this former rail route, now a scenic drive on a dirt road. Point Sublime is an archaic name that Jackson and his contemporaries used to describe this location, so we knew we couldn't count on finding a sign with those words on it. The first few miles of the road parallel the Front Range, gradually ascending to reveal spectacular views of the city and Great Plains to the east. We pulled over when we thought things lined up correctly, right where the road heads west up a large canyon and into once-gold-laden foothills.

Eric and I had to scramble 100 feet up a hillside to include in our view the railroad cut seen in the foreground of Jackson's photograph. This proved no small feat, given the erosive nature of the rock along the road. To negotiate dicey terrain such as this, during the project we always wore our most rugged hiking boots, with thick lug soles good for uphill traction. Unfortunately, like a four-wheel-drive SUV on ice, going up is easy, but the extra traction doesn't help much on the way down. (That's where pants with a reinforced rear come in handy!)

The dominant points of reference we employed were Broadmoor Lake, visible in both right-hand images, and downtown Colorado Springs and the escarpments on the edge of the slope in both left-hand images. Could the ponderosa pines in the foreground of Jackson's left-hand photograph possibly be the same trees as in mine? Ponderosas live to be several hundred years old, so they very well might be.

39

COLORADO SPRINGS

*Garden of the Gods,
Gateway Rocks, 1901*

p. 77

TN Thanks to the 1909 designation of the Garden of the Gods as a Colorado Springs City Park, these two photos do not differ greatly, except for the auto roads and parking lots serving one of Colorado's most visited natural attractions. The family of Charles Elliott Perkins, president of the Chicago, Burlington & Quincy Railroad, donated to the city the 1,350-acre park, with its fantastic, weather-carved, red and white sandstone formations.

After white settlement began in nearby Colorado City in 1859, Melanchton S. Beach gazed over the red rock formations and told his companions Lewis Tappan and Rufus Cable, "This would be a capital place for a beer garden!"

"A beer garden, indeed!" Cable replied. "This is a place for the Gods to assemble." So the park came to be called the Garden of the Gods. Despite that name, it did first flower as a beer garden, dance hall, and hodgepodge of commercial operations selling photos, rocks, and trinkets to tourists. Edwin L. "Fatty" Rice and his wife, Phoebe, opened Fatty's Place, a beer garden and curio shop specializing in gems and rocks. "Stop by and See the Fat Man," the bushy-bearded, 300-pound proprietor advertised. In 1907, Fatty's widow sold the place to Colorado Springs town founder General William J. Palmer, who worked with land donor Charles Elliott Perkins to acquire the entire garden and preserve it as a park.

A century ago, nationally noted author Julian Street called the Garden of the Gods "a pale pink joke," but it perennially ranks as one of Colorado's top 10 tourist attractions. Some 1.7 million visitors annually flock to see 1,000-year-old juniper trees and the spectacular rock formations popularized as the "Kissing Camels," "Irish Washerwoman," "Weeping Indian," "Baldheaded Scotchman," and "Cathedral Spires."

JF W. H. Jackson made many images of Garden of the Gods. I examined at least 30 of them, from which I chose a handful to rephotograph. Standing on the hill northwest of today's loop road presents this view to the southeast. I did not imagine that it would be difficult to find Jackson's spot — the subject rocks are obvious, and the horizon provides an additional perspective clue. But I did not expect to find living clues!

Of course, I can't guarantee that the piñon pines on the left- and right-hand sides of Jackson's image are the same trees framing my view. The availability of too few trunks and branches to examine lends scant evidence for making a positive identification, but the trees' positions *are* temptingly similar to those on the edges of my image. The proof that they might be the same trees is twofold: Piñon pines can live for a long time, and the juniper (also called cedar) in the bottom middle area is without a doubt the same tree in both photographs!

The juniper at the very bottom is actually a large branch growing off the main stem. See how many branches you can count that exist in both photographs. Junipers can live for more than 1,000 years, yet can appear almost unchanged from one century to the next. Piñons and junipers can survive with minimal water and, as a result, might grow less than an inch per year. The two plant species live together in the same arid ecosystem, or life zone, throughout Colorado and the West. Some people call such places "P-J" forests.

40

COLORADO SPRINGS

Garden of the Gods, Gateway Rocks, circa 1885

pp. 78–79

TN One of Colorado's signature landscapes consists of these red and white sandstone formations framing snow-capped Pikes Peak. One of the best views of Gateway Rocks is from the Garden of the Gods Visitors Center, a 10,000-square-foot visitors center, museum, and restaurant built in 1995 on the eastern edge of the park at 185 N. 30th St. The park offers many hiking, biking, and equestrian trails, as well as technical rock climbing. Living history exhibits and restored pioneer structures also make the nearby Chambers and White House ranches popular stops. Don't forget to bring your camera!

JR The spectacular rock fins and spires of the Garden of the Gods are carved from near-vertical layers of sedimentary rocks upturned 70 to 50 million years ago during the Laramide orogeny. Prior to the Laramide uplift, the soft-gray rocks in the immediate foreground lay near sea level in a nearly horizontal blanket that passed several thousand feet above the Precambrian granite on the future site of Pikes Peak. The rocks in these photos are about 6,000 feet above sea level; a few miles to the northeast, this same type of rock lies underground more than 1,000 feet below sea level. Pikes Peak tops out at 14,110 feet above sea level. Thus, the upheaval during the Laramide orogeny pushed the Precambrian granite that makes up the summit of Pikes Peak to a level more than 3 miles above the Precambrian rocks that lie beneath the Great Plains to the east.

Much of this uplift took place along a complex series of faults along this part of the mountain front. One of these, the Rampart Range fault, lies just west of (behind) the red Gateway Rocks shown here. As the block west of the fault moved up, the sedimentary layers east of the fault were bent upward to a nearly vertical position.

Since the uplift, erosion has removed the softer rock layers and sculpted these magnificent rock formations. The Gateway Rocks are carved from red sandstone in the lower part of the Lyons Formation;

the white rocks in the foreground are white sandstone in the upper part of the Lyons Formation. The Lyons Formation was deposited during the Permian period, about 260 million years ago. The gray rocks along the road in the foreground are limestone in the Morrison Formation, deposited during the Jurassic period about 155 million years ago. These photographs were taken from a ridge of limestone of the Niobrara Formation, deposited during the Cretaceous age about 90 million years ago. Therefore, the rock layers become younger toward the east, away from the Rampart Range fault. This pattern resembles a paperback book placed face-down on a flat table, with the pages bent up along the edge: The first pages (representing the oldest geologic layers) would be closest to the bent-up edge of the book, and the last pages (representing the youngest layers) would be farthest away from it.

As you drive through Garden of the Gods City Park from the east, the Gateway Rocks are the first major formation to appear. A long escarpment runs north to south a quarter-mile east of the Gateway Rocks—definitely the place from which Jackson photographed. Eric and I had only to park our vehicle and take a five-minute hike to the top of this ridge of rock and loose sediments in order to find Jackson's location.

Plentiful perspective clues facilitated our quest for Jackson's exact spot, especially the relationship between Pikes Peak in the background and the Gateway Rocks. Note that today's paved trail between the rocks nearly mirrors the road in Jackson's photograph. How close did I come to getting the snowpack on Pikes Peak in 1998 to match that in Jackson's scene around 1885? And thank goodness for color photography!

41

COLORADO SPRINGS

Pikes Peak from Austin's Bluff,
circa 1890

p. 80

JF As I explained in this book's Introduction, during most of the year 2000 I helped lead a campaign to stop sprawl in Colorado, and to better plan for and manage growth. Our organization, Coloradans for Responsible Growth, wrote an amendment to Colorado's constitution and collected more than 100,000 signatures in order to have it placed on Colorado's November 2000 ballot. It failed, for the most part because of a record $6 million developer-funded campaign to defeat it. A staggering number of TV commercials—unprecedented for any previous candidate or issue campaign in Colorado—were broadcast, most of them confusing and disingenuous. Ultimately, it was difficult for Coloradans to understand how effectively Amendment 24 would have fought sprawl and protected Colorado's unique quality of life.

This pair of photographs was used in the campaign to promote the Responsible Growth Initiative. We see in Jackson's image a rural landscape with Pikes Peak in the background. My photograph depicts sprawl development built not long before I arrived to remake the Jackson image.

Sprawl, which is not contiguous with existing development, consumes open landscapes and farm- and ranchland. It is expensive to service such areas with water, roads, sewers, and schools because they exist so far away from other infrastructure. Sprawl is particularly egregious when it occurs in natural landscapes with great scenic value. The high cliffs, scrub oaks, and stately ponderosa pines of Colorado

Springs' Austin Bluffs, which Jackson called Austin's Bluff, make this area particularly beautiful. To build symmetrical tract housing—an eyesore from the start—in such places should be a crime. Under our current system of land-use planning and enforcement, it is not, although growth-management bills continue to be presented in the state legislature.

Colorado is too beautiful for its citizens to allow sprawl to engulf its natural lands, and its beauty too valuable environmentally, emotionally, and economically. If we use up all of our landscapes, biodiversity will pay a large price; you and I will go crazy without such relief from all things urban, and we will have cooked the goose that laid the golden egg. Colorado's quality standards of living attract the kinds of people with the most mobility: highly educated and well-paid workers. Companies move to Colorado, or open branches here, because they know they can recruit such people away from their competitors in places like Atlanta or Los Angeles. If we continue to degrade open landscapes and wildlife habitat, and pave over our farms and ranches, we will be no better off than those cities, and we will have lost our competitive edge.

We must find ways neither to stop growth nor even slow it, but to direct future development within existing built areas—or at least contiguous with them—instead of leapfrogging to where the land is the cheapest and planning commissions the most lenient. We owe this stewardship of the land to future generations of Coloradans, and to Mother Nature.

JF Oh well, at least I got close enough to Jackson's photo location to make a political statement about sprawl development! Without the ridge trick, this site would have been impossible to find. The escarpment of white rock called Austin Bluffs runs north to south through Colorado Springs, east of Interstate 25, for many miles. Pikes Peak is visible from just about every point on top of the ridge. The alignment of foothills in relation to Pikes Peak, and even the position of the Garden of the Gods formations in the distance, allowed me to hit upon this spot in about five hours. The most difficult part was knowing how far east or west to stand, as the formation is a mile wide in places.

My first foray took me to the top of the ridge in the mid-ground of the scene, a location that did not reveal the valley in the foreground of Jackson's scene. I headed east to the next ridge, near the intersection of North Union Boulevard and Austin Bluffs Parkway, and eventually made my way to the top of the cliffband via Ridgecrest Drive. Private homes blocked access to the undeveloped part of the ridge that I needed to scout, so I knocked on one door—no one home—and then another. A man answered, and I explained the project to him. He produced from his library a couple of my books, which I autographed, and then with his graces I went on my search. One hundred yards south of his lot, I found the approximate place in which Jackson stood, but I never did locate the exact foreground rocks in the historic photograph.

42

COLORADO SPRINGS

Monument Park, 1874

p. 81

These curious pinnacles, like the arch called Elephant Rock (see Photo Pair 11), are carved in soft, feldspar-rich sandstone of the Dawson Formation, which is composed of debris eroded from Pikes Peak Granite. The coarse sandstone contains scattered quartz pebbles, some several inches in diameter — a number of which are clearly visible on the rock face along the right edge of the photographs. The rock that caps the pinnacles is a sandstone bed, 1 or 2 feet thick, that is cemented by brown iron oxide; solutions that percolated through the sandstone shortly after it was laid down 65 to 55 million years ago apparently deposited the iron oxide here. This tough, iron-cemented sandstone resists erosion extremely well. During the last million years or so, as Dry Creek cut down into the soft sandstone to form Woodmen Valley (occupied by the subdivision in the left mid-ground of the contemporary photo), remnants of the hard, iron-cemented sandstone layer protected the underlying soft sandstone from erosion, forming these strange pinnacles.

    Note that several pinnacles on which the protective caprock balanced most delicately in Jackson's photo have disappeared in the contemporary photo. Presumably, the hard caprock slabs tumbled, exposing the soft rocks to rapid erosion and leaving only the stumps of the old pinnacles behind.

JF Jackson's caption, "Monument Park," was a misleading clue. My first instinct told me that Monument Park must be near the town of Monument, in the same vicinity as the natural arch I photographed northwest of the town (see Photo Pair 11). However, I had my doubts because that arch is orange and these formations are gray. In addition, I remembered seeing a similar scene in *Second View*, a book of rephotography by Mark Klett, published in the 1980s by the University of New Mexico Press. The book identified the location as Woodmen Road in Colorado Springs.

So Eric and I headed to the Springs and proceeded east from Interstate 25 on Woodmen Road. A few miles farther on, we had spied no such formations, so we drove back to the west and across the highway. There we saw an assortment of these oddly shaped, eroded features — called hoodoos and goblins — in people's yards. Eventually, we noticed a suspicious hill next to the road, so we parked the Suburban and began to hike. The view on top revealed an array of hoodoos and goblins on the hill's southern backside, but none like the patterns seen in Jackson's photograph.

We had learned during this project that perseverance was a critical trait for effective "perspective detectives," so we continued to hike and climb among the unstable, slippery rocks. Eventually, I let out a victory shout and Eric came running to see the precarious perch on which I was standing, and from which Jackson had made his photograph. Further examination of the environs resulted in the discovery that the toppled ponderosa pine in my foreground was the tree in the middle of Jackson's scene. The dead tree's brown needles still clung to its branches, so the live tree Jackson photographed must have expired just a year or so before we arrived — 124 years later!

43

MANITOU SPRINGS

Manitou, circa 1890

p. 82

TN As both images attest, Manitou Springs remains a green, low-rise, rustic resort community. Manitou Springs is home to the natural mineral springs that lent Colorado Springs its name. Colorado Springs founder General William J. Palmer and Dr. William A. Bell, president and vice-president of the Denver & Rio Grande Railroad, respectively, established Manitou Springs in 1871 as a resort town. They platted the 640-acre site with, as Bell insisted, "streets and roads adapted to the contour of the ground." He explained that "the lots were made of large size and of necessity irregular, and were mostly intended for villa sites." A shortage of buyers inspired subdivision of the original large lots to accommodate more modest dwellings. To supplement the natural beauty of the wooded hillsides, landscape architect John Blair planned meandering roads and paths, two stone footbridges (1906–1907), and rustic seats placed to capture the views.

Note the picturesque Queen Anne–style house and hotel in Jackson's right foreground. Although many Queen Anne landmarks remain, especially within the downtown National Register Historic District, much new construction bears a less distinctive look—witness the Fielder photo.

 The drive along U.S. Highway 24 just west of Colorado Springs provides glimpses of Manitou Springs below. Unfortunately, the construction of the highway obliterated much of the landscape above Manitou. We pulled over a few times and hiked up the hillside south of the highway in order to reconnoiter. At about the correct latitude from which Jackson photographed, and right next to the busy highway, we spied a large, flat, and conspicuous balanced rock looming above us: a perfect place for Jackson's big camera.

Getting to the top required some boosting, but once there, we thought that we had found our place — the ridges of the foothills aligned perfectly with themselves and with Pikes Peak. However, our Polaroid test photos made it clear that the tree-covered ridge in our bottom right foreground did not match the one in Jackson's. We were standing about 100 yards east of Jackson's location, ultimately, the best we could do. This proved to be among several times that highway excavation prevented us from standing exactly where Jackson had.

44

MANITOU SPRINGS

Ute Pass, circa 1890

p. 83

EJ Long before Jackson crafted his view of this steep wagon road, American Indians followed the same route between South Park and dry prairies in the shadow of Pikes Peak. Comanche and Kiowa people, and later Cheyenne and Arapaho, climbed the rough canyon to collect lodgepoles and salt, to hunt plentiful game, and to carry out raids against their traditional enemies, the mountain-dwelling Utes. The Utes traveled downstream to raid Plains Indian camps and to soak in the bubbling mineral springs where the mountains met the prairie at the place known today as Manitou Springs.

French-speaking trappers who frequented the area before 1850 considered Ute Pass the best route from the beaver-filled mountains to the trading post at Bent's Fort, 100 miles southeast on the Arkansas River; they named the creek in Jackson's photograph "La Fontaine qui Bouille," or "Boiling Fountain," after the hot springs so loved by the Utes. The English name later was shortened to Fountain Creek.

In 1859, Colorado City was established 2 miles east of the pass. It was a booming gold-rush settlement and a staging ground for prospectors headed up the pass to the placer fields of South Park and Leadville. The next year, townspeople put up $3,000 for road construction on Ute Pass, replacing the ancient American Indian trail with a roadway more suited to wagons, oxen, and mules. More than 15,000 travelers made their way through the pass to the goldfields; nearly as many returned, empty-handed, the same way. Further improvements resulted from a $15,000 bond issue in 1871 that widened the road and eased the grade just enough to make heavy freight-wagon traffic possible — but 10 years later, two railroads reached Leadville from Denver, reducing freight traffic through the pass to a trickle.

Meanwhile, Ute Pass country and the wider Pikes Peak region saw increasing white settlement and steady growth in tourist trade. The town of La Font — later renamed Manitou and then Manitou Springs — was established in part by railroad magnate General William J. Palmer in 1871 to capitalize on the healing benefits of Soda Springs and other mineral baths. The Cave of the Winds attraction opened to the public in the 1880s, and tourist brochures extolled the scenery of nearby Rainbow Falls, Williams Canyon, and the Garden of the Gods. By the time Jackson made his photograph, the Ute Pass road had been rebuilt a third time to accommodate carriages full of tourists bound for resorts near Cascade and Green Mountain Falls — and onward to the crest of Pikes Peak.

Commercial traffic, tourism, and the gaming rooms of Cripple Creek continue to make Ute Pass a key route to the mountains west of Colorado Springs. The State Highway 24 bridge in Fielder's photo attests to the route's popularity — as does the gray cascade of dirt falling into the photo from the busy U.S. Highway 24 bypass, located outside the range of the picture, up and to the right.

━━━━━━━━━━━━━━━━━━━━━━━━━━━━

JF This scene required the better part of a day to locate. Jackson's caption, "Ute Pass," refers to the historic route that runs partly along Fountain Creek from Colorado Springs about 30 miles west to the town of Divide and beyond. We suspected that no such carriage road existed today, but were glad to have clues in the form of the rocks in the distance and what appeared to be a waterfall on the creek. Because the name of the town of Green Mountain Falls gave us a hunch that this waterfall might be in the vicinity, we initiated our search there and continued southeast to Manitou Springs. Not until we took the eastbound exit off U.S. Highway 24 into Manitou Springs did we find our waterfall. We might have missed it had it not been for the roar of falling water heard through our open windows!

We looped around to the highway in order to start tracking Jackson's footprints. It did not take long for us to realize that the entire landscape along the quaint carriage road had been obliterated to make way for four-lane U.S. Highway 24. Apparently, if anyone in the community of Manitou Springs cared enough to protect the historic road when the highway construction commenced, their efforts fell short. In addition, the resulting detritus from blasting away the mountainside had destroyed the ecosystem along Fountain Creek.

Though I've spent most of my life advocating protection of natural landscapes, this project encouraged me to consider the importance of historic human landscapes. While conducting autograph sessions at bookstores through the years, I've witnessed an incalculable amount of joy in the faces of people who exude pride in being native Coloradans. Safeguarding our historic landscapes is critical to creating the sense of place that makes us and our children proud to be Coloradans — and to establishing the sense of security that results from the feeling that one belongs somewhere on this vast planet. We must do better.

45

PIKES PEAK

The "W," Pikes Peak
Carriage Road,
after 1891

p. 84

TN The 1888 Pikes Peak carriage road, with its W-shaped hairpin turns, was converted to an auto road in 1915 by Spencer Penrose. Penrose, the mining tycoon who built the Broadmoor Hotel and transformed the Pikes Peak region into a tourist spa, built the auto road to test his new luxury automobiles and those of his friends. Penrose started the Pikes Peak Hill Climb, the annual summer auto race over what is now a 13-mile-long toll road owned and operated by the City of Colorado Springs. This still-grueling dirt highway has given new meaning to the old slogan "Pikes Peak or Bust." The 8,000-foot vertical rise, 10.5 percent grades, tight curves, and extreme elevation have busted thousands of automobile radiator hoses, engines, brakes, and tires.

The mountain that U.S. Army explorer Zebulon Pike called unclimbable has since been climbed, motored, or cog-railwayed by millions of people. Atop the peak, the 1964 Summit House sits above the retaining wall of the original cog railway depot. The Army Signal Corps opened a research station atop Pikes Peak in 1873. There, William B. Felts conducted Colorado's first winged craft experiments in 1897. He strapped himself into a giant mechanical birdlike contraption and made a running start that launched him from the roof of the Signal Corps station. Instead of soaring off Pikes Peak, however, Felts dropped a vertical distance of 12 feet and crashed into the rocks at the base of the building. Only Felts' pride was bruised, but his "aeroplane" never recovered.

At the High Altitude Research Facility on top of the mountain, scientists studying high altitude's effect on breathing have enjoyed more success. There, Professor Douglas of Oxford University tested his theory that people inhale oxygen and exhale carbon dioxide. Scientists have conducted many physiological studies there, including ongoing investigations as to why the elevation leaves tourists breathless.

Although snow, hail, and freezing rain greet some visitors to Pikes Peak, most draw inspiration from the mountain. No one, however, has found it more exalting than Katherine Lee Bates, an English professor from Wellesley College who guest-lectured at Colorado College. She rode a mule-drawn buckboard to the top of the peak on July 22, 1893. Later she published the song "America the Beautiful" and explained,

"The opening lines of the hymn floated into my mind as I was looking out over the sealike expanse of fertile country spreading away so far under those ample skies."

Many have suggested that this lovely hymn replace the bombastic national anthem. If so, we would hear more often the most famous words that Pikes Peak inspired:

O beautiful for spacious skies,
For amber waves of grain,
For purple mountain majesties
Above the fruited plain!
America! America!
God shed his grace on thee
And crown thy good with brotherhood
From sea to shining sea!

No mystery here. Eric and I hoped that simply driving to the top of Pikes Peak on the famous Pikes Peak Toll Road would reveal a landscape's worth of clues. Sure enough, the roadbed was basically unchanged in 100 years, and once we arrived above treeline we quickly found the rock clues. It was fun achieving perfection by aligning foreground rocks with mid-ground rocks laterally, and gaining the correct elevation by aligning the rock piles with the road's switchbacks in the distance. The icing on the cake was waiting for the right combination of modern vehicles to roll by, duplicating the carriages in Jackson's scene. Our Pikes Peak experience further sweetened when we arrived back at the bottom of the mountain without burning up our vehicle's brakes!

46

TELLER COUNTY

Anaconda, 1900

p. 85

As the black-coated man in Jackson's photo seems to appreciate, Anaconda thrived as a substantial town of 1,059, according to the 1900 U.S. Census. Founded in 1893, Anaconda lay 2 miles south of Cripple Creek. It sprouted up by and was named for the Anaconda Mine, the point at which the Florence & Cripple Creek Railroad arrived in the district. An F&CC train is visible in the Jackson photo, and the rail grade on which a summer tourist train from Cripple Creek now travels is prominent in the left center of Fielder's photo. The Cripple Creek and Victor Narrow Gauge Railroad excursion ends at Anaconda near the only frame structure still wearing a roof.

Both photos were taken along what is now State Highway 67. Although Anaconda has largely vanished, some ruins remain, as close scrutiny of the Fielder photo reveals. Cribbing and mill house ruins linger at the Doctor Jack Pot, Fauntleroy, Mary McKinney, and other million-dollar mines. False-fronted frame buildings, including the *Write Up the Camp* newspaper office, lined Anaconda's main street. Today, only the jailhouse foundation, fire hydrants, and evidence of streets survive. The district's last operating mill, the Carlton Mill (1951), on State Highway 67 a mile southwest of Anaconda, processes 1,000 tons of ore per day, dumped by trucks into the 16 bins that face the highway. In the 1950s, the 414-by-463-foot, L-shaped prefabricated steel structure was proclaimed to be the largest custom gold refinery in the world. During the 1980s, the Texas Gulf and Golden Cycle Mine reopened it as a cyanide leaching operation. Waste from these mills buries some of Anaconda as well as the old downhill town of Arequa, which now lies beneath a cyanide leaching pad. On the left horizon, note the 1900 head-frame that survives in Fielder's image.

JF Halfway between the historic mining towns of Cripple Creek and Victor once existed a town called Anaconda. Eric and I made a number of repeat photographs in those two communities, but were especially excited about finding one more of the sort that had disappeared completely. As we did not encounter the evidence of the townsite that Tom Noel mentions, we saw no sign of Anaconda's whereabouts.

The chief impediment to rephotographing this Jackson scene turned out to be a new forest of aspen trees. Although aspens rank as my favorite plants on the planet — they can be photographed so many different ways, and so artistically — this did not turn out to be the first time they created problems for us. There simply weren't as many around in Jackson's day. Note also how the tree cover on the distant hillsides has changed in 100 years.

As usual, the alignment of distant ridges got us close to what must have been Jackson's location. Note the railroad bed in the foreground of Jackson's scene; in my photograph, it's beneath the snowbank at the bottom center. To make the photograph, I actually stood on the old carriage road now hidden above State Highway 67 amongst the problematic aspen trees. Unfortunately, I could not replicate the positioning of the person or vehicle in Jackson's photo — I needed Eric by my side and traffic was light that day!

47

CRIPPLE CREEK

1900

pp. 86–87

TN   Although the street grid remains similar, most of the structures in Jackson's 1900 photo have vanished a century later. Visible survivors include some of the 1896 buildings lining Bennett Avenue (the main street) and St. Peter's Catholic Church in the center right. This photo pair dramatizes the fate of Colorado's boom-and-bust mining towns. Cripple Creek in 1900 was the world's largest gold district and Colorado's fifth-largest city, with a population of 10,147. Fifty years later, it was nearly a ghost town.

Ironically, the great Pikes Peak gold rush, which gave birth to Colorado, bypassed Cripple Creek — ultimately the richest goldfield of all — hidden just west of the peak. Cowboy Bob Womack scratched around the high-country cow pastures for years, theorizing that the surface gold he found would lead to richer deposits. Womack might have guessed, as geologists later realized, that the Cripple Creek District is one giant collapsed volcano, a bowl of gold created by volcanic pressures pushing gold upward into seams, cracks, and faults around the volcano's rim. In 1891, Womack found a pay streak, staked a claim, and built his shack in Poverty Gulch. During the subsequent gold rush, Cripple Creek was founded and in 1899 became the seat of a new county named for U.S. Senator Henry M. Teller.

Cripple Creek mushroomed as an instant city with two dozen satellite gold camps in a 24-square-mile district that by 1900 boasted 500 mines. They surrendered more than $18 million in gold, outproducing Australian, Canadian, Russian, South African, and U.S. rivals. Three railroads rushed in: the Florence & Cripple Creek, the Colorado Springs & Cripple Creek, and the Colorado Midland with its Midland Terminal extension from Divide to Cripple Creek.

After violent labor wars in 1903–1904, the district never recovered and by 1918 it found itself in the midst of serious decline. Cripple Creek's golden age is commemorated today by blast-and-pray prospect holes, mine head-frames, and immense mine waste dumps and mill tailings. These days, more people lie in the cemetery at the base of Mount Pisgah (the forested hill at center right) than live in this town of 1,115 residents.

In hope of reviving the economy and restoring the town, Colorado voters authorized limited-stakes casino gambling there, as well as in Black Hawk and Central City, beginning in 1991. The largest building in the Fielder photo is the 1996 Double Eagle Hotel & Casino, the giant among a dozen gambling havens that have transformed the town.

With plenty of mountains and ridges with which to employ perspective, Eric and I spent part of a morning investigating old mining roads southeast of Cripple Creek in order to find this Jackson location. One reasonably improved road in particular seemed to head in the general direction we desired. As we switchbacked up the mountain, we began to fear that the ubiquitous aspen trees might very well block the view that we needed. Sure enough, we ultimately were forced to place the camera higher up on the slope than did Jackson.

Notice that the distant ridges intersect the conspicuous mountain on the right at a lower point in Jackson's photograph than in mine — proof that we'd climbed too high. Nevertheless, if we'd remade the image from lower down, trees would have obstructed the view of the old buildings along the main street. Can you pick out any buildings that exist in both photographs? Note the great Sangre de Cristo Mountains rising in the background of my image.

48

CRIPPLE CREEK

Main St., circa 1892

p. 88

The Double Eagle Hotel & Casino, also visible in the first Cripple Creek duo (see Photo Pair 47), dominates Bennett Avenue in Fielder's sequel, which also captures an armored Wells Fargo money truck hauling casino earnings out of Cripple Creek. Since casino gambling began here in 1991, it has become the dominant industry, but is still a dicey one. Of some three dozen casinos to open in Cripple Creek during the past decade, 15 survive.

Smaller mom-and-pop casinos have been put out of business by huge operations, often backed by Las Vegas capitalists or other big shots. Typical of the new monsters, the Double Eagle Hotel & Casino opened in 1996 at the town's main intersection, the corner of Bennett Avenue and State Highway 67. This four-story, full-block, red brick development undermined any hope that casinos could be kept within the historic context and proportions of their environs, even if they display some neo-Victorian flourishes.

On the other (north) side of Bennett Avenue, the red brick buildings are vintage 1896 structures, starting with the Town Hall at right. Prominent in the distance are the three-story Gold Mining Stock Exchange/Elks Lodge and, a block farther west, the Imperial Hotel. The Gold Mining Stock Exchange is a distinctive 1896 landmark designed by prominent Denver architects John J. Huddart and T. Robert Wieger. As if to reassure investors, this sturdy red brick and sandstone Romanesque Revival building radiates wealth and permanence. From a massive, stone-arched, recessed entry a central bay rises above the sandstone cornice, dentils, and diapered stone frieze to a prominent parapet. This was one of three Cripple Creek mining exchanges at a time when the U.S. had about 200 mining exchanges. Ten years after it closed in 1903, the exchange became the Elks Club, which bought the building in 1913 for $20,000. The floor of the large, high-ceilinged exchange hall still contains electrical outlets for communications with exchanges in Colorado Springs, Denver, Chicago, and New York. The Elks maintain a bar, dining rooms, ballroom, and meeting rooms on the second floor and a grand hall and sleeping rooms on the third.

This stock exchange serves as a reminder that Cripple Creek was not a poor man's camp: By the 1890s, mining had become big business, controlled largely by out-of-town capitalists while the miners were reduced to $3-a-day drudgery. These economic circumstances are evident in the town's surviving residential architecture, which is characterized by modest homes rather than mansions.

Jackson's 1892 photo captures the one-year-old town when many of its buildings were still tents. If any of these structures survived until 1896, they were destroyed by the two great fires that ravaged most of the town that year. Subsequently, many downtown buildings bear the date 1896. Rebuilding occurred rapidly and usually in the form of substantial, stylishly designed masonry edifices, for Cripple Creek was producing millions every month in gold—enough to rebuild the town every year if need be.

JF Because every building in Jackson's old photograph seems to be made of timber, this photograph clearly predates the previous one looking down on Cripple Creek (see Photo Pair 47). None of the masonry structures had been built yet. Were it not for the ridge in the distance, I would have had no hint as to where Jackson's location might be hiding. Even then it was impossible to pinpoint his exact spot because there is no second feature with which to align the ridge, no way to employ perspective. I could only hope that the main street still pointed in the same direction, and that I was standing the same distance from the ridge in order to have it appear the same size as in Jackson's image.

I did think it appropriate to include in my photograph the armored truck in front of the modern casino. In Jackson's day, gold was king; today, it's gambling.

49

PUEBLO

circa 1910

p. 89

TN The relatively modest development seen here proves that Colorado's late 20th-century boom did not occur all over the state. Pueblo, Colorado's second-largest city in 1910, aspired to eclipse Denver when Jackson took his photo. Since then, the giant steel and smelter industries of the "Pittsburgh of the West" have shriveled to almost nothing. Pueblo, with 102,121 residents, has fallen to the seventh-largest city in Colorado.

Poverty, of course, is the best friend of historic preservation. Pueblo's stability has left it rich in Queen Anne–style houses, like the one decorating Jackson's foreground and Fielder's mid-ground, along with handsome red brick industrial and commercial buildings, like those in both foregrounds.

The drowsy city seen in Fielder's photo originated in 1860 as a sleepy trading post at the confluence of Fountain Creek and the Arkansas River. Pueblo awakened in 1872 to the steam whistle of the Denver & Rio Grande Railroad. Rising with the railroad age, Pueblo had erected 185 new buildings by the end of 1873. By the 1880s, the D&RG and its subsidiary, the Colorado Fuel and Iron Company (CF&I Steel Corporation), transformed the onetime adobe trading post into a bustling steel city.

Architect and Builder magazine noted in 1891 that Pueblo's "massive monuments of imperishable stone [put it] far ahead of many cities of a larger population." Many masonry edifices survive, giving Pueblo an unusually rich stock of older homes, public buildings, and commercial structures. As Colorado's industrial giant, Pueblo developed many ethnic, working-class neighborhoods. Italians initially clustered around the steel mill in Bessemer, while many Slavs worked at the Philadelphia Smelting and Refining Company and lived nearby amid the cottonwoods lining the Arkansas River in the area known as the Grove. More recently, Hispanics settled in Peppersauce Bottoms and along Salt Creek. Greeks, Japanese, and other ethnic groups also staked out turf in the steel city.

Pueblo aimed to replace Denver as the state capital and, in an effort to outdo Denver, hired Louis Sullivan, the celebrated Chicago architect, to design its Grand Opera House. This 1889 landmark burned

in 1922. Pueblo's hopes of superseding Colorado's Queen City were also short lived. Colorado's second-largest city from the 1880s until the 1960s, Pueblo today draws new industry, as well as retirees and tourists. And now that the steel mills are modernized and only partly in use, the air is clearer and sweeter.

<hr />

Not knowing Pueblo's streets well, Eric and I decided to look first for a high point from which to regard the city, and then to find the mesa in the distance. We suspected that the scene looked north. We exited Interstate 25 at Abriendo Avenue and by the time we reached Broadway Avenue, it was clear that we had found our mark. Notice that the house with the turret in Jackson's foreground is the same one as in my mid-ground. Can you match up some of the old buildings in the distance?

In order to make this photograph, I had to seek permission to climb onto the roof of The Bookery, a store that would later sell copies of *Colorado 1870–2000*. Notice, however, that Jackson appears to have been standing higher than we were. That's one reason why the house with the turret appears in the middle of my photograph, rather than at the bottom. I discovered later that we all had climbed to the top of the same building, but fire had truncated it by the time Eric and I arrived. The top floor now houses apartments, and a friend of a friend of mine resided in the unit that had access to the roof. Cold beer on a hot Pueblo day facilitated the making of this image, and extended the time it took to do so.

50

PUEBLO

Union Depot, 1900

pp. 90–91

TN Colorado's most distinctive railway station dominates both views. A century has erased most of the train traffic, industrial buildup, and smoky skies. The mural in the foreground of Fielder's photo adorns the cement retaining walls built after the disastrous 1921 Arkansas River flood. Begun in 1979, and still being extended, the mural has transformed the huge, ugly concrete retaining wall into "The World's Largest Mural," according to *The Guinness Book of World Records*. The mural got its start when University of Southern Colorado students began clandestinely painting large scenes on the levee to replace the random graffiti and tagging that had marked it for years. Working at night with paint rollers and flashlights, they evaded the police. Their work was good enough to spark considerable discussion as to whether it was graffiti or art. The popular and ever-growing mural gained respectability and, in 1988, a mural coordinator, Cynthia Ramu.

During her first year, Ramu tumbled straight to the algae-filled bottom of the Arkansas, but later got used to walking on an angle. She asks that all artists sign a release form endorsed by the Pueblo Water Conservancy District, which owns the levee, and then allows anyone to get to work. She says, "No matter how little you are, you can contribute to the biggest mural in the world. We haven't had a kid fall in yet."

The 65-foot-high mural now stretches for more than a mile along the levee. Thousands of individuals have contributed paintings, ranging from personal statements to large-scale projects such as an actual-sized airplane, a bathtub, lizards, a graveyard, and portraits of the Marx Brothers.

This mural and the recently opened Historic Arkansas Riverwalk of Pueblo have reenergized the long-declining downtown riverfront. With these and more new municipal amenities, Pueblo is undergoing a 21st-century urban renaissance.

Union Depot, another centerpiece of Pueblo's rejuvenation, was built in 1890 and restored in 1992. Like many American railway stations of its time, Union Depot was designed in a nostalgic, picturesque mode; it's a Neo-Romanesque–style castle with rectangular wings that flank a central entrance surmounted by a six-story mansard clock tower. Chicago-based architect Frank Newall used large, rough-faced blocks

of red Manitou sandstone, laid in both broken and continuous courses. Round-arched windows define the bays, while third-story dormers punctuate the steep-pitched roof.

Inside, cast-iron columns are painted and decorated to look like wood. Stained-glass Art Nouveau transoms, rich golden oak wainscoting and parquet ceilings, and hexagonal ceramic tile floors enhance this period piece. The addition of an Art Deco soda fountain updated the Victorian interior. Although it no longer sees the coming and going of train passengers, the depot retains its restaurant and other services, and features a trackside rail museum.

JF Also near Abriendo Avenue was the point from which Jackson looked over the Arkansas River toward Pueblo's train station. Jackson must have stepped far enough back from the edge of the bluff in order to purposely block the view of the Arkansas River below. Why didn't he include the river? All he had to do was walk forward a few feet. I preferred to include it and the form it has taken today — a conspicuously non-natural river channel with a retaining wall built after the early 20th-century flood that damaged much of downtown Pueblo. Pueblo Reservoir to the west controls flooding today, so the wall is not necessary. Faced with similar situations, other Colorado cities are working to return such landscapes to their natural condition: Grand Junction is restoring the Colorado River, and Denver is doing the same with the South Platte.

Notice that I stood to the left of where Jackson made his photograph. Dense trees blocked the view. Can you find the clues that corroborate this? What changes has Union Depot undergone? How many other buildings can you find common to both photographs? Can you spot the train in my photograph? Do you think Jackson would have preferred the yellow van over horse and carriage?

51

TRINIDAD

A Business Street, 1908

pp. 92–93

TN Born in 1859 as a trading center along the Santa Fe Trail, Trinidad boomed between the 1880s and 1920s. The then-thriving coal industry made it Colorado's fourth-largest city, noted for its brick streets and sidewalks with bricks stamped "Trinidad." Perhaps no town in Colorado has more fine structures of stone, many constructed with the local golden sandstone by master masons such as Trinidad stonemason/architect Charles Innes. Prominent local architects such as the Rapp Brothers and John Conkie, who designed the town's famed Columbian Hotel, make Trinidad an architectural historian's paradise. The town's golden age is preserved in the Corazon de Trinidad ("Heart of Trinidad") National Register Historic District, which centers on the Main Street and Commercial Street intersection, shown in both prints.

The balconied edifice on the left is the Columbian Hotel, built in 1879. Originally called the Grand Union Hotel, this three-story brick landmark trimmed in stone and pressed metal was renamed in honor of the 1893 World's Columbian Exposition. Heavily hooded and elongated windows in sets of two and three, polished stone quoins, an ornately bracketed cornice above a decorative frieze, and the flat roof with overhanging eaves typify the Italianate style. A terrazzo-floored lobby leads to a Rococo ballroom, a ladies' "retiring room," and a gaming room, saloon, and smoking parlor. Since the 1970s, this 100-room grand hotel has been vacant, undergoing a slow restoration.

The McCormick Building on the right retains its distinctive second-story bay windows and most of its rich architectural detail. Fielder's photo, unlike Jackson's, captures the unusual curved-glass window at the far right of the second story. Trinidad, as this little-changed streetscape comparison suggests, has remained remarkably unaltered during the past century. Just across the street from this scene, near where both Jackson and Fielder stood, is the photo studio of the Aultmans, father and son; it now serves as a museum property of the Colorado Historical Society, celebrating the great local photographers of southern Colorado.

JF Finding this location was a breeze, as downtown Trinidad is not large. What I did find difficult, however, was containing my emotions enough to make the photograph — look what I saw printed on the second-floor window on the building at the far right. Apparently, a dentist occupied the space in 1908 and so does one today! Actually, today's sign is one window to the right of Jackson's. Because I wanted to include this coincidence, I chose to frame the photograph slightly differently than did Jackson. Later in Denver, I called the phone number on the sign to inquire if there was a relationship between dentists, then and now. The answer was no, but the current dentists were aware of Jackson's photograph.

The next best part about remaking this image was the wonderful Mexican restaurant just behind where I was standing. Its refried beans were so delicious that I carried a quart home to Denver for later consumption.

Colorado 1870 - 2000 Revisited

Central Mountains Locations

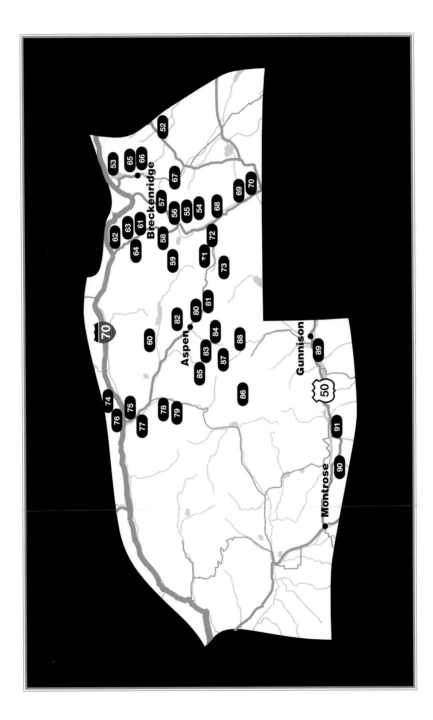

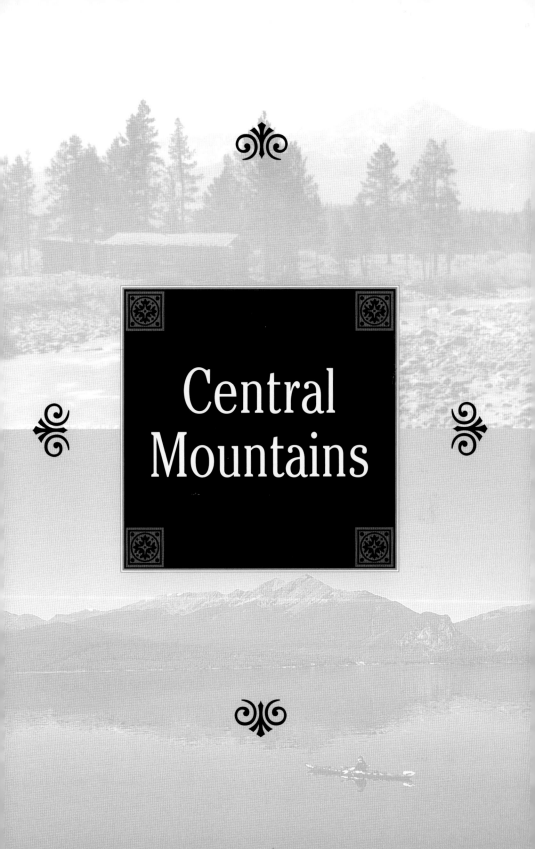

Central Mountains

52

KENOSHA PASS

Kenosha Hill, 1887

p. 97

TN The narrow-gauge path of the Denver, South Park & Pacific Railroad, with its roadbed still visible more than a century later, gave visitors one of Colorado's grandest views — an awesome panorama of the flat, verdant meadows of South Park rimmed by high mountains.

Former territorial governor John Evans and associates founded the Denver, South Park & Pacific Railroad in 1872. Denver mayor and brewer Joseph E. Bates, banker and U.S. Senator Jerome Chaffee, real estate tycoon Walter Scott Cheesman, banker Charles Kountze, and capitalist David H. Moffat, Jr., helped finance this railroad, the first to cross the Continental Divide.

The line began building out of Denver in 1873 and followed the South Platte River canyon through the mountains, reaching the slope of Kenosha Pass early in 1879. The 10,001-foot-high pass required grades as steep as the maximum 4 percent possible as construction crews muscled their way to the summit. The line reached the top of the pass on May 19, 1879, and crews paused to enjoy the panorama of South Park captured here.

The railway celebrated the triumphant view with a lavish description in its promotional booklet, *Picturesque Colorado*: "South Park! How the words thrill the memory and arouse the imagination. The place where every mood in man finds answering mood in nature. The glorious accomplishment of the painter's dream — the spot where serried peaks and variegated plain awake in the beholder sentiments of profound admiration.

"Imagine yourself standing upon the summit of a mountain overlooking a plateau nearly twice as large as the state of Connecticut. Surrounding this area, with its undulating hills, green meadows and many glittering lakes, are scores of mountains, whose sides are so steep that the early discoverers sought long and anxiously for a trail through the labyrinth of peaks .... In front, as far as the eye can penetrate, spreads out a carpet of green, yellow, brown and dark red, patches of the carpet representing the various phases of vegetation of this highly elevated region. In the east you behold the noble crest of Pikes Peak. In the west Mount Lincoln seems to gaze with benign countenance upon the entrancing scene, while in the

north looms up Longs Peak, and far away in the opposite direction the Spanish Peaks stand outlined in ethereal blue, completing an ensemble of transcendent beauty." Amen.

JF Eric and I assumed that the old railroad that once crossed Kenosha Pass must have followed the same route as today's U.S. Highway 285. A couple of trips up and down the pass revealed that we were wrong—we couldn't get anything to line up from the highway. A bit frustrated, I pulled over to the side, pausing where one first regards that well-known and infinite view across the vast intermountain basin called South Park. I was mostly just taking a break from making a decision about what to do next when I spied what seemed to be an old, unused road 300 yards below us. Eric and I gave each other the same look we always did when a clue came from out of nowhere: a kind of mischievous grin bubbling up from the thought that we were, once again, too smart for our own collective good.

A straddle of the barbed-wire fence and a short hike later, we reached the old road. It wasn't Jackson's location, but the elevation change gave us hope. We headed south, turning around every now and then to check the view against Jackson's photograph until we rounded a bend and looked back one more time. Success! The rails had been removed, but the roadbed and dirt-bank were just the same, and the peaks of the Mosquito Range in the distance aligned perfectly. Are the piñon pines the same? Probably, but larger after 111 years. And notice that between the two photographs, the clouds are about as similar as clouds can be.

53

DILLON

*Ten Mile Peaks, Blue
River Valley, circa 1883*

pp. 98–99

MP Colorado's population and water are reversed by location: More than 85 percent of the state's population resides east of the Continental Divide, but the vast majority of its water — 70 percent or better — falls west of the divide. The Rocky Mountains could pose an insurmountable obstacle to transporting water to the population centers, but early engineers quickly figured out the means — an elaborate system of tunnels that diverts billions of gallons annually beneath the towering peaks of the Continental Divide. The result is a crazy-quilt of pipelines, tunnels, canals, and reservoirs, all constructed with the goal of bringing the water wealth of Colorado's Western Slope first to the farms, and then to the cities, of the Front Range.

The Denver Water Board expeditiously moved to secure Western Slope water rights. Denver's earliest filings for water rights in the Blue River date to 1914, but the idea for Dillon Reservoir didn't take form until the 1940s. Once it was completed in 1963, Dillon Reservoir became the centerpiece of Denver's water supply as the largest reservoir in the system. Dillon Reservoir flooded its namesake town, creating a bucket to hold snowmelt from the Blue River and its tributaries. The Harold D. Roberts Tunnel bores under the Continental Divide and delivers water from Dillon into the South Platte basin. Travelers along U.S. Highway 285 near Grant often notice water rushing out of the tunnel's mouth, creating a raging torrent where a placid mountain stream used to flow.

The earliest transmountain water diversion to Denver took place near Winter Park. In the 1930s, Denver struck on a scheme to transport its newly found Western Slope water bonanza to the Front Range when it converted the pilot bore for the Moffat Railroad Tunnel into a water tunnel. Denver's first Western Slope water flowed east through the tunnel on June 10, 1936.

The Moffat Tunnel today diverts water not just from the headwaters of the Fraser River, but also from the Williams Fork drainage. Williams Fork water must be the best-traveled water in Colorado: It transits through the Continental Divide not once, but three times. One tunnel carries it eastward under the divide near Jones Pass into the Clear Creek watershed. A second tunnel transports this water back through the divide into the Fraser River drainage, where the Moffat Tunnel collects it for its final passage east into the Denver Water system and ultimately faucets, toilets, and sprinklers.

JP As with so many of the prospective Jackson photographs I reviewed, when I first saw this image I secretly hoped that some sort of sinister and significant change had occurred during the last century, enabling me to make a statement about how Colorado's landscape has been altered. In this case, I wondered if Dillon Reservoir might have inundated the valley. So it was easy to make this historic photograph one of the 300 I would seek during the project. Given the aggressive development of Summit County, I knew that even if the reservoir wasn't there, something conspicuous was bound to be manifest. My first thought proved to be true.

The Tenmile Range's Peaks 1 and 2, the tallest mountains in Jackson's purview, loom high as you drive west on Interstate 70 into the Dillon Valley. Easy clue to find. But where would I have to be in order for them to align as they do in Jackson's photograph? Eric and I first drove along the Swan Mountain Road east of the reservoir. No luck. We needed to move closer to the peaks, but miles of reservoir water blocked the way.

During the entire project, I don't think either of us had ever expected to do what we did next. On the other hand, from the start we had pledged to find all 300 places, come hell or high water! We made a beeline for the nearest marina and rented a motorboat. Thirty minutes later, a short distance north of where the mouth of Blue River enters the reservoir, we found a spit of land from which the two peaks lined up perfectly. The spatial relationship between the cliff on the right and the ridge behind it proves that Jackson's location now lies under the water, 50 feet below where I snapped my shutter.

While we were setting up the photograph, a man in his kayak cruised by. I convinced him to pose for us. The purpose was to highlight the difference in the economic base of this place, then and now. In Jackson's day, mining paid the way (note the miner's cabin in his scene), and today, tourism and recreation keep this valley afloat.

54

LEADVILLE

1885

pp. 100–101

TN Leadville, as you see here, is one of the few Colorado cities seemingly frozen in time. Even the one great change in the landscape, the creation of Turquoise Lake west of town at the base of the Sawatch Range, seems foreshadowed by the strange photographic "ghost" in the middle of Jackson's image — an aberration in his negative.

In Fielder's photo, sunlight shimmers on the shiny spire of the Annunciation Catholic Church, the pinnacle of Leadville's skyline. Two blocks away from the church, the Tabor Grand Hotel dominates Harrison Avenue, the main street, in both views. Many other Harrison Avenue landmarks linger, as do a good number of the outlying miners' cottages. Most of the mines in the foreground on Chicken Hill, however, are gone. An overly aggressive Environmental Protection Agency cleanup of the Leadville mining district reduced much of it to what town historian Neil V. Reynolds describes as golf-course greenery. Author Helen Hunt Jackson called 1880s Leadville "a Monaco gambling room emptied into a Colorado spruce clearing."

By 1881, when Leadville was four years old, it had 30 sawmills and four brickyards to feed its building boom. Frame construction and the need for charcoal to fuel 18 smelters denuded this 2-mile-high mountain valley of its once-dense Engelmann spruce forests. Evergreen trees, which originally dominated the picturesque headwaters of the Arkansas River, are slowly reclaiming what was Colorado's most devastated mining site.

JF We knew approximately where we should head to make a repeat photograph of this overview of Leadville — east of town. However, as with the Cripple Creek overview (see Photo Pair 47), finding the vantage point required exploring historic mining country, and that meant scouting many old roads. In 113 years, pine trees had grown up around the mine tailings in Jackson's foreground, precluding unobstructed views from most places. Eventually, Eric and I parked the car and climbed onto one of the old rock dumps. It would be a starting point.

Many buildings in Jackson's scene still exist. The church steeple in the middle right portion of the photograph came through for me as the best clue. I reached the correct longitude by lining it up with the same part of the lower ridge of Mount Massive as in Jackson's photograph. However, close inspection of the instant Polaroid test revealed several indications that we needed to relocate 20 feet higher up. Can you find those clues? Unfortunately, Mother Nature foiled us again — trees blocked the scene — so we settled for the view you see here.

Notice the addition of Turquoise Lake to the landscape since Jackson's day. The white cloud in the old photograph is actually an aberration on the glass-plate negative. How many buildings can you find common to both photographs? Notice how lodgepole pines have consumed the landscape west of town.

55

LEADVILLE

Fryer Hill, 1881

p. 102

TN These Fryer Hill photos, in which a residential neighborhood does a disappearing act, demonstrate Leadville's long decline and depopulation. Leadville was born in a prospector's pan. In 1860, the initial settlement of Oro City began in California Gulch as a gold camp. A decade later the black sand that had gummed gold operations proved to be high-grade silver ore, and in 1877 an instant city sprang up. By 1880, Leadville's 14,820 residents outnumbered those of every Colorado city save Denver. Two dozen surrounding camps and towns popped up as satellites of Colorado's greatest silver city.

Charles Boettcher, the German immigrant who became one of Colorado's most prominent industrialists and philanthropists, got his start selling hardware in Leadville. Upon his arrival in 1879, Boettcher found "The Magic City" infested with "any number of reckless people, lounging around doing nothing, just living on excitement…. People were living right on the streets. Many had tents, log cabins, or mere shelters covered with brush. The place was so crowded you could barely wedge your way through."

The highest and wildest of America's silver cities, Leadville still looks like a mining town. Pell-mell expansion over surrounding mine tunnels left the city plagued by disappearing backyards, sinking streets, and black holes that swallow everything thrown into them.

Leadville was a "git-and-git-out" town, where miners took out what riches they could find but put very little back into the community. The three railroads that rushed in during the early 1880s have all pulled out. Not until 1951 did Leadville build a citywide sewer system, and it had no zoning until 1990.

By 2000, Leadville's population sank to 2,821. A business district that once stretched for blocks in all directions has shrunken to hug Harrison Street. Yet the callused mining town refuses to knuckle under.

 Again, thank goodness for the ridge trick. If we had gone looking for a community (and a couple of boys sitting on stumps), this photograph would have defeated us. Once Eric and I had aligned ourselves with the north-to-south axis of the photograph by referencing the mountain with snow on it, we proceeded to drive north until we came upon the escarpment that must have underlain the Leadville suburb named Fryer Hill. However, getting there was no easy task. Initially, there were a number of ridges and valleys between us and our ultimate destination, and not necessarily roads on which to get there. Our path was circuitous at best, but within 30 minutes we arrived. In front of us was the California Gulch Road, which eventually climbs over 13,186-foot-high Mosquito Pass to the east. No buildings remained, the mine tailings were different, and no similar trees existed as clues, but the ridge trick worked.

W. H. Jackson often included people or other objects of known approximate size in the foreground of his photographs. This method allowed him to not only add a human dimension to the scene, but also to create a sense of scale — a feel for how large the rest of the landscape was. One of Jackson's objectives as a pioneer photographer was to acquaint people in the East with the grandness of the West. The use of scale in his photographs did just that.

56

LEADVILLE

Harrison Avenue,
circa 1885

p. 103

TN Harrison Avenue endures as the scaled-back main street of what was once Colorado's second-largest city. The avenue honors Edwin Harrison of the Harrison Reduction Works in St. Louis, who opened the first major smelter in Leadville in 1877. He sent James B. Grant, a graduate of the Freiberg School of Mines in Germany, to set up the plant that made Leadville silver pay off big-time. Grant later established Denver's giant Grant Smelter and became governor of Colorado.

Little of the wealth taken out of Leadville by dozens of millionaires, from the Grants to the Guggenheims, remained in the chilly silver city. Not until the 1980s were the sidewalks on Harrison Avenue aligned, in a main street facelift that unearthed multiple levels of wooden sidewalks.

Second Empire edifices, rare for Colorado, line Harrison Avenue (U.S. Highway 24). Residential side streets feature extravagant Carpenter's Gothic homes, such as those at 119 W. 3rd St. and 208 W. 6th St.; Mollie May's Brothel at 131 W. 5th St.; and the House with an Eye, 134 W. 4th St., named for its eyebrow dormer with an eye painted on the window glass. The town is particularly notable for many frame miners' cottages with exuberant Carpenter's Gothic entries, porches, and bays on the facades of what might otherwise be considered shacks.

Shown in the photographs, surviving landmarks on the left (west) side of Harrison include the Silver Dollar Saloon and the corner-towered Tabor Grand Hotel in the distance. The ornate mansard-roofed edifice dominating the streetscape in Jackson's photo is the old Lake County Courthouse, which burned down in 1942. On the right side of Harrison, Horace Tabor's Opera House, erected in 1879, stands prominently in the foreground. Many 1880s masonry buildings have prevailed, including the elegant Delaware Block and Post Office in the distance.

Of many memorable Harrison Avenue nights, one of the most noteworthy came in 1882. Oscar Wilde stepped onto the stage of the Tabor Opera House wearing a dark velvet suit, knee britches, and a Lord Byron collar. His full, sensuous lips parted in a smile, and he began to lecture the miners of Leadville on "The Practical Application of Aesthetic Theory to Exterior and Interior House Decoration, with Observations on Dress and Personal Ornament."

Like Wilde's lecture, this Italianate opera house, allegedly constructed in 100 days, epitomizes the mining frontier's rush to respectability. The three-story brick building incorporates a central pedimented

pavilion with a round-arched entry beneath a balcony. The entry is flanked by storefronts with their own recessed central entries. Flattened arches of sandstone top the windows of the third floor, while round arches with carved keystones grace second-floor windows. The little-altered interior contains a wobbly wooden balcony with some 700 Andrews patent cast-iron, plush-upholstered opera chairs, which were lugged over Weston Pass in wagons. Briefly known as the Weston Opera House, then as the Elks Opera House, the building has been owned since 1955 by local resident and author Evelyn Furman, who opens its doors for tours and performances.

In Leadville, the gold and silver have played out, tourists now support the economy, and many streets have been paved—but many of the same buildings persist. Therefore, I found this location as soon as I began looking for it. To remake the photograph, all Eric and I had to do was to avoid getting run over. On this weekend morning, Leadville bustled with the traffic of commuters headed to their jobs in far-off places such as Vail. Today, Leadville is as much a bedroom community for those who work in pricey ski resorts as it is a tourist attraction.

A brief stop at the sheriff's office and an explanation of the project resulted in our backsides being protected by flashing red lights—for a while. Just like the big city, Leadville has crime, even at 8 a.m. on a Saturday. Someone had just been shot! Off went the sheriff, and on-duty went Eric, warning folks not to run me over.

My favorite part of this photograph is the faded "Anheuser Beer on Draft" advertisement still visible on the side of the Tabor Opera House. Apparently, it had been painted over with another sign since Jackson was there, only to have the newer advertisement wash away just enough to reveal its precursor.

57

FREMONT PASS

1887

p. 104

TN The Denver, South Park & Pacific Railroad first puffed over 11,318-foot Fremont Pass in 1884. Here on the first mile of the Arkansas River headwaters, the town of Climax was established in 1887. The Climax Molybdenum Mining Company opened the Climax Mine here in 1916. It turned low-grade molybdenum ore into Colorado's richest mine and mill operation. Molybdenum, used as an alloy to harden steel, became crucial during World War I for armor plating and during the 1920s for automobile steel. World War II brought profits as well, and for several decades Climax produced more than half of the world's supply of molybdenum, along with by-products of tungsten, lead, and iron pyrite. Production peaked at 50,000 tons per day in what claimed to be the world's largest underground mine.

As the use of steel and molybdenum mining declined, this company town was dismantled, and many dwellings were moved to Leadville in the 1960s to become the nucleus of the West Park suburb. In 1982, Climax ceased production and laid off 3,000 workers. Hollowed-out Bartlett Mountain and miles of waste dumps remain. Fielder's photo captures some of the remnants of the Climax Mine, whose tailings spill down the northeast side of Fremont Pass for several miles as Colorado's most spectacular unnatural wonder.

The 14-mile rail line between Climax and Leadville has been miraculously preserved to this day and currently offers summer excursions aboard what is now called the Leadville, Colorado and Southern Railway. Train travelers, unlike motorists on the highway at the bottom of the watershed, enjoy the spectacular mountain scenery shown in both images.

JF   The discovery of Jackson's Fremont Pass photograph in the archives of the Colorado Historical Society was exciting. I did not immediately recognize the exact part of the Tenmile Range depicted in his purview, but could only hope that the contemporary Climax molybdenum mine was smack in the middle of the scene. At Climax, an open-pit operation about as conspicuous as any mine in Colorado, a whole mountain has been leveled for this ore that strengthens steel; it would have been fun to show the dramatic change.

Eric and I reached the top of the pass on State Highway 91 between Leadville and Copper Mountain on a glorious Colorado summer day. We soon realized that Jackson's photograph was made slightly south of the Climax Mine, in fact, by only one camera frame's worth. Unfortunately, we would not be able to show the mountain that had disappeared. Nevertheless, some of the mine's subsidiary buildings and a few older mine tailings appear in my repeat photograph, so all was not lost. The ridges of the Tenmile Range provided plenty of perspective clues with which to find Jackson's approximate location, but a new generation of spruce and fir trees mandated that we photograph from a few feet higher up than we would have liked.

58

TENNESSEE PASS

Crane's Park, circa 1887

p. 105

American transportation shifted from the railway to the highway in the 20th century. In Jackson's photograph, standard-gauge railroad ties are piled alongside the Denver & Rio Grande Railroad's narrow-gauge track over Tennessee Pass: The route was getting an overhaul to accommodate heavy traffic on the main line between Denver, the San Juan mining country, and Glenwood Springs. Colorado's railroads were vital forces in the state's economy — opening the Western Slope to farmers and fruit growers; hauling silver to Denver, coal to Pueblo, pianos and canned goods to Silverton, Aspen, and Telluride; taking tourists on jaunts through the mountains; and carrying workers from one job to the next. By 1930, Colorado's railroads had nearly 5,000 miles of track crisscrossing the state.

The railroad was king when Jackson made his photograph; there wasn't a car or truck to be seen, and fewer than 500,000 people lived in all of Colorado. Today, 4.3 million people call Colorado home, and they own nearly as many registered motor vehicles — almost one for each man, woman, and child alive in the state. But railroads operate only two-thirds of the track they ran in their heyday. No wonder the most striking thing about this pair of photographs is that the highway has replaced the railroad in the scene and pushed it into the background.

In the background of both pictures stand the quiet giants of Colorado's mountains, Mount Elbert (the state's highest) and Mount Massive. Limitations in Jackson's photographic process, as well as smoke from Leadville's smelters, heightened the distant haze in Jackson's view. The clarity of the skies in Fielder's picture is a product of cleaner air — Leadville's smelters are gone — and improved camera optics.

 Today, U.S. Highway 24 and the Continental Divide intersect at Tennessee Pass, located between the old mining towns of Minturn and Leadville. Jackson's view southwest toward the Sawatch Range and Mount Massive, on the right, and Mount Elbert, on the left, was simple to find. Aligning the foot of the ridge in the left mid-ground with the gap in between Elbert and Massive delivered me to the correct latitude. In addition, it seemed clear that U.S. Highway 24 coincided with the same bed as the Denver & Rio Grande Railroad in Jackson's scene, so I walked up the hill from the highway until I reached the correct elevation.

Notice that the modern railroad tracks (as of the writing of this book, abandoned) exist on the other side of what Jackson called Crane's Park. Note also the new population of coniferous trees that has grown on the hills in the middle distance of my photograph.

59

HAGERMAN PASS

Colorado Midland
Railway, circa 1892

p. 106

(Please see Colorado
1870–2000 *for the complete
series of photographs.)*

TN The dizzying switchbacks of the Colorado Midland Railway climbed over 11,980-foot-high Hagerman Pass. Named for Colorado Midland Railway president James J. Hagerman, the pass separates Leadville from Aspen and the Roaring Fork Valley. Colorado's two richest silver cities made it profitable to build and maintain this expensive mountain route, later improved with two tunnels under the pass.

As Jackson's photos show, railroad construction and fires set by coal-burning locomotives nearly deforested the pass. Trains and innumerable snowsheds are barely visible in Jackson's two-part panorama. In the left-hand image's lower left corner along the first big loop is the town of Busk, where the Busk-Ivanhoe tunnel opened in 1893. It ran under the pass and Mount Ivanhoe to Basalt and Carbondale on the Western Slope. From there, one branch ran to Aspen and the other to Glenwood Springs and Grand Junction, the end of the line for the Colorado Midland. The Midland, the first standard gauge (4 feet, 8 ½ inches) line to penetrate the Colorado Rockies, originated in Colorado Springs and represented that city's aspirations to match Denver's spiderweb of steel.

The Midland survived until 1918. Even earlier, the 1893 abandonment of the original pass route above the tunnel allowed the mountainsides to revegetate, the natural development now dominating Fielder's shot.

This Jackson panorama required an entire morning to find and rephotograph. Thank goodness that he captioned it "Hagerman Pass," the name we attribute even today to the low point in the Sawatch Range due west of Leadville between Mount Massive and the peaks of the Holy Cross Wilderness. Our drive west up Hagerman Pass Road (Forest Road 105) eventually led us to the conspicuous 90-degree bend seen in the bottom of the left-hand photographs that precedes the numerous railroad switchbacks leading to the top of the pass. However, from the road, we could not see the switchbacks in order to confirm that we were in the right place. We parked the car, packed up the camera and some lunch, and began to ascend the mountain due east of the crest of the Sawatch Range.

And mountain it was. A test shot taken with Polaroid film about halfway up confirmed my fear that we would have to climb all the way to the top in order to stand in Jackson's footsteps. Fifteen hundred feet of hard-earned vertical gain later, we were there. Eric and I walked back and forth along the flat mountaintop to find the correct longitude, using the bend in the road/railroad bed as the primary perspective clue. Unfortunately, trees blocked Jackson's original purview, requiring us to move 30 yards to the left of his location in order to make the two photographs.

Notice that, in the left-hand photographs, the lower bend in the railroad bed in Jackson's version is farther to the left of the low point in the Sawatch Range than it is in my photograph. The modern road does not follow the original railroad bed up the switchbacks seen in Jackson's photographs. Instead, it courses farther north as it approaches the top of the pass. The Colorado Midland reached the other side of the Continental Divide through a tunnel, now abandoned and inaccessible, where you see the rails disappear in Jackson's scene.

60

FRYINGPAN RIVER

The Seven Castles,
Colorado Midland
Railway, 1888

p. 107

MP   The Fryingpan/Arkansas Project represents one of Colorado's most ambitious undertakings of water engineering. Snowmelt destined for Aspen's backyard instead finds itself diverted through a maze of tunnels, canals, and reservoirs to Pueblo and points farther east. It's just one example of Colorado's enormous effort to replumb Mother Nature and force water delivery according to the patterns of human settlement, rather than those of gravity and topography.

Congress approved the Fry/Ark project in 1962. Its purpose was to transfer runoff from the deep snowpacks west of the Continental Divide and spread their life-giving sustenance to the dry prairies hundreds of miles east. The project's name is easily explained: It diverts water originating in the Fryingpan's watershed that naturally flows westward to the Colorado River, instead delivering it into tunnels that take the water to the Arkansas River and ultimately the Atlantic Ocean. Other transmountain water diversions tap the Colorado River's headwaters for the Cache la Poudre, South Platte, and Rio Grande rivers, as well.

The Fry/Ark project includes a half-dozen tunnels that lace the mountains between Independence and Hagerman passes. Constructed by the U.S. Bureau of Reclamation, these tunnels deliver water into Turquoise Lake near Leadville, where it is later released into the Arkansas River for summer irrigation and to fulfill Pueblo's municipal needs. Twin Lakes Reservoir comprises another feature of the Fry/Ark project. The Bureau of Reclamation raised the levels of the two original lakes and connected them by means of a dam.

The Fry/Ark project was part of a 1960s-era boom in transmountain water diversions. Denver completed Dillon Reservoir just as the Fry/Ark project was getting started. Aurora and Colorado Springs joined the water diversion parade with their own transmountain water supply project, the Homestead Project, which draws from the Eagle River's headwaters near Minturn and also tunnels the water to Turquoise Lake.

Transbasin water diversions rely on the peak of the hydrograph, the surging spring floods that rush downstream during the rapid burst of snowmelt. Their cumulative impacts are ecologically significant. High mountain wetlands previously flooded are now starved for water and shrunken in size. The native

fishes that evolved in the Colorado River system find their spawning beds no longer seasonally inundated by snowmelt. The total effects of these diversions — and of the vast quantity of water redirected to farms and cities in California and Nevada — reach as far as Mexico, where the Colorado River now often dries up before reaching the Gulf of California.

The Colorado Midland Railway descended the west side of Hagerman Pass after exiting the tunnel previously mentioned (see Photo Pair 59). It followed the Fryingpan River all the way to its junction with the Roaring Fork River. Today, Frying Pan Road (Forest Road 105) follows that same path down to the town of Basalt.

From the road, Eric and I spotted the cliffband named the Seven Castles, so all we needed to do was find a way up onto the hillside to the north. As luck would have it, Forest Road 510 soon led us to an open gate that accessed a ranch meadow. From there, we were able to drive to the edge of the bluff overlooking the valley. After a short hike, in a matter of minutes, Eric and I seemed to be in Jackson's exact spot — proof might be the relationships of the distant ridges with one another. A car traveling on the road duplicated Jackson's moment made historic by the train in his scene.

61

EAGLE COUNTY

Eagle Park, 1887

p. 108

TN This mountain valley known to Jackson as Eagle Park became the Pando stop on the Denver & Rio Grande Railroad line between Leadville and Red Cliff. During World War II, the U.S. Army selected the remote mountain valley as the training base for its first and only ski troops, the Tenth Mountain Division. Named for Colorado Spanish-American War hero General Irving Hale, the camp replaced an iceberg lettuce farm on the valley floor of the upper Eagle River. Constructed in 1942, Camp Hale ultimately housed 735 officers and 13,500 enlisted men.

Many skiers who trained here returned to Colorado after the war to launch ski areas at locations such as Arapahoe Basin, Aspen, and Vail. The camp was leveled in 1965 to its concrete foundations, spotlighted with sunlight in the middle of Fielder's photo. The concrete foundations are about all that remains of Camp Hale, a National Register Historic site. The site hosts reunions for the dwindling number of veterans who made this a major landmark for both Colorado's military and the ski industry.

 I had no idea how significant this Jackson photograph was until I explored my Colorado map for the location of Eagle Park, a name that, like so many others, might prove to be archaic. Guessing that it was along the Eagle River, I consulted my map and it did show an Eagle Park. I can't describe the tremendous elation I felt when I found the words "Camp Hale" in the same place. This valley was home to 10,000 ski troops of the Tenth Mountain Division during World War II. Jackson certainly had no idea just how historic Eagle Park would become more than a half-century after he made this photograph from the Denver & Rio Grande Railroad.

As a longtime backcountry skier, and an aficionado of Colorado's extensive system of mountain ski huts, I have always admired and idolized America's World War II ski troops. Camp Hale was the base from which they performed dangerous and challenging excursions into the frigid world of white, preparing for combats with Germans and Italians in an alpine environment. When I discovered the location of Jackson's photograph on the map, I did not worry as much about finding his place as I did about also unearthing a similar photograph of Camp Hale. Wouldn't it be interesting to have three photographs to manifest the history of Eagle Park—before, during, and after Camp Hale? Such a photograph proved elusive, so you must use your imagination by looking at images of Camp Hale made from other angles in the valley.

Forest Road 714 follows the old railroad bed. Five minutes after exiting U.S. Highway 24, we arrived at the approximate location from which Jackson made the photograph. Unfortunately, Mother Nature was up to her old tricks again in the form of spruce and fir trees impeding the correct purview. I could only see the valley through the new forest from one place, and it happened to be 30 yards to the left of Jackson's spot. Notice that the conspicuous hill in the middle of the valley lies a bit to the right of where it should be in my photograph. Notice also that the East Fork of the Eagle River has been moved from its natural location, a result of the construction of Camp Hale.

62

EAGLE COUNTY

*Gilman and Eagle River
Cañon, 1890*

p. 109

JR The rich ore deposits at Gilman were discovered in 1879 during the wave of prospecting that followed discoveries in Leadville. When Jackson took his photo, the mines had already been producing for more than a decade. By 1970, the mines had turned out more than 10 million tons of ore containing 393,000 ounces of gold, 66 million ounces of silver, 105,000 tons of copper, 148,000 tons of lead, and 858,000 tons of zinc. Production ended in 1984 when the deposits were exhausted; the electricity was shut off, the mines allowed to flood, and the town abandoned.

The lowest outcrops in this view of the canyon are Precambrian granite, about 1.7 million years old. The granite is overlain by layers of Paleozoic sedimentary rocks that were tilted gently eastward during the uplift of the Sawatch anticline, or arch, in the Laramide episode of mountain-building. Cambrian Sawatch Sandstone (about 510 million years old) forms the continuous cliffs running across the slope, about halfway between the town atop the ridge and the river below; the top of the light-colored mine dump in the left center of Jackson's photo abuts the base of the Sawatch Sandstone. The two light-colored dumps near the right side of the historic picture are in Mississippian Leadville Dolomite (about 335 million years old), which forms the discontinuous band of cliffy outcrops visible in the contemporary picture at the top of the steep slope.

Although some mineralization occurred in veins within the Precambrian rocks and the Sawatch Sandstone, by far the largest and most productive ore bodies here were irregular, tonguelike masses of sulfide minerals in the Leadville Dolomite. Some of these masses were more than 200 feet wide and 150 feet thick, and extended more than 4,000 feet down the slope of the layers; they were connected by cylindrical, pipelike ore bodies that cut across the rock layers. The deposits were apparently formed about 34 million years ago by hot solutions that emanated from a body of intrusive igneous rock somewhere to the east.

The Gilman mines employed hundreds of people for more than a century, supplying significant amounts of coveted copper, zinc, and lead during World War II. However, drainage from the flooded workings continues to flow into the Eagle River, severely damaging the aquatic ecosystem. Gilman is a classic example of how the activities of one generation, perhaps undertaken with the best of intentions, cascade down the decades to the detriment of succeeding generations.

JF We braved a steep and slippery slope down from U.S. Highway 24 to find this Jackson location. I could only hope that the ore-car rails and accompanying buildings in the foreground of his photograph were still intact. As ridge alignment clues show you, I was standing where I should have been, but no signs of the mine remain. Because of the hillside's extreme pitch, I can only assume that rockslides took their toll on most of this area's buildings during the past 100 years.

63

EAGLE COUNTY

Redcliff, circa 1887

p. 109

TN   Red Cliff, as it is now spelled, was a larger town in 1887 when Jackson visited than in 1998 when Fielder followed Jackson's tracks. From an 1890 population of 818, Red Cliff has dwindled to 289, according to the 2000 census. Miners founded the town in 1879 after silver strikes on Battle Mountain drew a swarm of fortune seekers. They found a plat level enough to situate a town where the Eagle River Canyon broadened at its junction with Homestake and Turkey creeks. By 1881, Red Cliff boasted a railroad, a sawmill, five hotels, and an opera house. Despite its fast start, Red Cliff never exceeded a population of 900 and, in 1921, lost the county seat to Eagle.

Metal-roofed, slab-sided buildings cling to the mountainside in disarray. Miner's shacks, log cabins, vernacular false-fronted commercial buildings, and a one-room schoolhouse make this a more authentic relic of the mining frontier than other mining towns reborn as fashionable ski resorts with streets of cute, colorfully frosted gingerbread buildings. Once a home for miners, the town now houses many service and construction workers who labor elsewhere, notably Vail and Beaver Creek.

JF A steep hike up the hill on the south side of the town of Red Cliff swiftly delivered Eric and me to Jackson's location for making this photograph. The basic street layout is still the same as when Jackson was there. How many buildings can you find that have endured since the 1880s? Perhaps a visit to Red Cliff would help you to answer that question.

64

MOUNTAIN OF THE HOLY CROSS

1873

pp. 110–111

RP The mountain with the cross on its flank was the stuff of legend for a few generations before Jackson managed to photograph it. It flickers in blue haze in the view from Mount Evans, some 50 miles away, and again from Grays Peak or from Shrine Pass, south of Vail. Trappers and explorers spoke of glimpsing it from afar, never quite believing what they had seen but taking it for a vision or a sign. In dry years or late, hot summers, it never appeared at all.

Jackson and his ghostwriter, Karl Brown, explained this mystery in Jackson's autobiography *Time Exposure* (page 216): "No man we talked with had ever seen [it]. But everyone knew that somewhere in the far reaches of the western highlands such a wonder might exist. Hadn't a certain hunter once caught a glimpse of it—only to have it vanish as he approached? Didn't a wrinkled Indian here and there narrow his eyes and slowly nod his head when questioned? Wasn't this man's grandfather, and that man's uncle, and old so-and-so's brother the first white man ever to lay eyes on the Holy Cross—many, many, many years ago?"

When Jackson found his way up Notch Mountain in the summer of 1873 and made a successful picture of the elusive peak, it made his reputation as a photographer. The poet Henry Wadsworth Longfellow wrote a poem about the place. Jackson's friends, the painters Thomas Moran and Helen Chain, painted it sight unseen. And when the photograph was displayed at the Centennial Exposition in Philadelphia three years later, visitors and reporters crowded the room to see the famous photograph.

Why the hubbub? The sign of the cross etched on a Rocky Mountain peak symbolized different things for different people. Christians viewed it as a divine gift, a sign of New Testament truths, and eventually succeeded in creating the short-lived "Mount of the Holy Cross National Religious Shrine." Romantics and American Transcendentalists saw it as the emblem of a constant, perfect "One" above the changing, inferior world of nature and man. And for those who staked their future on America's growth, the cross as a powerful emblem of Manifest Destiny—the idea that territorial expansion and settlement were our nation's God-given destiny—was real, correct, and true.

The story that Jackson retouched the cross to make it look more perfectly balanced is exaggerated. Some of Jackson's negatives and prints have been retouched—one adds a waterfall, another adds a

snowfield in the shape of a kneeling angel. But for the most part, the retouching seems intended to even the tones of the image, to make the snow look cleaner, and to distinguish the peak's high ridges from the surrounding sky.

JR This view of Mount of the Holy Cross from Notch Mountain probably ranks as Jackson's most famous photograph. In fact, the cross in his photo is so striking that he was accused of altering the negative! The spectacular cross reveals itself when snow accumulates in the steep couloir on the east face of the mountain and on the more-or-less horizontal ledges that constitute the arms.

The mountain is composed of Precambrian metamorphic rocks in the core of the large up-fold known as the Sawatch anticline, which formed during the Laramide orogeny. The couloir marks a nearly vertical fault; the ledges that make up the arms are controlled by joints, or rock fractures, that intersect the fault at nearly right angles. Depending on snow conditions, the cross might appear as vividly as it does in Jackson's picture, or it may vanish completely.

A glacier that probably disappeared only about 12,000 years ago occupied the valley between Notch Mountain and Mount of the Holy Cross. The lobate accumulations of talus on the opposite side of the valley are rock glaciers that formed since the large glacier retreated from the valley. Making exact comparisons between the photographs proves a challenge because of lighting differences, but it appears as though the rock glaciers have not moved appreciably since Jackson took his photo.

The early reports of the Hayden Survey listed Mount of the Holy Cross' elevation as 13,478 feet. The Hayden atlas published in 1877 revised the elevation to 14,170 feet. The U.S. Geological Survey map published in 1949 gave an elevation of 13,995 feet, thus removing Mount of the Holy Cross from the list of Colorado's Fourteeners. However, it regained Fourteener status with new surveys in the 1960s, which determined the elevation of the peak to be 14,005 feet. Of course, the mountain's elevation hasn't really changed — the figures merely represent improvements in surveying techniques. No doubt new surveys using laser and GPS equipment will further refine the elevation of this famous peak.

IF I knew that I'd have to hike high to find the site where W. H. Jackson shot his signature photograph, but I had no idea that I would have to make the trip three times! Jackson made this photograph from the top of Notch Mountain at 13,237 feet above sea level. Being the explorer and misguided individualist that I am, I rarely accept offers from others to tell me how to do something. I prefer making mistakes and enjoying successes on the road to discovery. I suppose that's gotten me to where I am going a bit more slowly than most people, but the joy and experience gained from living life by the seat of one's pants are unequalled by any other form of learning.

So I never bothered to ask anyone about Jackson's location for this image. In fact, there's a whole club dedicated to perpetuating Jackson's memory that makes annual pilgrimages to the spot I needed to find. But nooo… Would I call and ask for directions? Of course not. Instead, I pulled out my tattered copy of the White River National Forest map and looked for the nearest high mountain due east of Mount of the Holy Cross. Right where I needed it to be was a place called Notch Mountain. And there was a bonus — a trail right to the top! What more could you ask for?

On a cloudy day during the first week of July, Eric Bellamy and I set out to climb that trail, camp overnight on top of Notch Mountain, and, in the morning, make a beautiful photograph of Holy Cross from Jackson's location. The 5-mile hike to the top, and some 3,000 feet of vertical gain, put us right next to a stone shelter, which we interpreted to be a Jackson shrine. Unfortunately, the monsoonal clouds had descended low enough to just cover up the very peak we needed to photograph. And without the peak, we had no way to employ the ridge trick to find Jackson's approximate location and subsequently the specific rocks in his foreground. We went to bed early having never seen Holy Cross, and endured a scary thunderstorm during the night — we were in a tent with metal poles next to a stone building that was a perfect magnet for lightning, given that it was the highest thing around.

We survived the night and awoke to fresh snow on the ground, blue skies, and a clear view of Holy Cross about a half-mile to the west across the most beautiful alpine cirque valley you'll ever see. However, we immediately discerned that we needed to be a half-mile north of where we were in order to begin searching for Jackson's location. We set out across the long ridgetop of the mountain, but came to a halt 400 yards later when the ridge turned into a 100-foot cliff: the "notch" of Notch Mountain. The mountain is actually two peaks separated by a chasm that, without climbing ropes, would have required a 1,000-foot descent and then an ascent back up again to reach the top of "north" Notch Mountain. By then, the obligatory monsoonal clouds had begun to build, so we decided to leave this place and come back the following week. Eerily enough, the weather also thwarted Jackson's first attempt at photographing Mount of the Holy Cross.

With my son J. T., Danny Jones, and Eric in tow, we made a one-day hike to the top of the north side of Notch Mountain. Along the way, we discovered a fine trail not marked on the map; it took us right to the top and the very place where Jackson had made his image in 1873. His foreground rocks revealed themselves almost immediately, but when I looked up, Holy Cross was nowhere in sight. Again, monsoonal clouds had covered the peak. Nevertheless, I was determined not to have to make the climb again, and told the boys that we would wait there until the clouds lifted. A sandwich later, the peak appeared and we scrambled to make a number of color and black-and-white images like Jackson's famous photograph. Would you believe that within 20 minutes of finishing our work, the peak had disappeared again into the clouds?

A month later, the folks at KCNC-TV NEWS4 asked me to return to the top of Notch Mountain so they could film me "discovering" Jackson's spot for their weekly TV series about the project. Why not? Three's a charm.

65

BRECKENRIDGE

Hook Eye Curve, Denver,
South Park & Pacific
Railroad, circa 1885

p. 112

JP   Jackson made this high-angle view of the upper Blue River Valley on a summer afternoon just a few years after the Denver, South Park & Pacific Railroad completed its route over Boreas Pass from South Park. The tight loop of track in the foreground is Hook Eye Curve, which carried the rails down the last few miles to Breckenridge, in the distance on the left edge of the photographs.

The DSP&P was the brainchild of John Evans, a Denver businessman, ex-governor of the Colorado Territory, and onetime physician. Evans had taken a leading role in building the Denver Pacific Railroad that connected Denver with the Union Pacific's transcontinental line at Cheyenne, Wyoming, in 1870. He attempted to capture the rail freight markets of the Front Range's biggest ore-producers — Black Hawk, Central City, Idaho Springs, Georgetown, and Silver Plume — but was surpassed by W. A. H. Loveland's Colorado Central. With the best route to the nearest mining district tied up by the competition, Evans decided to build a new line to the next closest mining center, which was near Fairplay on the western fringe of South Park.

The DSP&P was organized in September 1872 by Evans and a *Who's Who* of Denver capitalists that included financier Walter Scott Cheesman, engineer Leonard Eicholtz, attorney Bela Hughes, bankers Charles Kountze and David H. Moffat, Jr., and many others. Construction began almost a year later, and the first steel rails were set down in May 1874. Local commentators, investors, and especially industrialists in the Fairplay district complained about the slow rate of progress, but to no avail: By June 1878, the end of track stretched just beyond Two Forks — a scant 35 miles from Denver.

The problem was that the route's difficult terrain required blasting, bridges, and culverts that quickly ran up the bills. In addition, poor planning, lax oversight, and a general economic slowdown that stretched out delivery times for steel rails, locomotives, and other essential equipment compounded the challenges. Just as distressing for Evans and his partners was the ever-shifting center of Colorado mining: By 1879, when the DSP&P actually approached its original target, Fairplay was small potatoes compared to the rich new strikes at Leadville and in the Gunnison region.

In 1880, the railroad started a short branch line from Como, in South Park, to the Lechner coal mine in the foothills of the Park Range. In April, the company's directors chose to push the branch line over the mountains to Breckenridge, where they hoped they might find ample freight business and an easy route to Leadville's riches. A month later, they sold the whole railroad to Jay Gould of the Union Pacific.

Jackson had met Gould the year before, just as the Hayden Survey was winding down. Gould remembered Jackson's 1869 photographs of the Union Pacific, and offered to contact "a number of railroad officials in Denver" on Jackson's behalf. Gould knew every railroad official in the state—he was hip-deep in business with the Colorado Central, the Denver & Pacific, the Denver & Rio Grande, and the Kansas Pacific companies as well as the DSP&P and his own Union Pacific; his good word helped to launch Jackson's Colorado studio and his career as a railroad photographer.

The DSP&P changed its name to the Denver, Leadville & Gunnison in 1890, then became part of the Colorado & Southern Railway system in 1908. The line was abandoned in 1937, but its route remains in use as a scenic auto road in summer, and a popular cross-country ski trail in winter.

JF My first guess about Jackson's location was the right one. Having driven Boreas Pass Road many times throughout the years, I knew that it would provide views over the town and perhaps Hook Eye Curve. As it turned out, the road follows the exact path of the old railroad bed for almost the entire way over the pass, down into South Park, and ultimately to the town of Fairplay. Eric and I merely had to travel the road until Jackson's view emerged. From that vantage point we discovered that the only change in the route had been the elimination of Hook Eye Curve. Boreas Pass Road now shortcuts the curve, which remains an access road to a local ranch.

Notice that the tree cover in the landscape today almost matches that of Jackson's day. This finding was an exception to the general pattern we had observed during the project: In the 19th century, cutting and fire had rendered the tree cover around mining towns more sparse than it is today.

66

BRECKENRIDGE

Rocky Point, circa 1885

p. 113

TN This railroad grade curve on a mountainside east of the town of Breckenridge overlooks what is now Breckenridge Ski Resort—note the runs visible in Fielder's photo. Rocky Point, a dramatic, rock-walled cut, lies on a dirt road between Breckenridge and Como in Park County. The road follows the bed of the Denver, South Park & Pacific Railroad, a narrow-gauge line that wound up 5 percent grades and tight S-curves. The 64-mile roadbed includes 435 curves, with the longest straight stretch measuring only 1.6 miles long.

Completed in 1882, the line was abandoned in 1937. Ruins of the engine house, boardinghouse, and snow sheds atop 11,482-foot Boreas Pass are disappearing, but the Section House has been restored, as has the Baker Water Tank (1882). Located 6.6 miles east of Breckenridge, this 9,305-gallon redwood cylinder was moved here in 1910 from its original site on the Denver, South Park & Pacific near the Alpine Tunnel. In autumn, the turning aspen leaves make this route a golden path to Breckenridge. In winter, cross-country skiers have it to themselves.

JF   Eric and I discovered a number of winter photographs in the Jackson archives, most made along railroads that operated year-round. We even dug up a few 19th-century skiing photographs depicting people on long wooden boards with staffs in their hands that they used to steer and slow down. Unfortunately, none of these contained an identifiable location, making rephotography impossible.

Because Rocky Point is an archaic name for this spot along the Boreas Pass rail route, Eric and I were at first unsure of its location. However, the drive to discover the area in the Hook Eye Curve photograph (see Photo Pair 65) suggested that we might continue up the pass in our search for the gap in the rock wall through which the train must have traveled.

In winter, snowplows clear Boreas Pass Road only for a short distance past the last homesite. Thereafter, the route is designated as a ski trail to the top of the pass, where sits a beautiful hut called the Section House. Part of the Summit Huts Association huts and trails system, the Section House is an old railroad building restored for the use of backcountry skiers and snowshoers. Eric and I parked our vehicle in the lot where the snowplow stops, and set off on snowshoes to see if we could locate Rocky Point. Two hundred yards up the trail it appeared, and we soon found and climbed the small hill on which Jackson stood to make his image. Regrettably, two fir trees had grown up in the middle of the scene, requiring us to move 10 feet to the right of Jackson's spot. Therefore, the prominent rocks in the foreground are out of kilter. Notice how the fire-damaged forest in Jackson's photograph has grown back, as well as how other trees fell to make way for the ski runs on Peaks 10 and 9 of the Breckenridge Ski Resort.

67

TENMILE RANGE

Blue River Range, 1873

pp. 114–115

JR   The jagged peaks of the Tenmile Range seen in this view are chiefly composed of Precambrian basement rocks — ancient metamorphic and igneous rocks that form the underpinning of this part of the continent. Here the basement rocks are principally gneisses and schists that formed about 1.7 billion years ago when high pressures and temperatures deep within the Earth's crust transformed volcanic and sedimentary rocks. About 1.4 billion years ago, the metamorphic rocks were intruded by the Silver Plume Granite that forms some of the light-colored outcrops in the left foreground of the photographs and the crisscrossing light-colored dikes near the center.

    Much later, a blanket of sedimentary rocks a few hundred feet thick — chiefly sandstone, shale, and limestone deposited in the shallow seas that covered this part of the continent during the early part of the Paleozoic era, between about 500 and 330 million years ago — covered the basement rocks. During the Laramide orogeny, the episode of uplift and mountain-building that first gave shape to the present mountains about 70 million years ago, the basement rocks and their cover of sedimentary rocks were raised into a great elongate arch, or anticline, that now forms the Sawatch Range. The Tenmile Range is part of the eastern limb of the Sawatch anticline that has been broken, uplifted, and tilted by younger faults that lie along the west side of the range. Quandary Peak on the right skyline in this view is capped with some of these eastward-tilted Paleozoic sedimentary rocks, and the eastward-sloping sedimentary layers are clearly visible in Jackson's photo. The same sedimentary rocks also top Mount Lincoln and form the debris in the foreground.

    Like most of Colorado's high mountain valleys, the one in the foreground and left mid-ground hosted glacial ice several times in the last million years or so, most recently only 15,000 to 12,000 years ago. Evidence of the work that glaciers performed here exists in the valley's U shape (in cross-section), the ice-polished rocks on the valley floor, the lakes such as Wheeler Lake (near the left edge of the photos) that occupy ice-scoured depressions, and the glacial amphitheater, or cirque, at the head of the valley. Talus (broken rock pried loose by frost action) that tumbled down-slope and accumulated in fanlike piles forms the smooth, light-gray aprons that festoon the sides of the valley. Notice that many of these talus aprons have spread out across the ice-smoothed outcrops on the valley bottom, indicating that most of the accumulation formed after the retreat of the last glaciers.

W. H. Jackson climbed some of Colorado's 14,000-foot-high peaks in 1873 and 1874 as the Hayden Survey's official photographer. I don't usually have time to climb Fourteeners during my nature photography excursions, and I'm not one of the goal-oriented hikers aiming to "bag" all of them. Nevertheless, I did look forward to ascending the ones that I had missed and on which Jackson had photographed. The *Denver Rocky Mountain News* was launching a weekly serialization of the book beginning in January 1999, so I thought it would be fun to take *News* reporter James Meadow and photographer Linda McConnell along with Eric and me to the top of Mount Lincoln (14,286'). James is about my age, physically fit for an old guy, and just plain fun to be with, and Linda's a fine photographer.

On a lovely August morning, the four of us hit the trail for the short but steep, 4,000-foot climb to the top to see if we could find Jackson's vantage point. Though Jackson's caption did not mention Mount Lincoln, the U.S. Geological Survey's Hayden Survey records indicated that the photograph was made there. It was logical anyway, as Lincoln is the next big peak due south of Quandary Peak (14,265'), seen in the right-hand portion of the photograph. The day glowed sunny until we arrived at the summit around 1 p.m., when the usual afternoon clouds began to roll in. We eschewed lunch until I could find and rephotograph the scene, not wanting to take a chance with "losing the light" or being struck by lightning! The ridge trick, as always, worked like a charm to indicate Jackson's location; in this case we used both the ridges in the distance and the one descending the north side of Lincoln, immediately in front of us.

Observe the similarity in the talus rocks at the bottom right-hand corner of the two photographs. This pair manifests very little change, aside from the new road to Wheeler Lake on the left. Though a bit more snow paints the mountains in the old photograph, I did duplicate the weather and clouds almost perfectly. As proud as I was of myself for being in the right place at the right time, we scarfed down our sandwiches and hustled back to the car before Mother Nature had the chance to teach us a little humility.

68

CHAFFEE COUNTY

*Great Morainal Valley
on the Arkansas at the
Mouth of the La Plata,
1873*

pp. 116–117

[JR] Clear Creek (Jackson's "La Plata") heads in a large basin along the Continental Divide that is ringed by high peaks, including La Plata Peak, Huron Peak, Missouri Mountain, Mount Belford, and Mount Oxford, all with elevations of more than 14,000 feet. The valley drains eastward through the crest of the Sawatch Range to empty into the Arkansas River about 2 miles south of the town of Granite. This view looks west up the valley of the Clear Creek from near its junction with the Arkansas River (foreground). Clear Creek Reservoir now floods the lower part of the valley.

The upper part of the Clear Creek Valley bears the distinctive U shape characteristic of glacier-carved valleys. The conspicuous, level-topped ridges on either side of the lower valley are moraines that mark the margins of the glacier that advanced down the Clear Creek Valley and into the Arkansas Valley.

Glaciers form where more snow accumulates in the winter than melts in the summer over a period of a few decades or centuries. The snow gradually changes to ice, which flows down-valley under its own weight, forming a glacier. The snout of the glacier advances down the valley until it reaches an elevation at which the amount of ice that is supplied by the flow of the glacier just balances the amount that melts during the summer. The snout of the glacier advances or retreats in response to this delicate balance, but the ice in the glacier always moves down-valley, even when the snout is retreating.

The moving ice carries rock fragments that have tumbled down the valley walls as well as debris incorporated into the ice. This load is released as the ice melts near the glacier's terminus and typically accumulates in prominent moraines such as those in this photograph. The high ridges on either side of the valley are lateral moraines that mark the edges of the ice tongue; the low, hummocky topography in the foreground is the terminal moraine that marks the glacier's front. These moraines were built chiefly during the last major glaciation, the Pinedale glaciation, which ended 12,000 years ago. At its maximum, the Clear Creek glacier measured 18 miles long and at least 900 feet thick at the upper ends of the lateral moraines. At that time, the glacier's snout extended beyond the present course of the Arkansas River and must have diverted the river through another channel along the east side of the valley floor.

The U.S. Geological Survey possesses the original glass-plate negatives that Jackson made during the Hayden Survey (notice the crack in the glass of this negative). The public can view and purchase copy prints of these images at the USGS photo library in the Denver Federal Center. Descriptions of the images derived from notes that Jackson made in the field, which helped Eric and me find the photographic locations, are also available. In this case, we learned that what Jackson called La Plata Creek is now called Clear Creek, and enters the Arkansas River along U.S. Highway 24, 13 miles north of the town of Buena Vista. I already knew that Clear Creek had been dammed to create Clear Creek Reservoir, so I thought it would be intriguing to see how much change a repeat photograph would manifest. Our goal was to find the specific rock and dead tree in the bottom right of Jackson's photograph high on a cliff—but this proved a challenge.

From the highway, Eric and I hiked across a trestle of the Denver & Rio Grande Railroad in order to cross to the east side of the Arkansas River. We then ascended the steep cliff that forms the eastern boundary of the river canyon from Leadville to Buena Vista. It consists of large rock outcrops mixed with piñon pines, junipers, and some grand fir trees. On this extremely hot day, two hours of scrambling around yielded no sign of the rock or tree, so we gave up and decided to use the "Dennis trick." Midway through the project we realized that instead of spinning our wheels and jeopardizing our undertaking's timely completion, we could just call my old friend Dennis Johns if we got stumped (so to speak)!

I hired Dennis, who was from Crested Butte, to sniff out some particularly hard-to-find places in the portfolio (sadly, Dennis died before ever seeing this book). He proved to have an uncanny knack for studying an old photograph, then a map, and finding on foot Jackson's spot. Two weeks later, Eric and I returned, but now with Dennis in the lead. The solution was distressingly simple: Jackson had photographed from the tip-top of the cliff, which was accessible, then and now, by way of an old wagon road that winds around the less steep east side. Once on top, Dennis had quickly discovered not only this location, but two others from which Jackson had photographed in the same vicinity. In this case, the dead tree had disappeared, but the rock remained. Dennis posed in the same place as had Jackson's companion.

69

BUENA VISTA

and Mount Princeton, 1887

pp. 118–119

TN The domed former Chaffee County Courthouse building occupies center stage in both photos. Built in 1883 at 501 E. Main St., it housed a safe full of county records stolen from Granite during a successful battle to replace that town as the county seat. Buena Vistans erected this ill-gotten, two-story brick courthouse with a stone inscribed, "Dedicated to Justice 1882." Leadville architect George E. King produced the design, executed by local builder Diedrich Fisher, complete with a matching jail, for $50,000. The classic Italianate edifice has central, pedimented bays on each side and a prominent octagonal cupola.

After Buena Vista lost the county seat in 1928 to faster-growing Salida, the courthouse became a school, to which a gym was added in 1937. The courthouse underwent yet another reincarnation in 1975, when it became the home of the Buena Vista Heritage Museum. The second floor contains a display with scale models of the Alpine Tunnel and the three railroads that chugged into Chaffee County. Despite some growth, including the new school in Fielder's foreground, Buena Vista remains a small town with many of the buildings constructed during its 1880s boom. Mount Princeton and Arkansas River Valley ranchland continue to dominate the background.

W. H. Jackson photographed from most of Colorado's railroads in the 1880s and 1890s. This image was no exception. From the Colorado Midland, he set up his 18-by-22-inch, glass-plate negative view camera and "snapped" this photograph of Buena Vista with Mount Princeton towering in the background. His wet-plate process utilized a silver emulsion that manifested higher contrast than today's black-and-white films — therefore, his bright skies and snow-capped mountains often disappeared from his images. Sometimes, to simulate the real sky that he saw, he would double-expose his photo paper and insert clouds from another image into the sky of the washed-out image. Most likely, that explains why the sky in this negative appears to have been "masked."

Eric and I drove County Road 304, the old railroad bed east of the town, in quest of Jackson's photographic site. Thank goodness at least one prominent building, the old, dome-topped courthouse, still exists. This structure acted as the key perspective clue: Aligning it with the correct spot on Mount Princeton allowed me to ascertain Jackson's location. Can you find any other buildings common to both photographs? Later that day, Eric and I climbed into the dome of the courthouse, now a gallery and museum, in order to duplicate a photograph Jackson had made from the same place in 1887.

70

BUENA VISTA

Main Street, circa 1885

p. 120

TN As the photos reveal, Buena Vista is one of the few Colorado mining towns to retain many frame buildings. Most communities, even if they did not suffer a disastrous fire, sought more stable brick and stone construction as they matured. The Railroad Hospital in the Jackson view serves as a reminder of how much railroads shaped Colorado. They gave life to towns like "Bue-knee," as locals call it, and when a railroad abandoned its tracks, it sent many a town to its grave.

Hospitals such as this one numbered among the many benefits of a railroad connection. Catholic nuns often staffed them. With their hospitals, schools, and orphanages, these sisters were unrecognized heroes on the Colorado frontier. The nuns were often German, Irish, or Italian immigrants, as were many of the miners and railroad workers to whom they tended. The Sisters of Charity and the Sisters of Mercy, who staffed many pioneer Colorado hospitals, looked after not only the physical health of their patients, but also their spiritual welfare.

 Thank goodness for historic preservation. I only wish there were more of it. In this case, the 1879 building that contained the "Black Hills Club Room" and the railroad hospital still exists. To find where Jackson had placed his tripod to make this view looking east down Main Street, I employed the building's northeast roof corner as the perspective clue with which to align the hilltop in the distance. Without it, I could have only guessed his location.

Did you notice that the building has an addition? And check out how I duplicated both the vehicular traffic and the laid-back atmosphere of Buena Vista, then and now.

NATURAL BRIDGE, LAKE CREEK.

71

LAKE COUNTY

Natural Bridge, Lake Creek, 1873

p. 121

Just above where Lake Creek empties into Twin Lakes Reservoir, it flows through a narrow gorge cut through the granite of the Twin Lakes pluton (a pluton is a fairly large body of intrusive igneous rock). The granite, about 64 million years old, was intruded into the surrounding Precambrian metamorphic and igneous rocks of the Sawatch Range during the Laramide orogeny, the episode that shaped the structure of Colorado's mountains. The Pinedale glacier that deposited the moraines around Twin Lakes (see Photo Pair 72) rounded and striated the upper surfaces of the granite outcrops flanking the gorge. The angular faces on the rocks in the gorge walls, however, indicate that glacier ice did not smooth them. Thus either Lake Creek cut the gorge since the glacier's retreat or, as seems more probable, a torrential stream flowing beneath the glacier largely carved the gorge, as is common in glaciers that exist today.

The huge chockstone that formed the natural bridge was probably a glacial erratic — a boulder carried on or in the ice and deposited here when the ice melted. The principal changes since Jackson took his photo have been the disappearances of both the chockstone and the upper part of the buttress, seen at the right side of the images. Early reports mention that blasting in connection with a placer mining operation prior to 1893 had destroyed a waterfall above Twin Lakes. It seems likely that this blasting accounts for the changes. Notice that the water levels in the historic and modern pictures are nearly the same, but in the Fielder photo, several large blocks of rock absent in Jackson's photo rest in the creek. These rocks may well be the remains of the chockstone. The block in the left foreground might be part of the missing buttress on the right.

JF Lake Creek is the beautiful stream that flows east out of the Sawatch Range along today's State Highway 82, the route that climbs over Independence Pass on the "back way" to Aspen. I had photographed the creek many times through the years — it is bounded by lovely aspen tree groves, and contains a number of photogenic waterfalls and cascades before it pours into Upper Twin Lake. Nevertheless, its canyon is steep and inaccessible in places, and I knew that finding this specific location would be tricky. If it had not been for the University of New Mexico Press' book *Second View*, which depicted this same scene, I can't imagine how long it would have taken to find the location. This book revealed that the boulder wedged in between the cliffs along the creek was no longer there. Even then, I knew this was a job for Dennis Johns, whom I asked to do the detective work.

As usual, Dennis found the spot. Three miles west of the town of Twin Lakes, we climbed down into the canyon and re-created Jackson's scene from the south side of the creek. Jack Reed's explanation that dynamite might have obliterated the chockstone that formed the natural bridge makes sense, especially if you inspect closely the disparity between the right-hand rock wall, then and now. Much rock seems to have been lost.

72

LAKE COUNTY

*The Upper Twin Lake,
1875*

pp. 122–123

The Twin Lakes originated as two natural lakes cradled in moraines deposited during the Pinedale glaciation. The main glacier flowed eastward out of the Sawatch Range from near Independence Pass through the U-shaped valley now occupied by Lake Creek (right mid-ground in the photos). Small tributary glaciers flowed down the two branches of Willis Gulch (left side of the photos).

The need to meet the demand for water has drastically altered the shape and character of these lakes in the 123 years since Jackson took his photo. In 1901, a dam was built across the outlet of the lower lake and a new outlet channel to the Arkansas River was constructed. In 1935, the completion of a tunnel through the Continental Divide allowed the diversion of water from the Roaring Fork River into Lake Creek, increasing the latter's flow by more than 40 percent. A channel connecting the two lakes was dredged, destroying the free-flowing stream seen in Jackson's photo and converting the lakes into a single reservoir. In 1981, the U.S. Bureau of Reclamation completed a power plant on Twin Lakes Reservoir, at the same time raising the dam at the outlet. All told, the water level in the lakes has risen by as much as 15 feet since the time of Jackson's photo. The moraines that pond the lakes are not conspicuous in these views, but they are just as high and continuous as those in the valley of the Clear Creek about 5 miles to the south (see Photo Pair 68).

 We did not have to expend much effort to find this location. The Twin Lakes, now Twin Lakes Reservoir, are just as conspicuous today as they were in the 19th century, as are Mount Hope on the left and the Twin Peaks in the middle of the scene. Our goal was to find a way to the east side of the lakes. A quick turn off State Highway 82 led to a road down to the outlet that connects the upper and lower lakes, at which point we realized that we were already drawing close to Jackson's vantage point.

These two lakes are reservoirs today because the Fryingpan/Arkansas water diversion project dammed the lower lake. As a result, the water level creeps higher than it ever did in Jackson's day — and on this day, it did. The ridge trick dictated that we should have stood about 30 feet to the south of where we actually made the photograph in order to duplicate Jackson's scene perfectly. Can you find the clues that prove this fact? The high water level widened the canal between the two lakes, precluding standing in Jackson's exact location. Observe that the rise and fall of the lake level has destroyed most of the vegetation present in Jackson's day, and has also created a "bathtub ring" around the lake. It was appropriate to include the family boat as evidence that this place still serves as a beautiful and enjoyable Colorado retreat.

73

SAWATCH RANGE

*View over the Summits of
the Sawatch Range, 1873*

pp. 124–125

Colorado's Rocky Mountains are not a single chain of peaks running north to south, but a complex mosaic of mountain ranges, high valleys, and deep canyons. If the Rockies could be said to have a backbone, however, many would claim that it is the massive Sawatch Range that stretches more than 100 miles from Wolcott in the north almost to the San Luis Valley town of Saguache and contains many of the highest summits in the state. The mountains and the town of Saguache both take their names from a form of the Ute Indian word—pronounced "sah-*watch*"—meaning "blue earth" or "water at the blue earth." The name of the mountain range was codified in the Hayden Survey's report in 1876; the report also fixed the title of La Plata Peak, which Hayden named in 1874 using the Spanish word for silver.

Jackson made this photograph after July 18, 1873, when he left the town of Fairplay with instructions from Hayden "to cross the Sawatch Range to the Elk Mountains between the Gunnison River and the [Colorado]...and then to wind up the season by photographing the Mountain of the Holy Cross" in the northwestern Sawatch. In his autobiography, *Time Exposure*, Jackson recalled that his small team rejoined Hayden and the rest of the survey outfit above the East River early in August. Shortly afterward, a cantankerous mule named Gimlet slipped his pack and broke many of Jackson's hard-earned negatives. A good number of the negatives survived this disaster unbroken, or just with minor chips around the edges—but Hayden and Jackson agreed that Jackson should retrace his steps for about two weeks and repeat the most important lost photographs in reverse order. At the end of the summer, Jackson made his renowned photograph of the Mountain of the Holy Cross (see Photo Pair 64).

Jackson climbed many of Colorado's highest peaks that summer and during the following two years, either to use them as vantage points or to create monumental portraits of the mountains themselves. His high-country photographs served several purposes at once: They supported the work of the Hayden Survey's topographers and scientists by documenting the lay of the land and geologic formations; they provided romanticized images for publicity; and they added to a broad, ongoing national conversation about nature, landscape, and art. In pursuit of these aims, Jackson climbed several Fourteeners besides La Plata: Capitol, Democrat, Evans, Grays, Lincoln, Longs, Pikes, Torreys, and Uncompahgre.

It is frustrating to think of those broken negatives lying in shards on an unnamed ridgetop in the Elk Mountains, but they are not the only ones "missing." A few years later, for example, Jackson tried some newfangled "gelatin dry plates" that, unlike the wet collodion negatives of the early 1870s, could

be carried around for days or weeks before they were developed; but processing errors and poor handling ruined a whole season's worth of work before Jackson had a chance to print it. Even using the wet collodion technique, Jackson could carry only so many glass plates into the field, so he had to edit his work late in the season, clear the second-rate negatives with an ether-soaked rag, and recoat the blank glass to make new photographs. This "field editing" involved difficult choices and more than a few trade-offs, as Jackson had to select images that satisfied his own artistic standards as well as the documentary and publicity needs of Hayden and the other survey members.

JF From the summit of Colorado's fifth-highest peak, La Plata (14,336'), both Jackson and I made our photographs. The fastest way to the top starts at the intersection of State Highway 82 and Forest Road 391, where the South Fork of Lake Creek enters Lake Creek. From the parking lot, a beautiful trail first winds through lodgepole pine, then spruce and fir, before entering the alpine zone on the north flank of the peak. Some 4,000 vertical feet of gain are required to reach the top by this route, which Eric and I hiked on a fine August day around noon. Once on top, it did not take long — perhaps 10 minutes — to find Jackson's spot.

Photographic locations from peak tops always proved easy to pinpoint — Jackson usually included rocks in his foregrounds, the sort of rocks that have been there for thousands, if not millions, of years. Can you locate the specific rocks that I knew I must find if I was to stand exactly in his footsteps? Once I spotted the rocks, it was only a matter of making a couple of Polaroids and comparing the then-and-now images in order to decide where I should plant the tripod legs.

I was lucky that my photograph mimics not only the place, but also the weather. Unfortunately, those clouds preceded lightning and thunder, so Eric and I quickly made our photographs, gobbled a sandwich or two, and then beat it back down to the car before the mountaintop became a lightning rod. Nevertheless, we had to don raingear during the last 2 miles to stay dry. That was okay with me, as hiking in the rain is one of the most sensual — and among my favorite — experiences in the Rocky Mountains.

74

GLENWOOD CANYON

The Walls of the Cañon of Grand River, circa 1891

pp. 126–127

JR   Glenwood Canyon is the spectacular gorge that the Colorado River cuts across the White River Plateau. At its deepest point, about 4 miles downstream from where these pictures were taken, the walls of the inner canyon rise more than 2,700 feet in about three-quarters of a mile. Most of the canyon lies in Paleozoic sedimentary rocks, but Precambrian granite, about 1.7 billion years old, is exposed in the deepest parts of the canyon. The cliffs in the foreground are Sawatch Sandstone of Cambrian age (about 510 million years old). Sandstone, shale, and limestone of Ordovician and Devonian ages (350 to 490 million years old) make up the broken slopes above the Sawatch cliffs. The upper part of the ridge in the background is Leadville Limestone (about 340 million years old). These represent some of the best exposures of these strata in central Colorado; in most places, either the erosion following the uplift of the Ancestral Rocky Mountains has removed them or younger rocks have covered them.

The present course of the Colorado River was apparently established about 10 million years ago when the river flowed across volcanic and sedimentary rocks that blanketed the White River Plateau. Subsequent uplift of the plateau caused the river to cut down through the blanket of relatively soft rock and into the Paleozoic rocks beneath. As uplift continued, the river kept up the pace, eventually cutting into the Precambrian basement rocks in the deepest parts of the canyon. Much of the inner canyon was probably carved in the last 5 million years. Volcanic ash that was deposited at river level at the eastern end of the canyon about 600,000 years ago now stands 300 feet above the river—which would indicate that during the last 600,000 years, the river has deepened the canyon at the rate of about a half-inch per century.

JF   One look at Jackson's photograph of Glenwood Canyon was all it took to fuel my passion for taking on this project. Finding just this one place would make all 25,000 miles and nine months of driving around Colorado on behalf of this undertaking worthwhile. How exciting it would be to ascertain just how much of that spectacular cliff on the river's right would have been excavated to clear the way for Interstate 70. Though I derive no joy from seeing Mother Nature abused, I did come to develop a perverse

sense of satisfaction in witnessing the degree to which we humans have altered the landscape. One of the broader goals of this project was to shock people into understanding that we had better change our ways before we pave over the very landscapes that brought us and keep us here in the first place.

Initially, I had no idea where this place was within the 20-mile-long canyon, so Eric and I began our search by driving back and forth on Interstate 70. Ultimately, the steepness of the canyon walls in Jackson's photograph, with or without so much rock removed, functioned as our best clue. After a few passes, we determined that our place was about a mile-and-a-half west of the Bair Ranch exit, but on the other side of the river, where the railroad tracks still carry trains! We walked west on the tracks, listening intently for train whistles, until the profile of the left-hand ridge appeared and intersected with the right-hand ridge at the proper point. A look across the river dumbfounded us both, for it became clear just how much rock had been obliterated to make way first for U.S. Highway 6, and then Interstate 70.

Another Jackson scene that I reshot in the canyon in June 1998 brings to mind a morbidly funny story. The location was farther west, about 2 miles from the Shoshone Dam. With permission from Public Service Company of Colorado (now Xcel Energy), Eric and I crossed the dam to the railroad tracks. There we found an enormous beaver, deceased and lying belly up between the two rails. Because it appeared to have suffered no trauma, we surmised that the animal was walking down the tracks when a train passed over it, scaring the hapless creature to death. (This could have been our fate when, 20 minutes later, we heard the whistle much too late and were almost flattened by a Union Pacific freight train.)

A year later in June 1999, I took a KCNC-TV NEWS4 crew down the tracks to record for its series my "discovery" of that same Jackson location. As I was telling the reporter about the dead beaver I had found the year before, I happened to look down just as we must have reached the place where the creature had met with its unfortunate fate. It was still there — lying on its back, skin intact, but now headless! A quick search divulged that the head lay below the tracks. We were all amazed that no scavengers, no single train out of the several thousand that must have passed over this spot in the past 12 months at high rates of speed, no rockfalls, and no weather or wind had removed the beaver from its exposed grave.

75

GLENWOOD SPRINGS

1901

pp. 128–129

TN   The U-shaped Hotel Colorado and the outdoor hot springs pool and bathhouse next to the Colorado River dominate both scenes. In 1887, the Denver & Rio Grande Railroad blasted its way through Glenwood Canyon, and the Colorado Midland Railway made its entrance via the Roaring Fork Valley. Both railroads promoted Glenwood Springs as a tourist destination while also tapping the rich coal deposits nearby.

Nowadays, the "world's largest outdoor hot springs pool," a restored Victorian bathhouse, and a grand hotel make Glenwood Springs the state's favorite place to "take the waters." The Yampa ("big medicine") Spring attracted the Utes for centuries before prospectors staked out a townsite at the confluence of the Roaring Fork and Colorado rivers in 1878. Walter B. Devereux, a mining engineer trained at Princeton and Columbia universities, arrived in 1883 and transformed the town into the "Saratoga of the West" by building the Hotel Colorado and the Hot Springs Lodge and Pool—still Glenwood's glories.

Amtrak passenger service continues to make Glenwood Springs a popular town for rail tourists, who travel more leisurely than motorists on often-congested Interstate 70 and State Highway 82, which intersect in the center of Fielder's photo. The highway and pedestrian bridge prominent in the contemporary photo have replaced the D&RG bridge, but the Colorado Midland bridge a half-mile downriver survives.

 Eric and I knew where we needed to perch in order to remake this Jackson view looking west down the Colorado River, but not how to get there. By May 1998, we had been practicing the art of being perspective detectives for two months. We believed that we had developed an instinct for seeking out Jackson's locations, if not just the knack for expeditiously finding the general vicinity without being distracted by obstacles. A lot of times, we probably just got plain lucky, too.

In this case, we drove a circuitous network of city streets toward the base of the hill east of town, only to encounter a dead end. However, right in front of us, Eric spied a sign that said "Scout Trail." We donned our packs and headed up, and up. This steep, dusty trail took us straight to where we needed to be. However, fir trees and piñon pines had grown up smack in front of Jackson's purview, requiring us to photograph to the right of his location by 15 feet. Which perspective clues tell you that we had to shift our positioning? How many then-and-now buildings can you find?

76

GLENWOOD SPRINGS

Bath House, 1891

p. 130

TN Interstate 70 and power transmission poles make Fielder's retake less idyllic than Jackson's unobscured, placid scene of the Colorado River and the hot springs pools. The railroad track along the south bank of the river is prominent in both scenes. The handsome, red-roofed depot in Fielder's photo was not built until 1904. Purple sandstone with gray sandstone trim forms the base of this depot, which rises into two brick towers that echo the towers of the Hotel Colorado. The three-story, recently restored Hotel Denver behind the depot houses the large, popular Glenwood Canyon Brewing Company and pub.

 The approximate locale from which we hoped to photograph Jackson's scene of the famous hot springs complex was obvious, but getting there was another matter. Still, we were honing our skills at picking the correct street from which to start a search on foot. Eric and I followed a couple of residential roads east from behind the Hotel Colorado in an attempt to position ourselves above the springs. By examining the Glenwood Springs overview photograph (see Photo Pair 75), you can see where we ultimately stood — on the right-hand side just above the powerlines and east of the last couple of homes on the hillside. With permission from the homeowner, we scurried out onto the ridge and set up the camera just about where Jackson did.

The round pool of water in both photographs is the original geothermal spring that supplies the complex. As Tom Noel mentions, notice a couple of additions to the landscape since the 19th century: Interstate 70 and the powerlines. Can you find any buildings in downtown Glenwood Springs common to both photographs?

77

GLENWOOD SPRINGS

Coke Ovens at Cardiff, 1893

p. 131

TN New construction caught in the act by Fielder's camera has obliterated much of the historic, once-extensive coke ovens at Cardiff, a now-defunct coal and coking town on the southwest outskirts of Glenwood Springs. The Colorado Midland Railway built Cardiff in the 1880s as a division point and coal and coking complex. Mining engineer Walter Devereux oversaw construction of the Cardiff coke ovens, as well as fuel smelters in Aspen and Leadville. Fifty-two rectangular Belgian stack ovens and 197 beehive-shaped coke ovens once connected by a stone wall lined a half-mile stretch of former railroad grade.

Because of its importance to Colorado's smelting industry, the town was named for the great smelting city in Wales. By 1910, Cardiff was a smoky village of 462 residents where coal brought by the railroad was fed into ovens to be cooked into coke. Last owned by CF&I Steel Corporation, which closed them in 1915, the Cardiff ovens produced more than 1.3 million tons of coke for smelters in Colorado and Utah. Colorado Midland conductors twitted tourists by telling them that the ovens were used to heat the water for "Glenwood's so-called natural hot springs."

 These old ovens once functioned on the southwest side of Glenwood Springs near today's airport. The town of Cardiff still exists on maps, so Eric and I quickly arrived in the vicinity. However, the row of ovens in Jackson's photograph has completely vanished, effectively eliminating my best perspective clue to tell us where to stand.

Nevertheless, the ridge trick once again saved the day. I believe that I made my photograph within feet of Jackson's location because of the precision with which I was able to employ perspective, using the three ridges in the photograph as reference points. Today this property is home to a steel company. A few "beehive"-style ovens around the corner from this site still linger, now protected as a historic monument.

78

CRYSTAL RIVER

Mount Sopris, Valley of the Roaring Fork, circa 1901

p. 132

EP The snow-capped peak in the distance is 12,953-foot Mount Sopris. The name Mount Sopris first appeared on Frederick J. Ebert's 1865 *Map of Colorado Territory, Embracing the Central Gold Region*, which Ebert drew under the direction of territorial governor William Gilpin. The difference in elevation between the valley floor near Carbondale and the summit of the peak — about 6,500 feet — lends such majesty to Sopris that it often is mistaken for a much higher summit.

The mountain is named for Captain Richard Sopris, who explored the Roaring Fork Valley with 14 other people in 1860. The sketchy, often conflicting accounts of the expedition are a historian's nightmare: Some versions of the story say Captain Sopris' party set out from Denver, but others claim they embarked from Black Hawk; most say they were miners, but one simply calls them "adventurous spirits," suggesting something more carefree than a search for precious metals.

Apparently, the group made its way through South Park and over the mountains to the area of present-day Breckenridge. From there, it went down the Blue River, up Tenmile Creek past what is now the Copper Mountain ski area, and — most likely — over Kokomo Pass to the Eagle River. The story gets murkier after that, but all accounts agree that the party reached the Roaring Fork/Crystal River valley, and many of them credit it with being the first group of white men to explore the area. A 1931 attempt to rename the peak "Mount Roosevelt" failed.

Jackson listed this as a Denver & Rio Grande Railroad photograph in his 1901 Detroit Publishing Company catalog. This same general vantage point was popular among railroad photographers for years afterward: Lewis Charles McClure in the 1900s, George L. Beam in the 1910s, and Otto Roach in the 1920s.

JF   We made this photograph of the Crystal River a few miles outside the town of Carbondale along what is now State Highway 133. In fact, the 1901 version of the highway appears in the foreground of Jackson's photograph on the opposite side of the river from where the highway runs today. With only a bend in the Crystal River as a perspective clue, Eric and I utilized the ridge trick (the ridge on the right intersecting with Sopris' north flank) once more to help point us to the vicinity of the scene. At the correct juncture, we turned off the highway at a sign that said "Crystal River Inn," and proceeded across the river and up a driveway to the inn. A man installing new driveway lights told us it would be all right to hunt for Jackson's location. Within minutes, we determined that to make his photograph Jackson had stood just about where the driveway makes its last switchback to the inn.

Today, cottonwood trees dominate the scene, a fact that we had learned, and would continue to observe, all around Colorado — especially along rivers and creeks in montane valleys of lower elevations. Notice that today's concrete bridge is in the same spot as Jackson's span, and a ranch still occupies the foreground. Considering how so many Roaring Fork Valley ranches have made way for golf courses and housing developments, I wonder how much longer this vista will remain intact.

79

CRYSTAL RIVER

Crystal River Railway,
Mt. Newman, circa 1905

p. 132

Jackson often photographed along Colorado's railroads — it was his main source of work from 1881 to 1894 — and he was not above applying the same formula to picture after picture. Many of Jackson's railroad views depict lofty, snowbound peaks at the head of a summery valley, with a river flowing into the foreground and a railroad alongside the stream. Leaning trees often frame the view, as they do here, and people stand — or, in this case, sit and fish — in the foreground to suggest the scale of the surroundings and to act as stand-ins for the viewer.

The railroad is barely visible in this view: Across the river and not quite halfway up the left-hand side of the photograph, note the glinting dots where sunlight bounces off a row of wooden ties. This is the Crystal River & San Juan Railway, built in 1905 under the direction of Colonel Channing Frank Meek, president of the newly founded Colorado-Yule Marble Company. A tireless promoter and tactician, Meek developed the astonishing marble beds on Yule Creek in the upper reaches of the Crystal River drainage, and built a huge mill in the town of Marble so that the pure white stone could be cut, finished, and polished before it made the long trip out of the mountains to every part of the globe. Meek supervised construction of an odds-defying electric trolley line to haul blocks of marble to the mill, and built the CR&SJ line from Marble to Redstone, where it joined the Denver & Rio Grande Railroad.

The Lincoln Memorial in Washington, D.C., and the Tomb of the Unknown Soldier in Arlington, Virginia, are made of Colorado-Yule marble. Highly valued for its sparkling grain and pure white color, the stone served as the primary material for such monuments of architecture as Los Angeles' Merritt Building, the First National Bank of Portland, Oregon, and the Salt Lake City Stock and Mining Exchange. Colorado abounds with gravestones and monuments carved from the snowy rock, and many buildings of Colorado-Yule marble survive in Denver to this day: The Denver Post Office (now Federal Courthouse) building at 19th and Stout streets, and the old Colorado State Museum at 14th Avenue and Sherman Street are but two examples.

The Colorado-Yule Marble Company struggled through the Great Depression, only to close in November 1941. Much of Colonel Meek's establishment was torn up and salvaged to fuel military and industrial efforts during World War II, and hundreds of quarry workers dispersed. For many years

afterward, blocks of marble left standing on the mill site were crushed into ornamental rock chips—but the quarry reopened on a modest scale in 1990 and continues to produce high-quality stone for buildings and sculpture.

We simply continued driving southwest along State Highway 133 after making the photograph of Mount Sopris (see Photo Pair 78) in order to locate this scene. The road follows the river all the way to the town of Marble, so it was just a matter of time before we identified Mount Newman.

The scene ultimately revealed itself about 7 miles to the east of the town of Redstone. However, this place served as a fine, though dreaded, example of both tree growth and highway excavation conspiring to hide or erase all perspective clues. The cottonwood trees along the river now concealed the left-hand ridge, and the cliffs on the right in Jackson's photograph had apparently been excavated to make way for the modern highway, if we were in the correct location. These factors made it impossible to know exactly from where Jackson had photographed. Just to double-check, Eric and I hopped into the car and surveyed the highway for a few miles in each direction, searching for any other place that would provide the same view of Mount Newman. No such place existed, leaving us confident that we had found the right place on the first try.

80

ASPEN

circa 1895

p. 133

Horse manure on Main Street and false-fronted frame buildings have vanished from Aspen, a long-busted silver city that evolved after 1945 into Colorado's trendiest resort town. The state's most affluent community started out in 1879 as a tent-and-shack mining camp called Ute City. Silver seekers from Leadville struck pay dirt in the broad valley where the Roaring Fork of the Colorado River is fed by Castle, Hunter, and Maroon creeks. After the Utes were dispossessed, the town was platted and incorporated as Aspen. Aspen Mountain south of town and Smuggler Mountain to the east boasted fabulously wealthy mines such as the Durant, the Little Nell, the Midnight, the Mollie Gibson, and the Smuggler, which produced the world's largest silver nugget, 93 percent pure and weighing 2,060 pounds.

Initially, Aspen grew slowly. It was a remote, out-of-the-way place. Miners paid as much as $100 per ton to transport silver by burro over Independence Pass to Leadville's smelters. Then the Denver & Rio Grande Railroad steamed into town in 1887, followed by the Colorado Midland in 1888. Jerome B. Wheeler of the Colorado Midland Railway built a fine hotel and an opera house, which he both named for himself, and a Queen Anne–style mansion that now houses the Aspen Historical Society. Such antiques stand out today in a town of much new construction, typified by the A-frame chalet with stone chimney at the right and the boxy modern building on the left in Fielder's photo.

JF   Thank goodness that the researchers for the Denver Public Library's Western History Department had determined that Jackson made this image at the corner of Main and Monarch streets. Otherwise, I would never have known where Jackson had placed his tripod. None of the buildings remain, and that ridge in the distance is not a conclusive clue. Nevertheless, when I got to that corner, the gently sloping northern flank of Aspen mountain to the northwest did match the slope of the ridge in Jackson's purview.

Now all we had to do was walk across the street and find a safe place to plant the big camera. Here, however, that turned out to be a chore. In today's Aspen, no longer the happy-go-lucky ski town it was in the 1960s, process and order now supersede a laid-back attitude. Too many new people, too many people in one place, and a general lack of appreciation for the environment in which Aspen dwells make it, in my opinion, a less desirable place today than perhaps it was in Jackson's day. As Eric and I walked along the crosswalk of Main Street, with the stoplight red, proceeding slowly while scrutinizing the view down Main for the photograph, suddenly I found myself 3 inches in the air with my heart pounding at 120 beats per minute. An Aspen cop seated in his Aspen-cop Saab must have thought Eric and I were walking too slowly, so he let off a 120-decibel siren blast that could very well have affected the genetic integrity of any creature within 50 feet for thousands of years. When the adrenaline rush died down, I could only smile at the irony.

81

ASPEN

*Cooper Avenue West
from Post Office Block,
circa 1898*

p. 133

TN   Some of the corniced Victorian commercial buildings of the 1880s survive on the left side of Cooper Avenue, while modern buildings prevail on the right side. Among downtown's venerable frame buildings is the *Aspen Times* building. The *Times* asserted on August 24, 1888, that Aspen "is far beyond her most formidable rivals...no city of corresponding age in the U.S. can compare."

From the beginning, Aspen seemed ambitious. Its broad, 70- to 80-foot-wide streets were laid out according to the compass rather than on the stream-oriented plat of many mining camps. Townsfolk planted trees along the streets and formed a literary society and a glee club. Aspen's population peaked in 1893 at around 12,000 as it briefly surpassed even Leadville in silver production to become the nation's number one silver city. In 1892, Aspen and Pitkin County produced more than $7 million in silver, compared to $5.1 million for Leadville and Lake County.

Aspen boasted Colorado's first electric lights and the first electric mining tramway. By the early 1890s, Aspen had a streetcar system, an opera house, and trailed only Denver, Pueblo, and Leadville in population. In 1893, the Silver Crash and subsequent repeal of the Sherman Silver Purchase Act of 1890 changed all that. The price of silver sank from about $1.32 an ounce to $0.59 an ounce. Aspen silver production sank to about $3.7 million in 1894, half of what it had been in previous years. The town's population also tumbled, reaching a low of 705 in 1930.

JF Again, the research conducted by the Denver Public Library swiftly delivered Eric and me to our destination, in this case Cooper Avenue and the view to the northwest. This scene did contain one building that still existed, and it became my perspective clue in relation to the steep north ridge of Aspen Mountain in the distance. In fact, I was able to "wedge" the ridge up under the gable of the building to match that same intersection in Jackson's photograph. I had to have been standing exactly in his location!

Note the modern post office behind the American flag. Based on Jackson's caption, an older version must have existed on this block in his day. Can you see the American flag in the old Cooper Street photograph? My version captures Eric crossing the street, in an attempt to mimic the pedestrian in Jackson's scene.

82

ASPEN

1887

pp. 134–135

TN   Aspen of 1887, as these views suggest, was more populous than it is today. Mines and miners' cabins even crawled up Aspen Mountain in the background, where skiers now pay $60 a day for a lift ticket. Aspen's great boom ended abruptly with the Silver Crash of 1893. One old miner, Jacques Bionis, supposedly blew himself to heaven. Bionis put three sticks of dynamite under his hat, then lit the fuse—a fuse long enough to allow him to finish his last pint of beer.

During the drowsy decades, the Hotel Jerome was about the only place for visitors to stay. There, a few miners lingered in the Hotel Jerome Bar or sat out front on the church pew that still serves as the town's loafers' bench.

"Hey, pops," a 1930s visitor asked one of the old codgers on the hotel bench, "have you lived here all your life?"

"Nope, not yet."

"What makes this town so slow?"

"Well, sonny, I'll tell you. The people in Aspen are all mineralized. They've got silver in their hair and lead in their pants."

After the 1893 Silver Crash, Aspen saw little construction until the late 1940s, when the ski era dawned. Newcomers acquired silver bonanza structures for back-taxes unpaid since 1893. Since the 1950s, steady growth has brought Aspen back from a 1930s low point of 700 residents to a 2000 population of 5,914.

JF We knew where we needed to head in order to duplicate Jackson's great overview of Aspen. Between the city and Red Mountain to the north lie foothills that provide a fine view south toward Aspen Mountain and the peaks of the Maroon Bells–Snowmass Wilderness. Unfortunately, residential streets and large homes cover just about every square inch of these hills. Eric and I set out to find access to the southern edge of the escarpment in order to look down on the Roaring Fork River as had Jackson. We soon came across a street named Ridge Road, packed densely with homes right on the edge of the bluff. We cruised back and forth in an effort to achieve the correct latitude, straining to see the view between the homes. When we believed that we had reached the proper spot, we parked the car and knocked on the door of the appropriate home whose back porch we needed to visit.

I discovered long ago that a smile can literally open doors. This case proved no exception. The caretaker for this residence gladly accepted my explanation and allowed Eric and me to access the south-facing porch. Once there, we instantly realized that we had hit the nail on the head: Jackson must have stood 20 feet below us on the hillside itself, for everything seemed to align perfectly. Our major hint was the intersection of the right side of Aspen Mountain with the ridge behind it on the right, very faint in Jackson's photograph, but still usable as a clue. Notice that the Roaring Fork River has changed course and that cottonwood trees now dominate the riparian area. Can you find Hallum Lake in both photographs?

83

PITKIN COUNTY

Castle Peak, 1873

p. 136

JR Castle Peak — the high peak on the left skyline — and the ridges and peaks in front of it are composed chiefly of interlayered red-brown sandstone, shale, and conglomerate of the Maroon Formation. These sedimentary rocks were deposited here during the rise of the first major mountains in central and western Colorado, the Ancestral Rocky Mountains, which were uplifted 300 million years ago. The sediments represent materials eroded from these long-vanished mountain ranges. The sedimentary layers visible in Jackson's photo are emphasized by relatively thin, light-colored sills — sheetlike bodies of igneous rocks injected parallel to the sedimentary layers — which were intruded about 34 million years ago, after the episode of geological uplift known as the Laramide orogeny. The rounded white outcrops in the basin at the bottom of the photographs make up part of a large body of igneous rock called the White Rock pluton, emplaced at about the same time as the sills.

The area with the hummocky surface and lobate outlines, which appears medium-gray in the center of the photographs, is a rock glacier — a jumbled mass of angular boulders and rock fragments with an ice core that moves gradually, much like a normal glacier. Some rock glaciers here in the Elk Mountains move as much as 1 or 2 feet per year, but I can discern no appreciable changes in the outline of this one during the 125 years between Jackson's photo and the modern photo. Some rock glaciers in this part of Colorado formed after the end of the Pinedale glaciation, but before a warm period that ended about 7,000 years ago. Others seem to have formed during the "Little Ice Age," an interval during which fluctuations in the unstable climate included many extremely cold periods between about A.D. 1400 and 1850.

JF Finally, Eric and I were in our element: the heart of the Colorado wilderness. In my day job, I am a nature photographer. The then-and-now project was a way to help pay college tuition for three kids! Ever since January 1998, when we found a handful of Jackson's images taken in what is today the Maroon Bells–Snowmass Wilderness, I had dreamt of making the backpacking forays necessary to rephotograph these sublime places. In 1992, I had photographed in this wilderness for an entire book, *To Walk in*

Wilderness: A Colorado Rocky Mountain Journal. Friend and writer T. A. Barron accompanied me on the adventure, and together we published the book, derived from a 30-day hike through most of this wilderness' 181,000 acres. So I was chomping at the bit all year in anticipation of returning to some of the places I already knew and loved, and that Jackson had visited 125 years before.

As much as we wanted to spend significant time in this wilderness, we had 300 other places to find and photograph in less than a year. It was one thing to approximate a Jackson location when I could use a building or two as perspective clues, but entirely another when the clues were remote topographical features. Finding our mark quickly would be a challenge if we relied on reconnoitering on foot — the mountains are too steep, the obstacles too numerous, and the distances too great. Therefore, Dennis Johns scouted for Jackson's Maroon Bells locations before Eric and I arrived. Ultimately, he found all of the Jackson locations before he ever left home by first identifying specific physical features on both the old photograph and a modern topographic map, then connecting the points on the map and extrapolating a straight line back to some other high point on the map where Jackson might have stood. The three of us were able to make a beeline, albeit with some serious and steep hiking involved, to each of the remote locations.

To find this particular place, the three of us backpacked 4 miles to camp at Twin Lakes at the head of the Middle Fork of Brush Creek. The next morning, we climbed to a ridge east of Triangle Pass at 13,000 feet, which Dennis had previously identified on his map. The lack of a foreground in Jackson's photograph mandated the use of the ridge trick (as you can see, there are plenty of ridges) in order to know where he stood. Eventually, we noticed a conspicuously flat spot that seemed like a typically convenient Jackson tripod foundation—assurance that we were within feet of his remote photographic location. The view looks east toward Castle Peak (14,265'), the high point in the photograph.

84

PITKIN COUNTY

Maroon Mountain
National Range, 1873

p. 137

MP The Maroon Bells' brilliant red hues and distinctive silhouettes make them one of America's most-photographed landscapes. The peaks' parallel striations canted slightly upward bespeak their origin as sediments at the bed of an ancient ocean. Few events so vividly demonstrate the immense power of geologic forces and the inconceivably long duration of geologic time than the uplifting of seabeds to lofty peaks, today almost 3 miles above sea level.

As Jack Reed explained previously (see Photo Pair 83), the Maroon Formation's history began 300 million years ago atop an ancient mountain range raised in central and western Colorado. As erosion wore down the so-called Ancestral Rockies over millions of years, iron-bearing sediments washed into an inland sea where the reddish sands and muds compacted thousands of feet thick. When the modern Rockies began uplifting 65 million years ago, these sand and mud seabeds underwent terrific heat and pressure, hardening into the Maroon Formation.

Unlike the firm granite that marks many other mountain peaks, the rocks of the Maroon Bells more easily crumble and break. The "rottenness" of the rock makes the Bells one of the most difficult and dangerous climbs among Colorado's 54 peaks above 14,000 feet. Climbers must exercise extreme care not to dislodge rocks onto fellow climbers below, or lose their footing on the loose talus that covers the steep slopes and knife-edged ridges.

Early explorers considered the Bells one summit — "Maroon Mountain." By the time climbers began to seriously pursue its summit, around 1908, the northern peak was noted as a subpeak of the main mountain, and common terminology came to call the northern summit "North Maroon Peak" and the main summit "Maroon Peak."

The U.S. Forest Service early recognized the appeal of the peaks and surrounding terrain for sightseers seeking scenery and mountaineers honing their climbing skills. The range's designation in the 1930s as a Forest Service "Primitive Area" emphasized the opportunities here to enjoy natural beauty and primitive recreation. When the Wilderness Act was passed in 1964, the Maroon Bells became one of the nation's first official wilderness areas. The boundary initially encompassed a relatively small area centered

on the Maroon Bells. The wilderness area later doubled in size, in 1980, to include more of the valleys on the range's west side.

JF Using the map technique described in the previous Maroon Bells entry (see Photo Pair 83), Eric, Dennis, and I were also able to find this Jackson location quite easily — albeit on another backpacking excursion. In this instance, we departed from the Trail Rider Pass trailhead in the Lead King Basin of the Maroon Bells–Snowmass Wilderness and ended up camping high on a ridge at just under 13,000 feet, below the place depicted in the photograph. That afternoon during the first week in August 1998, we climbed the ridge in search of the foreground rocks in Jackson's scene. By the time we reached the top of the ridge, the temperature dropped to below 32 degrees Fahrenheit and, of course, it began to snow! Though you cannot see the flakes, my photograph was made while it was snowing.

From 13,300 feet above sea level stretches a fantastic view of this serpentine ridge, which divides the headwaters of Snowmass Creek and the North Fork of the Crystal River. The ridge ends at the wilderness' two namesake peaks, North Maroon Peak (14,014') on the left and Maroon Peak (14,156') on the right. This color image gives you an idea why photographers love this place so much: the chromatic diversity of the complementary colors in the red rocks and green vegetation.

85

GUNNISON COUNTY

White-House Mountain and Elk Lake, 1873

pp. 138–139

JR Light-colored, granite-like rock — part of the Snowmass stock, which was emplaced about 34 million years ago — makes up Snowmass Mountain (left skyline), Hagerman Peak (right skyline), and the ridges to the right of Hagerman Peak. Maroon Formation conglomerate, composed of material eroded from the Ancestral Rocky Mountains about 300 million years ago, forms the smooth, ice-scoured outcrop in the foreground. The pebbles, cobbles, and boulders in the conglomerate are chiefly sedimentary rocks from older Paleozoic formations, but some are metamorphic and igneous rocks from the Precambrian basement, exposed during the Ancestral Rocky Mountain uplifts.

The valley above the lake bears the typical U shape of a glacial valley; the amphitheater between Snowmass Mountain and Hagerman Peak cradles a large rock glacier that formed after the Pinedale glaciation. Large, light-colored fans of talus festoon the lower valley slopes above the lake. No appreciable difference in the outlines of the rock glacier and the talus fans shows between the two photos. However, the disappearance of the large, rectangular block of conglomerate — probably a glacial erratic carried and deposited here by ancient ice — sitting in the left foreground of the Jackson photo is a real mystery!

After rephotographing the previous scene, the three of us spent a lovely, but cold, night sleeping under the stars once the snowstorm abated. The next morning, we packed up camp and hiked 4 miles to Geneva Lake, which Jackson called Elk Lake. Though I'd visited Geneva Lake many times before, I never tire of its setting at treeline and its reflections of Snowmass Mountain (14,092'), at left. We quickly found Jackson's location, but decided to have lunch while waiting for the sun to shine on the peaks before remaking the photograph.

This pair of photographs manifests one of the great mysteries of the project: Where is the large boulder in the bottom left corner of Jackson's scene? The boulder appears in the repeat photograph made in the late 1970s and published in the aforementioned book *Second View*, so it disappeared sometime during the past 20 years. I estimate that it must have weighed several hundred pounds, and could not have moved without the help of humans. After taking the photograph, I checked in the willow bushes in the foreground, in the lake (very cold water!), and under the spruce tree on the left — no boulder. Given that the location is a long way from a road, I don't think that the boulder was transported by any earthly means, therefore leaving only unearthly answers to the mystery. I do believe that we are not alone in the universe. My best guess is that this rock had some cosmic importance that we humans could never comprehend, and that it was beamed up for preservation by another civilization that must have paid a visit to this place sometime since the late 1970s. Do you have a better explanation?

Note the tundra growing on the foreground rocks in both photographs. The amount and shape of these three batches of plants have barely changed in 125 years! We know that driving our SUVs in high-country tundra can damage it, and we've heard that it takes 100 years or more for it to grow back, if at all. Perhaps this scene confirms that tundra grows extremely slowly. Notice also that we were able to duplicate Jackson's monsoonal cloud patterns.

86

GUNNISON
COUNTY

*Lake Brennand,
circa 1880*

pp. 140–141

I've mentioned that some of Jackson's captions contained archaic place-names — deeming the images mystery photographs — and if we did not recognize something in the scenes, only luck would allow us to stumble across their locations. The most enigmatic of these photographs also happened to be the most beautiful mountain reflection scene of the entire 22,000-image Jackson collection. It had a caption, but no one had ever heard of the place or identified the location.

From the moment I saw this image at the Colorado History Museum, I knew that I had been to the lake and mountains it depicted, yet for the life of me I could not recall where they were (I rarely forget a place that I've photographed). The image haunted my mind every day of the project, and I hoped that I would accidentally encounter it in my far-flung travels. By the end of August 1998, I had been just about everywhere I could possibly guess that it might be. No luck.

I was losing confidence in my intuition, and finally convinced myself that these mountains must grace the landscape of another state. "So be it," I rationalized. I had accomplished just about all that I had set out to do at the beginning of the year, so how important was the failure to find one scene?

One day early in September 1998, I was having breakfast in Leadville with Eric Bellamy and Dennis Johns. By then, Dennis had found each of the 10 obscure places that I had presented to him during the course of the summer. It never occurred to me to show Dennis the Lake Brennand photograph because I thought that few people knew mountain lakes in Colorado as well as I. Why bother? As soon as that photograph hit the breakfast table, Dennis proclaimed that he knew where the clandestine scenery was located. Eric and I both looked at him in disbelief, despite his unblemished record that summer.

"John," he said, "this is Lake Irwin." Well, I know Lake Irwin, having photographed all around it, but never quite at it, during the years that I taught photography workshops at the Irwin Lodge near Crested Butte. I've probably driven 100 times on the Gunnison National Forest road that circumvents Lake Irwin. I looked at Dennis and said, "We'll see."

Two weeks later, Eric and I were standing on the eastern edge of Lake Irwin as an invisible sun began to color the clouds pink above the Ruby Range. From that side of the lake, the three mountains appear separate from one another. From the western side, where I had always photographed, the three mountains seem as one. No wonder I did not recognize the scene. Driving around the lake after making

the mystery photograph, I looked at the sign that for 20 years had announced in big letters: "LAKE IRWIN." For the first time in my life I read the small print underneath: "Once called Lake Brennand." It dawned on me that if I had only taken the time, one moment in the past two decades, to read the fine print, I would not have been frustrated for the better part of a year trying to find Jackson's elusive photographic location!

The story gets worse. I traveled back to Crested Butte a year later, on a break from promoting *Colorado 1870–2000*, and went hiking in the tundra above Lake Irwin. After my hike, I drove back down the road from the Irwin Lodge and past the Lake Irwin sign. Do you know, and probably just to spite me for the fun I had completing the project, that the "powers that be" had changed the sign from the year before? It now read, "LAKE BRENNAND (formerly Lake Irwin)." Go figure!

87

GUNNISON COUNTY

View Down East River, 1873

p. 142

FP   Jackson photographed this splendid view down the East River in the summer of 1873, when a Hayden Survey team was mapping and exploring the Elk Mountains. Among the many chemicals and bits of paraphernalia he carried up the hill in order to create this image was a bottle of silver nitrate that he used to make his glass plates light-sensitive. If Jackson had been less preoccupied with his work, or interested in a different kind of silver, his career might have taken off in a new direction.

Six years later, two old hunter-prospectors, John and David Jennings, walked up this same valley and found a lump of "arsenical iron" at the foot of a talus slope; drops of glistening silver sweated out of the rock when they heated it with a blowpipe. So they picked their way up the slope, looking at loose rocks, until — 1,000 feet above their first find — they discovered a fabulous lode of silver ore that they named "The Sylvanite."

News of the rich ore strike spread like wildfire to other mining camps in the Gunnison River drainage, and back over the Continental Divide to Cañon City, Denver, and the world. Late in July, more than 100 new buildings had been tossed up in the valley below the Sylvanite; two sawmills and a 10-ton smelter chugged away around the clock, and several supply stores whittled their margins to win business from several hundred prospectors. The throbbing new town was named Gothic and, when it was incorporated a month later, every lot in town was sold in less than a day. The town doubled its size in the following month, and added a church, a hotel, and six commercial buildings. More than 100 mines opened in that and following years, and Gothic saw a steady stream of new arrivals bent on fortune — and an equal stream of disappointed seekers leaving for home or the next big "show."

This sudden burst of toil and hope was characteristic of Colorado's 19th-century mining towns. So were the snarled lawsuits and countersuits over mineral rights and landownership, and the fickleness of stock speculators who poured money into a mine one year and pulled it all out the next, so that even some very rich lodes sat idle for lack of steady capital. Gothic's boom tapered off in the 1880s and went flat in the 1890s. By 1930, the place was only a memory. It has drawn ghost-town buffs for years since World War II — including artist Muriel Sibell Wolle, who often sketched and painted there. On many days the valley probably is as quiet as it was when Jackson camped there.

 Dennis Johns found all the Crested Butte–area photographic locations for us. He had lived in "The Butte" for 20 years and was the obvious choice to save us time by doing the detective work before Eric and I arrived with cameras and equipment. I, too, love this area with a passion and had been making the pilgrimage there for many years. Wilderness surrounds the town: Maroon Bells–Snowmass, Raggeds, and West Elk; its ski area is my favorite; and Crested Butte is home to some of the most biocentric individuals, staunch environmentalists, I've ever known. The old town of Gothic, which bears the same name as the conspicuous mountain on the right in the photographs, hosts the Rocky Mountain Biological Laboratory, one of our nation's premier high-altitude biological research institutions.

As it turned out, this Jackson location was only 30 yards below Crested Butte's beloved "401 Trail," Gunnison National Forest Trail 401, which skirts the head of the main drainage in the area, the East River. So Dennis, Eric, and I made a direct assault on the place. Ultimately, a "misplaced" spruce tree required us to move 20 yards north of Jackson's location to photograph this scene looking southeast toward Crested Butte, the mountain in the middle. The only change in the scene is the addition of Gothic Road, which leads over Schofield Pass and on to the towns of Crystal and Marble.

88

GUNNISON
COUNTY

Red Rock Falls, 1873

p. 142

JR This small cascade on East Brush Creek northeast of Crested Butte marks the place where the stream encounters some especially resistant layers of rock in the Maroon Formation. These outcrops consist mainly of coarse sandstone and conglomerate formed of debris eroded from a mountain range to the southwest, once part of the Ancestral Rocky Mountains. These materials were deposited about 300 million years ago in gently sloping, fan-shaped accumulations around the margins of the mountain ranges, much like the alluvial fans in Nevada's basins.

The climate during these geologic events was probably arid or semiarid, with periodic torrential floods during the wet season. Occasional flash floods probably carried down the pebbles and cobbles visible in one of the conglomerate layers in the left foreground of Jackson's picture. Several sandstone beds display faint diagonal striping at low angles to the bedding planes. These manifestations are cross-beds produced as sand was deposited in the channels of the streams that built the alluvial fans. The rocks more fully reveal themselves in Jackson's photo because of better lighting and lack of vegetation — apparently the result of a forest fire that left the many standing dead tree trunks noticeable in the background of his image.

 The U.S. Geological Survey archives contain extended captions for most of the photographs Jackson made during the Hayden Survey. These bits of information especially aided us in finding the locations of photographs like this one, which offered no recognizable features as clues. This particular caption identified the spot as in the Crested Butte area. In addition, I thought that I recognized the rocks, even in black-and-white, to be of the Maroon Formation, the red sandstone that prevails in this region. Then we left it up to Dennis to isolate this creek and waterfall out of the several dozen creeks that drain from the surrounding wilderness!

Dennis was nothing if not persistent. After much searching, he found this waterfall along the East Fork of Brush Creek, which drains from the Pearl Pass area of the Elk Mountains to the north. The location lies just off the Pearl Pass four-wheel-drive road, not far from the junction of the East and Middle Forks of Brush Creek. Today, willow bushes have grown up in front of Jackson's purview, making the new photograph impossible to take unless in winter, when the limbs bear no leaves.

89

GUNNISON

*La Veta Hotel,
circa 1884*

p. 143

TN Comparisons such as this one call into question the idea of "progress" as the theme of Colorado's development. The La Veta, a palatial public hotel, has been replaced by much more modest private housing. This grandiose, four-story, Second Empire–style hotel opened in 1884 at the corner of South Boulevard and Gunnison Avenue. Built at a cost of $200,000, the hotel called itself "the grandest in Colorado." It was not, but did rank in the top tier of hotels with its 40-by-60-foot rotunda and grand black walnut, oak, and ash staircase under glass skylighting. The La Veta Saloon boasted six billiard tables and a splendiferous back bar with "the largest plate-glass mirror in Colorado."

After Gunnison faltered as a mining hub in the 1930s, the La Veta went downhill fast. A lone bidder bought it in 1943 for $8,350. He knocked down the upper three stories and tried to maintain it as a bedraggled one-story apartment house.

 A visit to the county clerk's office in October 1998 yielded the former address of the grand La Veta Hotel. When we arrived, we discovered that a couple of new homes had sprung up among the bricks and rubble from the demolished hotel. Apparently, the first floor of the building had endured as late as that very summer, and had recently served as a municipal building. As Tom Noel explains, the upper floors had been razed long ago. If Eric and I had rephotographed this scene a few months earlier, we would have captured on film what remained of the hotel.

As it was, the rubble and associated foundation of the hotel still allowed us to ascertain exactly where it had stood. The cliffs seen in the distance on the right in Jackson's photograph functioned as the perspective clue that made it possible for us to position the camera almost exactly where Jackson had. We did not even need to reference the West Elk Mountains on the left, now hidden by cottonwood trees. What a shame it is for Colorado to have lost this landmark hotel.

90

MONTROSE COUNTY

A Cattle Ranch on the Cimarron, circa 1885

pp. 144–145

EP Most of Colorado's bison herds had been hunted to oblivion by the time of statehood in 1876. Coloradans raised cattle in their place.

Stock raising got off to a slow start in the years just after the 1858 discovery of Colorado gold. Although Hispanic farmers in southern Colorado kept modest herds to supply their families and communities, large-scale cattle operations grew up along with the booming mines and towns of the 1860s and 1870s. Texas cattlemen drove large herds of rangy cattle up the Goodnight-Loving Trail, over Raton Pass, and north to Denver in 1864; local dealers bought the livestock and fattened it up for sale to miners, railroad crews, restaurants, and families. When railroads reached Denver and Cheyenne, they opened lucrative access to markets in the East and inspired the territory's stockmen to build their herds — from 147,000 head in 1867 to more than 800,000 in 1880.

The unsettled plains of eastern Colorado and the grassy, unfarmable mountain valleys offered easy chances for profit. Grass was free, expenses were few, and the men and women who controlled land along watercourses where cattle could drink found that a steer raised to market weight for $2 could fetch $25 or more. Stock growers turned their cattle out to forage on open range each winter, then rounded them up, cut them into herds according to their owners, and fattened them up on bottomland grass through the summer.

County cattlemen's associations that formed in 1870, and the Colorado Stock Grower's Association a year later, fostered cooperation among independent operators, circulated favorable publicity, lobbied the territorial legislature, and controlled the health and safety of their herds by publishing brand books, posting rewards, and hiring health inspectors and detectives. Their business succeeded so well and turned such nice profits that investment syndicates jumped into ranching in the 1880s.

But the 1880s cattle boom fell flat. Beef prices dropped almost 40 percent over 10 years. Overgrazing and a harsh series of droughts and tough winters littered the rangeland with emaciated carcasses. The relatively few cattlemen who stayed in the business abandoned the old open-range approach to invest in fencing, wells, and alfalfa fields that supported sedentary ranching with carefully bred, high-quality herds.

In the 20th century, rising land prices and other costs made ranchers increasingly reliant on public lands for summer pasture. The U.S. Department of Agriculture has issued permits for grazing on Colorado's 13 million acres of National Forest since 1899. The Taylor Grazing Act of 1934 set aside other public lands for use by stock growers on 10-year permits issued by the Bureau of Land Management. Such uses of public lands, and the fees cattle ranchers pay for their privileges, have generated heated debate in recent years.

JF Jackson photographed along most of the Gunnison River, including the area where the Cimarron River enters it near the old town of Cimarron. This town marked the exit point from the Black Canyon of the Gunnison for the Denver & Rio Grande Railroad. Jackson photographed the fall roundup on this cattle ranch a short distance upstream from the confluence.

A casual drive along U.S. Highway 50 and the use of the ridge trick expressly revealed this location. Disappointingly, Eric and I could not stand where Jackson did because the hillside on which he climbed had been partially removed to clear the path for the modern highway. Therefore, we had to photograph this scene looking west from 30 yards to the north of the correct location. Can you find the clues that indicate our shift away from Jackson's spot? Notice how the cottonwood trees rule the riparian area in 1998, just as along other rivers we encountered during the project.

91

GUNNISON RIVER

*Chipeta Falls, Black
Cañon of the
Gunnison, 1883*

pp. 146–147

TN Chipeta Falls was named for the wife of the Ute Chief Ouray, whose people once occupied the Gunnison River Valley. The Gunnison River is now dammed and the Denver & Rio Grande scenic route that Jackson captured on film now hides under the water. In 1971, the U.S. Bureau of Reclamation built the 469-foot-high, 740-foot-long Morrow Point Dam, the country's first large, double-curvature, thin-arch dam. Its dramatic, free-falling spillway measures three times the height of Niagara Falls, and the underground power plant has a 120,000-kilowatt capacity.

A relic of the railroad days has recently been built at Cimarron, once a major livestock loading depot. A 119-foot-long section of a four-span bridge over the Cimarron River has been recycled as a pedestal for D&RG narrow-gauge locomotive #278, with an attached boxcar and caboose. This rail remnant in a rugged, remote canyon commemorates the D&RG's engineering feat in building through the Gunnison River's valley and canyons. It also speaks of the larger search for a rail route west, beginning with the epic railroad survey of Captain John W. Gunnison in 1853. The National Park Service, which erected and maintains the Cimarron trestle train, also opened a small museum, visitors center, and exhibit of D&RG freight and stock cars at nearby Cimarron.

JF A phone call to the National Park Service's Curecanti National Recreation Area offices answered all questions about this location. When we mentioned Chipeta Falls, it evoked an immediate identification of this place: Today it is Morrow Point Reservoir, one of three reservoirs built along the Gunnison since the 1970s as part of the Wayne Aspinall Project. I made arrangements with the park service to tour the reservoir later in the summer (four more Jackson scenes were made here).

We launched a boat large enough upon which to set up my tripod and large-format view camera. Chipeta Falls tumbles down at the eastern end of the reservoir, not far from another famous landmark photographed by Jackson, the Curecanti Needle. By the time we arrived at the falls, I had already gained skill photographing with the large camera from a rocking boat, which proved unnecessary for this scene. We discovered a narrow ledge of rock on the north side of the reservoir on which I could just barely set up the camera. Can you find the perspective clues that reveal that I was about 10 feet higher than Jackson and a bit to the right of where he stood? Notice Jackson's personal railroad car that contained his dark-room and studio. He often set up his largest camera, which used an 18-by-22-inch glass negative, on the flatbed car in order to record the scenery.

Colorado 1870 - 2000 Revisited

Southern Mountains Locations

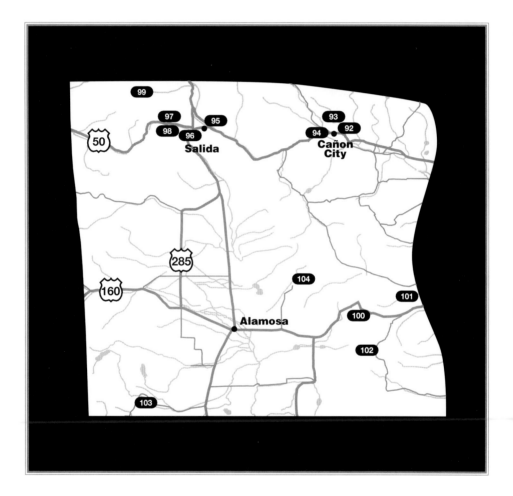

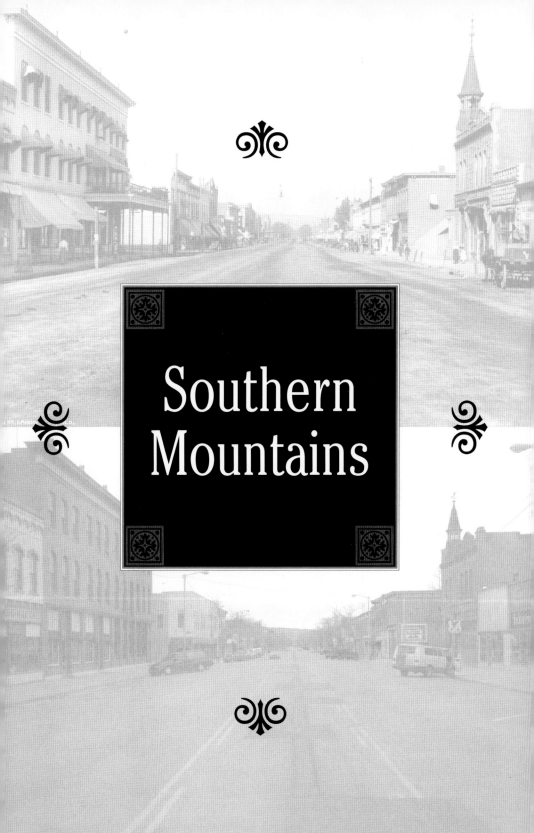

Southern Mountains

92

CAÑON CITY

Main Street, circa 1900

p. 151

TN Main Street retains such landmarks as the steepled Raynolds Bank Building in the right of both photos. Built in 1882–1883 at 330 Main St., this Gothic Revival gem's corner entry features a second-story turret crowned with a slender, 20-foot-tall spire, a reconstruction of the original.

Cañon City originated in 1859 as a supply camp for the upper Arkansas River mining towns. Cañon City led an up-and-down adolescent career as a mining supply town during local gold, coal, oil, tin, and zinc booms. The Denver & Rio Grande Railroad, which demanded and received $50,000 in bonds and town lots before building to Cañon City, made the town a rail hub.

Cañon City was a contender in the race for designation as Colorado's capital until it backed Denver's bid in exchange for a lesser political plum — the state penitentiary. Cañon City residents reckoned that the state prison would be better attended than the other possible second prize — the state university. Furthermore, prisoners, who in those times were rented out as cheap labor, were considered more productive than professors and students.

The town's well-preserved Main Street and residential areas reflect past economic booms. The Downtown Historic District, stretching from 3rd to 9th streets between Main and Macon streets, contains 80 brick and stone commercial buildings.

JF Main Street actually lies one block north of U.S. Highway 50, which some people might think is the main street in Cañon City because it carries so much traffic. Thank goodness for utility lanes in the middle of the street, designated for serving delivery trucks — Telluride's main street has one, too. They made it easy to set up the camera without getting run over and without having to ask the sheriff to protect our backsides!

As you can see, Main Street has changed very little during the past century: The street is now paved, but many buildings persist. How many of them can you find common to both images? Notice that the steeple on the right prevails in both photographs. The Raynolds Bank Building was built in 1882–1883, but its steeple was removed in 1924 and replaced with a replica in 1982. Is it the same design?

93

CAÑON CITY

Skyline Drive, circa 1900

p. 152

TN   Skyline Drive is one of Colorado's best examples of old-fashioned, scenic auto roads. Located a mile west of Cañon City off of U.S. Highway 50, the drive was built by convict labor around the turn of the last century for $6,400. It offers a 2.5-mile excursion along the ridge of Cañon City's western hogback, with its precipitous drop-offs and fine views.

Opened as a two-way buggy drive, it was converted to a paved, one-way auto road with deep dips and steep hills. The 1932 arch at the west entrance of Skyline Drive contains rocks from every state in the nation. Unlike modern highways, which straighten out curves and level the route with cuts and fills that scar the terrain, antique highways like Skyline Drive follow the contour of the land.

I was excited to have unearthed the Skyline Drive photograph from the archives. For 20 years, my family and I have enjoyed cruising along Skyline Drive whenever we are near Cañon City. Built during the last years of the 19th century atop a long, narrow, and precipitous ridge, this road parallels U.S. Highway 50 on the west side of town. It definitely can create "willies" in your stomach as you look simultaneously down both sides, several hundred feet. Until I found the Jackson photograph, I had no idea that Skyline Drive was historic.

This was an easy location to pinpoint, merely requiring that we drive until we find the remains of the rock wall fortification and certain natural rock clues on the hillside. Can you see that the location of the wall has changed? What ridge trick clues confirm that I stood in the correct place and that the wall had been moved?

94

ROYAL GORGE

circa 1888

p. 153

The thousand-foot-deep chasm of the Royal Gorge formed as the Arkansas River cut through the Precambrian basement rocks of the De Weese Plateau, the northwestern extension of the Wet Mountains. Metamorphism of volcanic and sedimentary rocks deposited about 1.75 billion years ago during the initial development of this part of North America formed the gorge's dark schist and gneiss. Soon after these volcanic and sedimentary rocks were deposited, they were plunged to depths of more than 7.5 miles, where they reached temperatures of more than 1,000 degrees Fahrenheit—so hot that the rocks flowed like soft putty!

The gorge's pink rocks chiefly consist of granite injected into the metamorphic rocks during their conversion to schist and gneiss. Much of the granite in the gorge's cliffs came from intruding offshoots of nearby masses of 1.7-billion-year-old granite, but some of it might have originated when the metamorphic rocks partially melted.

These basement rocks have been uplifted at least four times: initially more than 500 million years ago, prior to the deposition of Paleozoic sedimentary rocks like those at Gilman and Glenwood Canyon; once during the uplift of the Ancestral Rocky Mountains about 300 million years ago; again during the Laramide orogeny 70 to 50 million years ago; and finally during the uplift of Colorado's entire mountainous region between 10 and 5 million years ago. Before this last period of uplift, the Arkansas River flowed at the level of the prominent tableland at the rim of the gorge. During the uplift, the river maintained its course by cutting down through the tough Precambrian basement rocks, forming the Royal Gorge. This carving action would require that the river deepen the gorge 1 inch in about 400 years — quite slowly by human standards, but quite rapidly in terms of geologic time!

JF The alarms went off in my head when I first laid eyes on this Jackson photograph. I did not recognize the precise location — I have not spent a lot of time at the Royal Gorge, considering my tendency to avoid such tourist attractions — but knew that it would be fun to track down the exact spot, with all of the same rocks and cracks. And I was especially interested in discovering if I would be lucky enough to find the Royal Gorge Bridge, a modern structure, in the middle of Jackson's purview. As was the case throughout 1998, certain fortuitous events happened that made it clear to me that this project was just *meant* to happen — and the existence of the bridge in the contemporary view ranked high among them.

Can you point out the rock clues that delivered me to approximately the correct place? Can you find clues to prove that I perched too high up, compared to Jackson's location?

SALIDA

circa 1890

p. 154

TN These views from atop Tenderfoot Hill reveal that Salida has remained fairly stable in its buildings and town plan. Although the Denver & Rio Grande Railroad station in Jackson's photo on the east (near) bank of the Arkansas River is gone, the V-shaped configuration of the two major streets remains.

Salida, the county seat of Chaffee County, takes its name from the Spanish word for "exit" or "gateway" because of its location near the west end of the Arkansas River canyon. D&RG town developer and former territorial governor Alexander C. Hunt laid out the V-shaped town grid bounded by the converging Arkansas and South Arkansas rivers. The D&RG built a splendid depot, roundhouse, hotel, hospital, and some shops in Salida, a strategic division point for trains headed south over Poncha Pass to the San Luis Valley, west over Marshall Pass, or north to Leadville. The large, two-story, Queen Anne–style D&RG depot at the foot of F Street (the main street) was replaced by a 1930 Streamline Moderne depot, also now gone.

Local granite quarries and three brickyards fed a building boom that continued until the early 1900s. Salida became a major rail, smelter, and supply town, with a population peaking at 5,065 in 1930. A low rate of growth since then has left Salida with one of Colorado's most intact downtown historic districts. The town boasts a fine collection of masonry buildings, many showcasing splendid brickwork and rich stone trim.

JF It was evident that Eric and I would look for Jackson's location to the north of Salida. It took us awhile to find the nearest road across the Arkansas River, and longer still to hit upon the road that spirals to the top of Tenderfoot Hill. The hill contains the big "S" that stands for Salida. We needed only to set up the camera in a place that kept the angles of the various Salida streets in line, and to determine the appropriate elevation on the hill from which to shoot.

I suspect that we were at the correct latitude, but on second thought, perhaps we stood too high up (I had assumed that Jackson would have photographed from on top). Can you find the clue that indicates why we should have relocated a little bit lower? Notice that Chipeta Mountain, the snow-capped peak in the left background of my photograph, is missing in Jackson's image. His film emulsions could not effectively reproduce high-contrast scenes, therefore some mountains and many clouds disappeared from his negatives.

96

PONCHA PASS

*Mt. Shavano from
Poncho Pass, circa 1890*

p. 155

TN   Note the narrow-gauge locomotive and solitary passenger car in the Jackson photo. This might be the deluxe coach that Jackson traveled in, along with other publicists and officials, as he toured the line while photographing for the railroad. Today, as Fielder's follow-up photo shows, the railroad is gone, but you can still view its grade and many handsome stone retaining walls and trestle foundations during the scenic drive over Poncha Pass along U.S. Highway 285 between Poncha Springs and Villa Grove.

Poncha Pass, the northern gateway to the San Luis Valley, attracted stage lines and the Denver & Rio Grande Railroad. Despite booster railroad and real estate prospectuses, which sometimes featured Jackson's photos, the pass and the valley remain little developed, as Fielder's image suggests.

The word "poncha" could bear Spanish or Ute origins. Some authorities think it is related to the Spanish word "pancho," meaning paunch or belly, referring to the hump of the 9,010-foot-high pass. Commanding the background is Mount Shavano, a giant of the Collegiate Range at 14,229 feet high. It was named for a war chief of the Tabeguache band of Utes.

 I assumed that what Jackson called "Poncho Pass" was actually today's Poncha Pass, so we headed south on U.S. Highway 285 from the town of Poncha Springs. We soon decided that we should hike or drive to the top of the ridge just southwest of the little town in order to find Jackson's location. Sure enough, County Road 206 took us to a cemetery atop the ridge from which we quickly discovered Jackson's purview.

The railroad is gone today, but the bed remains. Can you identify some of the individual piñon pine trees that appear in both photographs?

97

MONARCH PASS

*View from above Chaffee
Looking Down, 1880*

p. 156

EP   Jackson's photograph of Chaffee City dates from the summer of 1880 — the year the town was named, and the summer before the railroad arrived to provide an easy conduit for the district's rich gold ore. But sources indicate that Jackson was not on the scene that year, so although he published the picture himself, it probably was made by someone else.

The most likely ghost photographer was a young man named George E. Mellen, who ran a photography studio in Gunnison in the early 1880s. Mellen wandered throughout the Western Slope for about three years, plying his trade in mining camps and new towns from Monarch Pass to the Elk Mountains and west to Grand Junction. In 1888, he opened a Colorado Springs studio that closed in less than a year — a failure that sent him to work for Jackson until he got back on his feet. He apparently never did: He worked in Jackson's studio until 1896, and photographed for the Detroit Publishing Company after Jackson joined the firm in 1897. Sometime in the 1880s or 1890s, Mellen turned over his stockpile of negatives to Jackson, who published them under his own name.

Regardless of its authorship, the 1880 view of Chaffee City portrays Colorado's boomtown glory in all its scruffy charm. Named for Colorado's first senator, Jerome B. Chaffee, the little village at the foot of the hill saw an influx of more than 3,000 gold seekers in 1878 after a prospector named Nicholas C. Creede hit pay dirt. Renamed Monarch in 1884, the town thrived until the Silver Panic of 1893 destroyed metal prices and plunged the nation into a five-year depression. Most residents left when the last train passed through in 1893; those few who remained tore down buildings for firewood. Snowslides and the construction of U.S. Highway 50 nearly completed the demolition job.

The CF&I Steel Corporation operated a limestone quarry on the hill south of Monarch in the late 20th century, hauling the rock to Pueblo for use in blast furnaces at steel mills. By that time, the town of Monarch had slipped quietly into oblivion — the quarry workers commuted from Poncha Springs or Salida. Some vestiges of cabins and a schoolhouse are all that remain.

I first came across this Jackson image at the Denver Public Library. Its associated caption told that Jackson had taken the photograph on the east side of Monarch Pass, and I deduced that the location was somewhere along today's U.S. Highway 50. Jackson had made a number of photographs along this route, so Eric and I spent a couple of days searching for their whereabouts. Despite the amount of landscape that had been excavated for CF&I Steel Corporation's limestone quarry, seen on the right in my photograph, we quickly recognized this particular valley in the long drainage. We would clearly have to climb above the highway near the entrance to County Road 231.

It was a steep climb. Eric and I scouted for a while for the rock outcrop on the left in Jackson's scene, but once we spotted it 300 yards above the highway, we knew how to duplicate his photograph exactly. Our tasks at hand were aligning the large boulder with the background and framing an adequate amount of landscape in order to contain Jackson's image area. We would crop my photograph down to precisely match the area shown in Jackson's image later on the computer, as we did for 95 percent of all the repeat photographs. Apparently, nothing remains of the town of Chaffee except for the few ruins that Eric Paddock mentions.

98

MONARCH PASS

Arboursville, 1880

p. 156

EP   George E. Mellen probably made this image in the same week that he photographed Chaffee City (see Photo Pair 97), and later turned it over to be published by Jackson. Arboursville — also known as Arborville, Arbourville, and Arbour-Villa — sprang up 5 miles below Chaffee City/Monarch on the heels of Nicholas C. Creede's 1878 gold strike. Unlike Chaffee, which was cheek-by-jowl with the rich mines upriver, Arboursville served more as a gathering place for miners, traders, and freighters who convened to exchange goods and stories, or to board stagecoaches bound for Cañon City or Alamosa. A few successful mines cropped up within a mile of town, and modest smelting operations processed ore from the surrounding hills, but Arboursville had one type of business that its wealthier neighbor did not: a brothel.

Colorado's early mining camps swarmed with men who drifted in great waves from one new strike to another. Most of them never struck it rich, and the majority went home after a year or two or found other lines of work. The steady supply of hopeful tenderfeet who arrived by wagon or stagecoach, horse or mule, provided muscle for heavy or dull jobs; others — blacksmiths, loggers, sawyers, harness makers — fell back on their old, useful trades to get by, and hunted for silver or gold during their off-hours. Many discovered that what now might be called "service industries" were steadier — and often more lucrative — than work in the mines. Storeowners who sold dry goods and groceries followed close behind the itinerant mass of would-be mining barons, as did engineers, lawyers, and the occasional preacher or two; together with the more successful miners and tradespeople, these folks formed the staunch core of the new communities.

Prostitutes and saloonkeepers, too, trailed close behind the first wave that rushed from place to place, and were considered as necessary as their counterparts in other professions. Some — such as Denver madam Mattie Silks — used their money, power, and business acumen to build small fortunes; others entered banking or politics to become pillars of their communities. The dance hall at Arboursville attracted its clientele from an area of 50 square miles or more and flourished with the local economy until ore prices fell or other, richer strikes drew people and their money away. But the music fell silent and the liquor stopped flowing there more than 90 years ago. Arboursville's fortunes declined along with those of other towns in the Monarch district.

JF The drive along U.S. Highway 50 west toward Monarch Pass eventually revealed the view of these peaks in the distance. But we needed to get down to the valley south of the highway, ultimately by way of County Road 226. A right turn off this road took us onto what appeared to be private property, and a quarter-mile later, we found ourselves in the middle of this valley. As the opportunity to align old buildings with mountains failed to present itself, we employed the ridge trick to decipher where to stand. We came within a couple of feet of Jackson's location.

Neither hide nor hair remains of Arboursville! Notice, too, how few coniferous trees remain, with aspens now ruling the landscape. This was not the only time we found evidence that Colorado contains more deciduous trees — aspens and cottonwoods, especially — today than in the 19th century. In the multicentury cycles of forest destruction from fire and cutting and subsequent regrowth, domination of tree type rotates back and forth from deciduous to coniferous. I am glad that I have photographed in my time — I don't know what I would have done without my beloved aspen trees! And I suppose that Jackson did not care much artistically about aspens anyway, as he only photographed in black-and-white.

99

GUNNISON COUNTY

The Palisades, Alpine Pass,
1883

p. 157

TN Note the dry-stack stone retaining wall that has held up well since 1881, when the Denver, South Park & Pacific Railroad built through the Palisades on its way to Gunnison. Italian or Cornish stoneworkers may have constructed this hand-laid rock wall, which measures 2.5 feet thick, 33 feet high, and 452 feet long. Crews had to blast and carve this roadbed out of the Palisades, a smooth, almost vertical wall of solid granite 400 feet wide and almost as high.

Located 164 rail miles west of Denver and a mile-and-a-half below the west portal of the Alpine Tunnel, this stretch took much of the year 1881 to construct. Despite the relatively high wages of $5 a week plus board and lodging, railroad workers kept disappearing. Many took railroad picks and shovels with them as they struck out to become miners in the nearby gold, silver, and coal camps.

Not until the summer of 1882 did the Palisades and the entire stretch from the west portal of the Alpine Tunnel to Gunnison open for regular train service. Boasting the first railroad tunnel completed under the Continental Divide, this route enabled the Denver, South Park & Pacific to beat its rival, the Denver & Rio Grande Railroad, into mineral-rich Gunnison County.

Former territorial governor John Evans, banker David H. Moffat, Jr., water and real estate tycoon Walter Scott Cheesman, and other Denver capitalists headed the Denver, South Park & Pacific, a line based in Colorado's capital city. The steam-powered, narrow-gauge line never reached its nominal goal — the Pacific Coast. It ran out of steam in 1883 in a remote mountain valley 40 miles north of Gunnison and 200 miles southwest of Denver. Nevertheless, the Denver, South Park & Pacific served Denver well, bringing in South Platte River Canyon lumber, Morrison sandstone, South Park hay and cattle, and Gunnison granite, coal, and gold. The Denver, South Park & Pacific became part of the Colorado & Southern Railway, which abandoned the dangerous and difficult-to-maintain Alpine Tunnel route in 1910 after a tunnel caved in.

The removal of rails in 1923 transformed the roadbed into a popular backcountry auto road. The tunnel has never been reopened, but the auto road and hiking trails lead over and around it. During the 1990s, the National Forest Service constructed a small museum at the tunnel, 19 miles northeast of Pitkin via Quartz Creek Road (Forest Road 839). The museum celebrates the Palisades as one of the largest, hand-fitted stone feats of railroad construction in the American West.

As the Fielder photo shows, only the capstones have been removed from the dry-stack stonework that still elegantly and stoutly holds up what now serves as an automobile road. Below the railroad grade is the old Williams Pass stage road, which descended into Brittle Silver Basin (also known as Missouri Gulch). Paywell Mountain rises in the background.

JF   I had been to the west entrance of the Alpine Tunnel in the Sawatch Range before, so I assumed that Jackson's "Alpine Pass" was one and the same. Forest Road 839 near the tiny community of Pitkin provides access to the tunnel's west portal. It did not take long to hone in on this location, made obvious by the sheer cliff shorn away in order to accommodate the railroad. Though the rails are gone today, the roadbed makes it possible to travel in a two-wheel-drive vehicle all the way to the tunnel, which has caved in on both sides of the range.

We handily ascertained Jackson's exact location by aligning the numerous rocks and cracks in the foreground with the ridges in the distance. Can you find the old roads, among which some seem unusable, that still exist today?

100

LA VETA PASS

Dump Mountain, 1881

p. 158

EP This heroic photograph is emblematic of the railroad's conquest of the Rocky Mountains — and of its unequaled power to shape the settlement and economic growth of Colorado.

The Denver & Rio Grande Railroad completed its narrow-gauge line over Dump Mountain, on the east side of La Veta Pass between Walsenburg and Alamosa, in 1877. At the time, the route astonished the railroad world by reaching the highest elevation over the steepest grades of any railroad in North America. Jackson photographed this sprightly, double-headed, passenger train — on its way down from Dump Mountain to the town of La Veta — on one of his first commissions after he left the Hayden Survey and established his photography studio in Denver.

Passenger service opened Colorado to settlers and tourist traffic in a way that no other conveyance ever had. With the 1870 arrival of the first train to Denver, travel time from Chicago or St. Louis was cut to just two days; it was possible to arrive from New York, Philadelphia, or Washington, D.C., in only three or four. Shortened travel times and intensive advertising by railroads and civic boosters contributed to rampant growth that expanded the territory's population from just 39,000 in 1870 to nearly 200,000 a decade later.

Railroads vaulted Colorado into the forefront of the nation's tourist industry at the same time. The state attracted more than 100,000 tourists two years after statehood, and twice that many by 1885. These visitors arrived by railroad, stayed in Front Range hotels and inns, then ventured into the mountains on narrow-gauge railroads to take in the scenic splendors of Boulder Creek, the South Platte River, and nearby mining towns such as Central City and Georgetown. Others frequented the soothing mineral baths at Idaho Springs, Glenwood Springs, Mount Princeton Hot Springs near Buena Vista, or Soda Spring in Manitou. Colorado Springs, though springless, grew into a large, fashionable, and "dry" resort for well-heeled tourists — mainly through the advertising prowess of William J. Palmer, head of the D&RG and one of the state's canniest land speculators.

Freight traffic was another mainstay of Colorado's railroads. Trains did away with long, slow, ox- or mule-drawn wagon trips, and slashed the cost of moving ore, refined metals, lumber, and coal to Front Range cities or on to the Midwest or the East Coast. Freight expenses for machinery, canned goods, shoes, pianos, and oysters "imported" from other parts of the country fell at the same time. In the 1880s and

1890s, the added speed and heavier payloads of the region's trains supported pell-mell development of new mining districts at Leadville, Silver Cliff, the San Juan Mountains, and Cripple Creek, powering Colorado industries to new heights of productivity that guaranteed continued business for the railroads.

For many years, railroads triggered economic growth wherever they went in Colorado. The D&RG, for example, linked far-flung raw materials with a substantial workforce to create Pueblo's booming steel industry and exploit the coal beds of Huerfano and Las Animas counties; it opened the San Luis Valley to large-scale farming, the North Fork and Grand Junction districts to fruit growing, and nearly all of the land within its service area to cattle and sheep ranching. Other railroads spurred similar growth throughout the state and connected growers to markets on both coasts.

The power of the railroad waned with the 20th-century advent of the automobile, the long-haul truck, and the airplane, but Colorado relies just as much on transportation today as it did in Jackson's day. New development around the once-isolated Denver International Airport, dense growth along the Interstate 70 corridor from the Eisenhower Tunnel to Rifle, and population spikes near recently widened highways demonstrate that Colorado's future is tied to the way people, goods, and materials move around.

JF I knew already that the train that crossed La Veta Pass on its way west into the San Luis Valley, both in Jackson's day and through much of the 20th century, followed a route south of U.S. Highway 160's present path over the pass. In fact, the highway pass is called North La Veta Pass. Just to the southeast of North La Veta Pass, a left turn onto County Road 443 leads to the old rail route and La Veta Pass.

Conspicuous Dump Mountain, to which most maps still make reference, made it easy to find Jackson's general location, but nailing the exact location proved impossible. Much excavation along the old bed hindered my ability to gain the correct elevation and latitude. I did the best that I could. Find the old railroad bed (and County Road 443) winding its way to the top of Dump Mountain.

101

SPANISH PEAKS

and Lake Miriam,
circa 1887

p. 159

The snow-capped Spanish Peaks, both more than 12,000 feet high, stand serenely over the arid canyons and grasslands of southeastern Colorado. Often visible from 100 miles away, they have been important landmarks since the time when Comanche people wandered the prairie more than three centuries ago—and probably for many generations before that. Plains Indians called the mountains "Huajatolla," and regarded the peaks and the land around them as the rain gods' home and the "breasts of the world," where clouds and rain were born and from which all living things received sustenance.

It is likely that the Spanish soldier Juan de Ulibarri spied the twin peaks when he crossed the high mesas of what now are the Colorado–New Mexico borderlands on his 1706 expedition to found the settlement of Santo Domingo near the Smoky Hill River in present-day Kansas. His guide, the frontiersman José Naranjo, probably had enjoyed this view already. Governor Valverde of New Mexico camped at the feet of the peaks in 1719, when he led 600 soldiers and Apaches along the mountain front in pursuit of raiding Comanches. Settlers later arrived from New Mexico to farm and raise livestock on the upper Apishipa and Cucharas rivers north and east of the Spanish Peaks—some of the northernmost outposts of Spanish Mexico.

The Spanish Peaks region served as a cultural crossroads throughout the 19th century. Influenced by the presence of Bent's Fort, the Santa Fe Trail, and Hispanic settlements near present-day Pueblo, Walsenburg, and La Veta, American Indians—Comanche, Apache, Kiowa, Ute, and Arapaho—mingled and traded with French, African-American, and Euro-American trappers and traders, Hispanic farmers, and soldiers. After the 1858 discovery of Colorado gold near Denver, Euro-American settlers arrived in ever-growing numbers.

Gold and silver seldom occurred in the rock formations of the Spanish Peaks, sparing the region from the sudden influx of miners and hangers-on that attended major ore strikes elsewhere in Colorado. The Denver & Rio Grande Railroad's 1877 arrival in the area was a boon to agriculturists who shipped produce and livestock to market in Alamosa, Pueblo, and Colorado Springs. The rail line also opened the

foothills of the Spanish Peaks to large-scale coal mining that fueled Pueblo's steel mills and drew workers from throughout the world. As coal mining waned in the mid- and late 20th century, the area became a new kind of cultural crossroads, where Hispanic farmers, Euro-American cattle ranchers, and miners' descendants rub elbows with hippie communes, retirement villages, urban refugees, and methane prospectors.

JF As distinctive as the Spanish Peaks are, finding this Jackson location proved problematic. The twin peaks stand isolated in the southern Colorado landscape and appear to be aligned like they are in this Jackson scene for many miles on an axis to their northeast. Few reference points exist in front of the peaks to help determine just how far away Jackson had placed his tripod, and we had obtained no information about a Lake Miriam. However, we did know that if we could detect some very large rock outcrops sticking up from the flat landscape, we just might be able to hit our mark.

After cruising back and forth on U.S. Highway 160 west of Walsenburg for a while, we decided to head north to Lathrop State Park and examine the scenery around Martin Lake. Once there, we had a hunch that this might be the place. On the north side of the large lake, much larger than Jackson's Lake Miriam, a cliffband descended into the lake. After an hour of climbing around, Eric and I concluded that the specific rocks in Jackson's view had either been excavated or were underwater. Nevertheless, we did our best to find the rocks that most faithfully duplicated the scene.

102

CUCHARAS PASS

Culebra Mountains,
circa 1885

p. 160

JR   This view looks south-southwest up the valley of the Cucharas River from near the town of Cuchara. The snow-covered peaks on the skyline lie along the crest of the Sangre de Cristo Mountains. Precambrian basement rocks, chiefly schist, gneiss, and granite formed about 1.7 billion years ago, make up these high peaks. All of the forested foothills in this view are carved in the red sandstone, conglomerate, and shale that constitute the Sangre de Cristo Formation. Like the Maroon Formation in the Elk Mountains and the Fountain Formation along the Front Range, the Sangre de Cristo largely consists of debris eroded from highlands that were part of the Ancestral Rocky Mountains between about 300 and 250 million years ago.

The source of the Sangre de Cristo sediments in this area lay to the southwest, in what has been called the San Luis highland. Subsequent erosion completely leveled the San Luis highland. However, during the early part of the mountain-building Laramide orogeny, sometime before 70 million years ago, the old San Luis upland was resurrected as a new highland, and the rocks of the Sangre de Cristo Formation were crumpled and pushed eastward. These are the rocks that make up the wooded foothills pictured here. Later in the Laramide orogeny, faults broke the new uplift, and the Precambrian basement rocks that now form the crest of the range were uplifted relative to the Sangre de Cristo Formation on the eastern slopes of the range.

Beginning about 28 million years ago, long after the close of the Laramide orogeny, the Earth's crust in this region began to pull apart, forming a great rift that extends from near El Paso, Texas, all the way into central Colorado. This feature is known as the Rio Grande rift because its namesake river follows it for much of its course. The rift also forms the San Luis Valley, which lies just west of the mountains in this view, and the upper Arkansas Valley between Salida and Leadville. The rift is bounded on one or both sides by a series of faults along which the valley floor has dropped thousands of feet in relation to the rocks on the rift margin. When the rift floor was subsiding, the rocks flanking the rift tended to rise, warmed by escaping heat.

More than half of Colorado's 14,000-foot peaks lie along the margins of the Rio Grande rift; the highest peaks follow the rift margins in central Colorado, where the rift is most active. The Sangre de Cristo Mountains form the eastern margin of the Rio Grande rift from Glorieta Pass near Santa Fe,

New Mexico, to Poncha Pass near Salida, Colorado — a distance of 220 miles, making it one of the longest rift-margin mountain ranges on the continent.

The name "Dakota Wall Ranch" seen on the sign in the contemporary picture no doubt refers to the cliffs formed by outcrops of Cretaceous Dakota Sandstone on the east side of the valley, outside of the photographs' range.

As soon as I saw this Jackson image, I realized that he had probably made it along what is today State Highway 12, south of the town of La Veta on the way up to Cucharas Pass. The Culebra Range is the portion of the Sangre de Cristo Mountains south of La Veta Pass.

After photographing Jackson scenes of the Spanish Peaks ultimately not included in *Colorado 1870–2000*, we headed up State Highway 12 in quest of this location. The major clues turned out to be both the first good view of the snow-capped mountains and the bend in the highway. The valley looked similar, and the bend was situated in the same place as the bend in the carriage road in Jackson's photograph. Regrettably, the high contrast inherent in Jackson's negatives precluded using his peaks in relation to the tree-covered ridges as effective ridge-trick clues. Still, I think we struck close to his location. Courtesy of Land Properties, Inc., an aggressive Colorado Springs subdivider of Colorado ranchland, we found ourselves just inside the gate of the first major ranch to be subdivided into ranchettes in what for many years had remained an undeveloped, bucolic valley.

103

CONEJOS COUNTY

*View West from Los Pinos
Cañon and Toltec Gorge,
circa 1883*

p. 161

TN William Henry Jackson stood above the Toltec Tunnel and pointed his camera west for this view featuring the Toltec Gorge of the Rio de los Pinos. The severe climate of this timberline setting is recorded in the badly cracked and fractured outcrops of Precambrian granite, gneiss, and schist in the foreground.

Jackson had been hired by William J. Palmer of the Denver & Rio Grande Railroad to help publicize such dramatic railroad scenes. Fielder's photo celebrates the little-altered natural setting of a picturesque rail line slithering through Colorado's silvery San Juan Mountains — the D&RG's Toltec Gorge section on the San Juan Extension. Constructed in 1880, this extension connected Alamosa with Durango, Silverton, and the booming silver and gold mines of the San Juan Mountains. The Alamosa-to-Durango line was abandoned in 1970, but part of it — from Antonito, Colorado, to Chama, New Mexico — was reconstructed by the states of Colorado and New Mexico as a summer tourist excursion. The Cumbres & Toltec Scenic Railroad is America's highest (Cumbres Pass is 10,022 feet high) and longest (64 miles) narrow-gauge, steam-powered passenger train.

Toltec Gorge lies at the west end of the Toltec Tunnel, 315 rail miles from Denver. The gorge is narrow, deep, and V-shaped because the Rio de los Pinos had a difficult time eroding the hard, resistant crystalline rocks. Newspaper correspondent Jackson D. Dillenback described Toltec Gorge rail construction in 1880: "The Denver and Rio Grande is a romantic, ambitious and adventurous road, and must be searching for new fields...untouched by railroads, in whose mountains and streams are inexhaustible treasures of silver and gold — the great San Juan country.... Having allured the railway into their awful fastnesses, the mountains seem determined to baffle its further progress. But it is a strong hearted railway, and although a little giddy at a thousand feet above the stream, cut its way through the crags.... At one point the canon [sic] narrows into an awful gorge, apparently but a few yards wide and nearly a thousand feet in depth, between almost perpendicular walls of granite. Here a high point of granite has to be tunneled, and...the rock men are at work drilling and blasting.... The frequent explosions of the blasts echo and re-echo among the mountains until they die away in the distance."

 If we had not spied from a mile away a white pickup truck kicking up a cloud of dust as it passed through a gate along a remote mountain road, we would never have found this Jackson location. However, I suppose we could have ridden the Cumbres–Toltec train to the Toltec Tunnel (immediately below where we stood to take the photograph) and asked the engineer to drop us off and pick us up later. On the other hand, the railroad operators might not have welcomed that idea. So Eric and I floored the Suburban in a frenzied attempt to catch up with the pickup.

We must have scared the driver and his passenger to death as we pulled up alongside them at 45 miles an hour on Forest Road 103. Nevertheless, they graciously pulled over. We peppered them with questions as to the whereabouts of the Toltec Gorge and Tunnel, and if the ranch they had just left accessed the place we desired to go. It turned out that they owned a piece of the property in question and that, yes, the tunnel was nearby, and that, yes, they would grant us permission to explore the area while they went grocery shopping in Antonito. With the combination to the gate lock, we headed back to remake two Jackson photographs in the area, this one and another image (not included in this book) that we shot at the bottom of the gorge.

Eric and I parked, then headed south about a mile on a long bench to what we guessed would be the entrance to the Toltec Gorge, albeit 1,000 vertical feet above it. For the next two hours we climbed down the steep slope to Rio de los Pinos, completed the first repeat photograph, then trekked back up to the top of the gorge in an effort to find the scene above the tracks of the Cumbres & Toltec Scenic Railroad.

Thirty minutes later, as we set up the view camera above the tunnel, we heard a faint whistle. Eric and I glanced at each other as we simultaneously realized that we had an opportunity to photograph the tourist train as it exited the tunnel, if only I could act fast enough to get the scene aligned and focused properly. As the train left the tunnel, I snapped two black-and-white pictures and then two in color as the train disappeared around the bend. Can you find the train in my photograph? What rock clues indicate that I had missed my mark slightly in my haste to capture the train on film?

104

SAN LUIS VALLEY

Sand Dunes near Mosca
Pass, 1873

pp. 162–163

JR The Great Sand Dunes form part of an extensive blanket of windblown sand that has accumulated in a recess in the western flank of the Sangre de Cristo Mountains on the east side of the San Luis Valley. The sand covers more than 300 square miles in this part of the valley, but the highest and most active of the dunes cover only about 30 square miles. These most active dunes, the tallest sand dunes in North America, all exist within Great Sand Dunes National Park (Congress designated this former national monument a national park at the beginning of 2001). The highest dunes tower as much as 750 feet above the San Luis Valley floor, and some of the dune ridges stretch as far as 2 miles.

The prevailing winds, which blow across the floodplain of the Rio Grande, now lying about 25 miles to the southwest, carried the bulk of the sand here. At the end of glacial time, about 12,000 years ago, the river apparently followed a course that lay much closer to the dune field, so it seems plausible that much of the sand accumulated then. The sand in the dunes is largely composed of grains of quartz and small fragments of volcanic rocks that came from the upper reaches of the Rio Grande on the eastern slopes of the San Juan Mountains. The sand was deposited where the prevailing southwest wind funnels into the reentrant in the mountain front and loses velocity as the mountains push it up and over them. The long axes of many of the dune ridges lie approximately perpendicular to the prevailing wind, but strong northwest winds and occasional east winds reshape the dunes into complex patterns, including some star shapes. Although the dunes are constantly changing, they migrate very slowly, only 1 or 2 feet per year. In fact, these two images demonstrate that although many details have changed, the general shape of the sand accumulation in the contemporary photo is remarkably similar to what it was when Jackson took his photo.

Recently, it has been recognized that streams play a significant role in recycling the sand and maintaining its accumulation. Medano Creek (in the middle distance of the photos) flows down the western flank of the mountains and along the southeastern edge of the active dunes; Sand Creek flows out of the mountains and around the northwestern edge of the dunes. Both creeks eventually disappear as their waters sink into the porous floor of the San Luis Valley. During high water, the streams transport sand from the dunes and deposit it on their floodplains as the water seeps away. As the floodplains dry out, the

prevailing wind carries the sand back and redeposits it in the dunes, helping to maintain the sand supply. In the photos, whose direction of view points toward the northwest, the prevailing wind would blow from left to right.

JP Of all the places that Jackson had photographed, none, I thought, would manifest more geological change than these dunes, today located in Great Sand Dunes National Park. The dunes would not only show change over the past 125 years, but constantly do so on a daily basis—the winds that sweep across the San Luis Valley move grains of sand with ease. Ever since Eric and I had encountered this Hayden Survey photograph in the U.S. Geological Survey archives in Lakewood, we had eagerly anticipated updating it.

My familiarity with this place, which I had been photographing for 25 years, and my knowledge that a once-historic road over Mosca Pass connected the Wet Mountain and San Luis valleys (now it's a foot trail), helped me find Jackson's location with ease. Eric and I made the photograph from a ridge a little to the south of the trail, in between piñon trees that tried to block the scene. Though Jackson probably stood slightly below where we did (notice the cottonwood trees looming in his scene), I believe that we had at least gained the correct latitude from which to shoot by using ridges in the distant Sangre de Cristo Mountains as perspective clues. Can you find any dunes that are the same today as they were in 1873?

Colorado 1870 - 2000 Revisited

Southwestern Mountains Locations

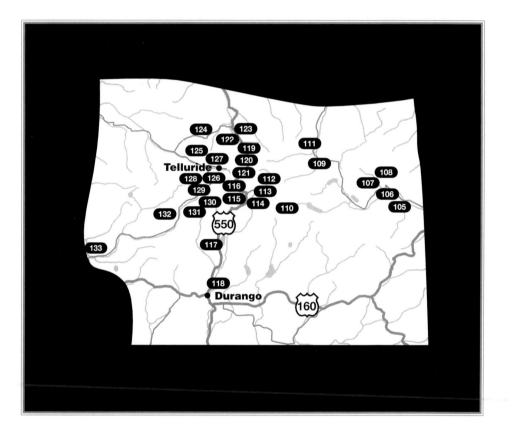

Southwestern Mountains

105

MINERAL COUNTY

Wagon Wheel Gap,
circa 1885

p. 168

EP   Wagon Wheel Gap was a well-known location long before Jackson photographed it. American Indians — especially Utes — made summer camps there for generations before Spanish explorer Juan de Oñate passed through in 1592. Other explorers, including Jacob Fowler, George Baker, and John C. Frémont, camped or hunted there between 1820 and 1850; after 1840, they were likely to meet settler Tom Boggs, a brother-in-law of Kit Carson. By the time the Hayden Survey arrived to map the area, Wagon Wheel Gap already was an established and rather prosperous settlement that consisted of a handful of farms and a busy stagecoach station, where gold-rush hopefuls rested before jolting through the San Juan Mountains.

Jackson's most memorable photographs of the area date from the 1880s. His best-known photograph of the place, *Trout Fishing at Wagon Wheel Gap*, dates from 1881, when Jackson toured southern Colorado and parts of New Mexico with writer Ernest Ingersoll and painter Thomas Moran to work on a series of illustrated articles for *Harper's Magazine*. The traveling party included Ingersoll's wife, a manservant, and several Denver artists and literati, such as regionally celebrated landscape painter Helen Chain. The group traveled in a special train (supplied by the Denver & Rio Grande Railroad in return for Moran's and Jackson's work on a booster book called *Colorado Tourist*), stopping to paint, sketch, photograph, and play. They fished for trout at Wagon Wheel Gap — the women in hats and long buttoned dresses, the men in tweeds, the water blurred by a long exposure time — and Jackson captured their graceful ease. The photograph continued to appear in guidebooks and brochures long after the subjects' clothes went out of style.

 On the way to Creede, Eric and I made a quick stop along State Highway 149, less than a mile to the west of the town of Wagon Wheel Gap. Jackson's prospective location seemed obvious, and the ranch road in my photograph provided quick and direct access across the Rio Grande. We were able to find our target after a 400-yard hike up the ridge to the west, but low-lying clouds prevented us from immediately using perspective clues. Eventually, enough of the ridges in the distance revealed themselves, allowing us to put the ridge trick into action. Ultimately, we must have stood within feet of Jackson's location. In my photograph, notice the new meander of the Rio Grande and the obligatory growth of cottonwood trees along the river.

106

CREEDE

Lower Creede, circa 1891

p. 169

TN One of Colorado's most spectacularly sited towns is wedged into a narrow canyon carved by Willow Creek, 2 miles north of its junction with the Rio Grande. As you can see, the town has not changed that much during the past century. Perhaps the most notable difference here is that stone and brick buildings have replaced many frame ones.

Nicholas C. Creede found a silver lode here in 1889. His Holy Moses Mine started a rush that brought an estimated 10,000 people into this remote chasm and led to the establishment of Creede in 1891. Nicholas C. Creede sold his Holy Moses Mine (whose ruins you can still see 3 miles up East Willow Creek) to David H. Moffat, Jr., president of the Denver & Rio Grande Railroad, which built a spur line to Creede in 1891 from Wagon Wheel Gap.

As Richard Harding Davis wrote in *The West from a Car Window* (1892), Creede had "hundreds of little pine boxes of houses and log-cabins, and the simple quadrangles of four planks which mark a building site....There is not a brick, a painted front, nor an awning in the whole town. It is like a city of fresh card-board."

This "card-board" town squeezed in between towering basaltic spires was scorched by fires and drowned by several major floods. But nothing stopped the eternal hubbub of mining and ore processing, or of gambling and carousing in some 30 saloons strung out along Willow Creek. Creede attracted a rogue's gallery of Western characters, including Poker Alice Tubbs, Bob Ford, Calamity Jane, Bat Masterson, and Soapy Smith. Cy Warman, editor of *The Creede Candle*, wrote of the frenetic frontier boomtown that "it's day all day in the daytime, and there is no night in Creede."

Awesome milling and mining structures for the Amethyst, Last Chance, and Commodore mines top the five- to seven-story-high cribbing at the upper end of Main Street. Creede's subterranean heritage — some 2,000 miles of underground mining tunnels — is commemorated by an underground community center, mining museum, and fire station at 9 Canyon Rd. at the northwest end of town. Much of modern Creede spills south to open terrain that captures more sunshine, leaving the old town to its narrow, spooky canyon.

JF   Discovery of the numerous Creede photographs in the Jackson archives at the Colorado History Museum thrilled me to no end. During the summer of 1969, my freshman year of college, I worked in CF&I Steel Corporation's geology department as a junior geologist. Among other things, I traveled around the West with company geologists, prospecting for precious minerals such as gold, silver, and molybdenum. For almost two months of that wonderful summer, I lived at the Snowshoe Lodge in Creede. Each morning, third-generation Creede miner John Jackson would pick me up and deposit me high in the mountains above Creede with a shovel and small bags. These were the tools I used to perform geochemical surveys that might reveal minerals beneath the surface of the earth. I loved my summer in historic Creede, and was anxious to find all of the Jackson locations there 29 years later.

Remaking this scene required the assistance of Sheriff Phil Leggitt to protect my backside on Main Street on July 4, 1998. Because no buildings seemed to remain from Jackson's day, my best perspective clue was the intersection of ridges in Willow Creek Canyon. In retrospect, I probably should have stepped a few feet farther forward and a bit to the left of where I made the photograph. Can you see why?

107

CREEDE

Upper Creede, 1892

p. 170

EP | Jackson perched his camera above the confluence of East and West Willow creeks to make this bird's-eye view of Creede. Although he gave it the title *Upper Creede* to distinguish it from Stringtown, Jimtown, and other camps downstream, the place in the photograph is the original townsite.

The rocky cliffs in the center and upper left of the photograph form the southern end of Campbell Mountain, site of famous early lodes such as the Holy Moses, the Big Chief, the Argentine, and the Eldorado. Nicholas C. Creede struck pay dirt at the Holy Moses after he left the Monarch district, making his own fortune and those of his partners, George Smith and Charles Nelson. West Willow Creek twists to the left and out of the frame; mines named the Bachelor, the Commodore, the Last Chance, and the Amethyst—which produced ore until it closed in 1976—were scattered along its banks and in the hillsides above. The flanks of Mammoth Mountain, whose name was more impressive than its ore, rise in the distance.

In the foreground of Jackson's photo is an odd mixture of tents, log cabins, and frame buildings that shows the make-do approach of mining camp architecture. Also evident are a few improvements to the structures: Two of the newest-looking tents have stoves and stovepipes, some of the cabins have glass windows, and except for one cabin with a pole roof, most of the buildings have shingles. Rocks and logs have been thrown down to channel the creek, though later experiences showed that when Willow Creek wants to flood, there is very little that can stop it.

In the historic image, downtown Creede, strung along the canyon floor to the right along the banks of East Willow Creek, is a double row of buildings crammed elbow-to-elbow on the only ground that passed for level. The Denver & Rio Grande's narrow-gauge tracks, which arrived in December 1891, creep up the street, where a straggling crowd appears to be posing for the camera. Jackson stood too far up the hillside for us to be able to read the signs on the buildings, but other photographs and early business directories help us start a list. Going up the street, one passed Regan & Davis's Junction Saloon, the

Miners Bank, the Ouray Saloon, R. G. Atkinson Real Estate & Insurance, the Last Chance Restaurant, the Cliff Meat Market, the Silver State Saloon (and across the street, the Silver State Restaurant), the Rio Grande oyster and chop house, and a store selling liquor and cigars.

JF Updating the two Upper Creede photographs required a drive from Lower Creede up Willow Creek Canyon to the confluence of East and West Willow creeks. Here begins one of the best four-wheel-drive loop tours in Colorado mining country. On this tour, you can witness some of the most historic and dramatic mine structures built anywhere in the state during the 19th century.

Though only one building from the old town remains (see Photo Pair 108), ridges in the distance once again allowed me to get within feet of Jackson's location. A steep climb up a talus field to the west of the confluence quickly delivered Eric and me to the spot. A couple of Polaroids later, we made the final repeat photographs. Obviously, Jackson's photographs of Upper Creede, also called North Creede, were made in winter when snow blanketed the ground. Eric and I were there in the summer.

108

CREEDE

*Main Street,
Upper Creede,
1892*

p. 170

Once Creede boomed, it seemed that everyone got into the publicity business. Denver's Oxford Hotel gave away copies of a booster book titled *Creede Camp: The Great Mineral Discovery* to raise interest among miners and investors in 1892. The author, C. J. Kelly, speculated about the limitless wealth that lay in the mountains up Willow Creek and enthused about the chances one had for striking it rich—if not in mining, then in freighting, railroading, or running a store. With Kelly and others like him as its touts, the Creede district saw a steady flood of new arrivals.

But Kelly understood the effects of the mass migration. "Chaos come again is the way to describe Creede," he wrote. "There is scarcely a foot of ground left whereon to plant a post, for it is an old settled locality—nearly a year—and real estate is valuable." Jackson's photograph shows how people crowded into the narrow canyon, stuffing their overflow between the buildings and the street: logs, sawn lumber, barrels, boxes, an old sluice, trash. You can barely decipher two men working in the sunlight, behind the wagon in the center of Jackson's photograph; they probably moved their workshop outdoors to take advantage of the wider space and the warmth of the sun.

Upper Creede looks brand-spanking new in Jackson's view. Untouched by the 1892 fire that turned Lower Creede to cinders, Upper Creede continued to prosper until the Silver Crash of 1893 knocked the wind out of its sails. Although several of the nearby mines continued to produce quantities of high-grade ore, the national downturn of the 1890s lowered prices, and wages, so that many who rushed to Creede in the boom years drifted away in the following decades. Mining surged again during and after World Wars I and II, but slumped during the Great Depression and in the late 1970s. Few new buildings went up in the boom periods, and hardly any during the busts; flooding along Willow Creek, heavy snows, and disuse wiped out much of Upper Creede, and Lower Creede became the center of the local population.

JF In order to make this repeat photograph, Eric and I drove a little way up East Willow Creek, seen to the right in the other pair of Upper Creede photographs (see Photo Pair 107). Ultimately, we stood in a place looking back toward the camera location for that pair.

If Upper Creede had not still housed a few residents, and if one of those, Robert Sullivan, had not been hanging out nearby that day, I would never have known that a perspective clue existed other than the ridges in the distance. I showed Jackson's photograph to Robert, who immediately told me that the A-frame building in my purview was the same one as on the right-hand side of the street in the historic image, and that he actually lived there. What a great clue! I think that I missed my mark by a few feet to the left, and that I should have moved back a few feet, too. Can you discover why?

109

HINSDALE COUNTY

Lake San Cristoval, 1887

p. 171

JR   Moraines left by the Pinedale glaciers dam most natural lakes in Colorado's mountain valleys. However, Lake San Cristobal near Lake City has a much different history. A large earthflow landslide, which blocked the channel of the Lake Fork of the Gunnison River about 700 years ago, impounded the lake. This slide, called the Slumgullion Slide, originates in a basin surrounded by unstable cliffs of broken and altered volcanic rocks on the west slope of Mesa Seco. The toe of this nearly 3.6-mile-long slide buried the river channel for a distance of almost 2 miles and to depths of as much as 230 feet. When it first formed, the lake measured about 2.5 miles long and almost 90 feet deep. Subsequently, the river has built a sediment delta into the upper end of the lake that has reduced the length of the lake to about 2 miles. Parts of the delta barely show through the trees on the small point near the middle of the historic photo, but trees in the contemporary photo completely hide the delta.

Recent studies of the slide show that parts of it moved as long ago as 1,600 years, and that much of the movement took place during the last 1,100 years. Some of the slide's upper part still moves at rates of as much as 18 feet per year.

Members of the Hayden Survey noted and photographed the Slumgullion Slide in 1874, but the local miners who gave it its name already knew it well.

 Lake San Cristobal (called Cristoval by Jackson) is geologically unique in Colorado and scenically spectacular. Though I had not often photographed it, I had been traveling the historic Cinnamon Pass mining road, seen to its left, for 25 years. In order to find this location, Eric and I drove south from the town of Lake City to the Lake Fork of the Gunnison River turnoff and proceeded around the east side of the lake. Though the distant ridges of the Continental Divide might have been clues enough to find Jackson's spot, we coveted the large rock on the edge of the lake next to the dead tree in his scene.

When we arrived at what we thought was the approximate location, we pulled the car over and got out to look for the rock. Guess what was lying behind the bush in the bottom right-hand corner of my photograph. The rock! You can see its top through the bush. With this additional perspective clue, we made our photograph. Notice the growth of conifers around the lake today compared with the scene in 1887.

110

HINSDALE COUNTY

*The Rio Grande near
Pole Creek, 1874*

pp. 172–173

JF Though this location is remote, I knew immediately where to go in order to begin the search for the rocks in the right foreground. The Colorado Trail, which I had hiked in 1990 and 1991, follows Pole Creek down to the Rio Grande. Forest Road 520 proceeds west from Rio Grande Reservoir to this location and on to Stony Pass before dropping into the Animas River drainage near Silverton. So the easy part was getting to this general vicinity. The hard part was getting the weather to cooperate.

In June 1998, Eric and I made our way to this place in the pouring rain. For three days, we rephotographed Jackson scenes all around the Rio Grande drainage. Each time we returned to this locale during the trip, clouds covered the peaks along the Continental Divide in today's Weminuche Wilderness. Without those peaks, we believed that the repeat photograph would be vacant and ineffective. Frustrated and needing to move on to other places, Eric and I gave up and vowed to return in the fall.

We came back to this place the first week in October. Still no peaks! An early-season snowstorm shrouded the peaks. Determined this time not to leave until we got our photograph, Eric and I set up camp along the river. Every 15 minutes we would peek outside the tent, hoping each time to see clear weather. We performed this act for an entire day and part of the next morning. By then, including the summer trip, we had invested four days of patience. I was beginning to get angry.

Finally, around 11 a.m., Eric and I hiked up to our location one more time. We set up the view camera and I silently asked the powers that be for mercy. These are the same unknown powers that have allowed me to be at the right place at the right time for the past 25 years' worth of nature photography. Within 10 minutes, the clouds parted just enough to reveal most of the peaks. Ten minutes later, the clouds swallowed them again. Effectively, loyal Eric had posed on that rock for four-and-a-half days during 1998!

Notice how the aspen trees have grown in since 1874. Notice also that I stood to the left and slightly forward of Jackson's camera location. A tree had sprouted exactly where I needed to position the tripod.

Observe how many more aspen trees exist in this view today. As I have explained previously, deciduous trees succeed conifers in the cycle of forest destruction by fire and subsequent regeneration. Fires were allowed to burn in the 19th century, and the remaining trees were cut for fuel and construction. Aspens occupy much more of the landscape today than they did in Jackson's day. Thank goodness I live now, not then—I've sold a lot of aspen tree photographs through the years!

111

LAKE CITY

circa 1887

p. 174

TN   Counting the number of roofs in these two photos suggests that Lake City has grown smaller while its trees have grown larger. Its 1890 population of 607 climbed to a peak census-year population of 700 in 1900. A century later, only 377 residents lived in the hamlet.

Lake City followed the Western custom of kiting, or tacking "city" to a name as a tail is added to a kite. Proponents of this measure believed that the extension made a town sound bigger and gave it a better chance to fly. Enos T. Hotchkiss founded the community in 1875 as a stop on his toll road between Saguache and the new San Juan mountain mining centers. Hotchkiss lingered at Lake City after he discovered the Golden Fleece lode. He platted the town on the usual grid, in the valley where Henson Creek joins the Lake Fork of the Gunnison River. The remote town, isolated by high peaks, was named for nearby Lake San Cristobal, the second-largest natural lake in Colorado.

Typical of Colorado mining towns, Lake City started off fast, then experienced a long decline in terms of population and prosperity. During the initial 1877 boom, an estimated 136 buildings were completed, including two smelters, a courthouse, and a dozen businesses. A second boom in the 1880s produced the Hough Block, a now-vanished $30,000 brick school, and a number of stylish brick residences. The 1893 Silver Crash and depression nearly drowned Lake City, although the Denver & Rio Grande Railroad spur line endured until 1933.

Now primarily a summer town, Lake City has installed plank sidewalks and preserved many of its silver-era structures. Stone and false-fronted frame buildings, generally in the Italianate style, characterize a well-preserved business district. Lake City remains one of Colorado's most scenic mining towns, with tight local preservation guidelines as well as National Register Historic District designation.

Plenty of ridges allowed us to employ perspective to find the vicinity of this Jackson photograph. Eventually, we had to ask permission from a Texas family to drive through their property, where Jackson's hillside was located. As was always the case, these nice people were fascinated by the project and happy to accommodate our needs. The bonus gift of one of my books or calendars never hurt either!

Unfortunately, this hillside northwest of town had either eroded naturally or been excavated in the past 111 years. The volcanic rock on which we stood was very friable. Eric and I never could get quite far enough to the left to duplicate Jackson's perspective. Can you find the proof that corroborates this fact? Some of the buildings in downtown Lake City seen in his purview still exist in mine.

112

ANIMAS FORKS

circa 1896

p. 175

TN   Animas Forks (1875–1915) lies 13 miles northeast of Silverton on the Engineer Pass/Cinnamon Pass loop road. Accessible only by four-wheel-drive vehicles, this is one of Colorado's most picturesque ghost towns, with a breathtaking, 11,200-foot-high site at the confluence of the north and west forks of the Animas River. The hamlet once boasted some 200 residents, plank sidewalks, and a main street lined with hotels, saloons, and the highest newspaper in the United States, *The Animas Forks Pioneer*. The stout old jail (1882), made of 2-by-6-inch planks stacked flat to create stronger walls, survives.

In the Fielder photo, note the prominent William D. Duncan House (a.k.a. Thomas Walsh House) with its distinctive bay window, located at the northwest end of the old Main Street. The San Juan County Historical Society and Bureau of Land Management have undertaken efforts to preserve Animas Forks and some of the surrounding mines and mills. Among many ruins are the concrete foundation of the three-story Gold Prince Boarding House, the skeleton of the Gold Prince Mine's steel-frame concentrating mill, and remnants of the 12,600-foot-long tramway with steel cables suspended from 33 towers. Skeletal towers and strands of cable still exist between the Gold Prince Mine and ore-loading operations up in Placer Gulch. Little remains of the Silverton Northern's 50-foot turntable (1904), where railroad locomotives were turned around in Animas Forks for the trip back to Silverton.

IF I had hoped that the famous, oft-photographed house with the bay window seen in my image actually existed in Jackson's. No such luck! However, given that fire frequently and repeatedly destroyed the wooden structures in many a 19th-century mining town, I deduced that the town of Animas Forks I saw must have been a later generation than Jackson's town.

Animas Forks is one of Colorado's choice ghost towns. On the popular and most scenic Engineer Pass/Cinnamon Pass loop road that reaches almost 13,000 feet in elevation, it's a favorite stop of tourists four-wheeling San Juan mining country. I have journeyed here dozens of times, so the discovery of this image in the Jackson archives had me excited from the start to find out why the house with the bay window was not in his purview. Once we had the ridges aligned properly, and we knew that we stood where Jackson did, it was clear that the house simply had not yet been built.

113

HOWARDSVILLE

Baker's Park, circa 1896

pp. 176–177

TN   Five miles above Silverton along State Highway 110 and the Animas River lies the original San Juan County seat of Howardsville. George R. Howard settled here at the confluence of Cunningham Creek and the Animas River in 1872 and located the Sunnyside Mine, the area's leading gold producer from the 1870s until the 1980s.

George Howard, at least in legend, had a sneaky streak that doomed his town to fall behind the younger, upstart town of Silverton. He had been a co-conspirator with Captain Charles Baker in the Baker's Park Humbug of 1860. Baker was determined to launch a gold rush, whether or not there was any gold in or along the Animas River. In letters to the *Santa Fe Gazette*, Baker boasted that Baker's Park (the future site of Silverton) had "extensive gulches and bar diggings richer than any mines hitherto discovered." A large party, including women and children, set out from Denver in 1860 for the promised land. After enduring the bitter cold and heavy snows of the San Juans, as well as poor prospecting, the argonauts returned to Denver sadder and wiser. One of them told the *Rocky Mountain News*, as it reported on February 9, 1861, that "the San Juan is a humbug," and urged that Baker be hanged.

Howard, however, remained confident that he could lure others to the San Juan Mountains. He cut and piled up logs and then displayed a barrel of whiskey. As fortune seekers came through the Animas River Canyon, he invited them to join him for a drink. After guests became duly warm and appreciative, Howard asked if they would mind helping him lift several of the heavier logs into place. Thus he built his log cabin, an inn, a store, the San Juans' first post office, and much of Howardsville. When guests grew disenchanted with Howard's hospitality, they would leave and he would await the next arrival.

Howard not only exploited people, but also sold town lots at exorbitant prices. Many newcomers pushed farther down the Animas to Silverton, where friendly old Frank Snowden had built the first cabin — all by himself — in 1874. Snowden welcomed one and all to join his community, which also erected the first smelter in the San Juan mining region. Silverton soon outgrew Howardsville and replaced

it as the San Juan County seat in 1876. Howardsville remained a small mining community until 1939, when its post office closed. It has been a ghost town ever since, although summer tourists and a few fair-weather prospectors have kept the site active, as Fielder's photo shows. One or two old log cabins survive and Howardsville's famed Old Hundred Mine now offers tours.

Like Animas Forks, Howardsville is another famous old town north of Silverton on the way to Engineer and Cinnamon passes. The ridges in the distance proved to be good perspective clues, but the bridge across Cunningham Creek in Jackson's scene did not. Once I had the ridges aligned properly, it became clear that the new bridge had been built to the left of the old one. But the bonus clue for this repeat photograph turned out to be a building. Can you find the only building in Jackson's photograph that still exists today? I was able to align it with the ridgetop in the top left-hand corner of the scene in order to discover exactly where Jackson had stood.

114

SILVERTON

and Sultan Mountain,
1883

pp. 178–179

TN   Cradled in a 9,300-foot-high mountain valley, Silverton remains a small town where only the main street is paved. The census-year peak population of 2,152 came in 1910 during an early 20th-century building boom that erased many of the log and frame structures in Jackson's 1883 photo of the infant town.

Of 16 post-office towns once active in San Juan County, only Silverton has escaped becoming a ghost. Even this sole surviving town has experienced a population drop in recent decades, tumbling to only 531 year-round residents as of 2000. Silverton has been well preserved by its economic poverty and geographic isolation. Hollywood producers looking for a quaint, picturesque mining town have used it as a set for many films, including *Naked Spur*, *Ticket to Tomahawk*, and *Maverick Queen*.

After a false start with the 1860 Baker's Park Humbug, the town, founded in 1874, blossomed. The Greene Smelter (1874) briefly made Silverton the smelting capital of southwestern Colorado. Then the Denver & Rio Grande Railroad arrived in 1882 and carted off both the smelter and Silverton's rich ores to Durango. By shifting its emphasis to gold and other metals, Silverton survived the 1893 Silver Crash. Mining fed the town and the county until 1991, when the Sunnyside Mine closed. After that, the mining industry hit rock bottom.

Tourism is the mother lode today. The Durango & Silverton Narrow Gauge Railroad carries some 200,000 summer tourists here annually between May 1 and October 31. Many more arrive via U.S. Highway 550, the "Million Dollar Highway," which angles across Sultan Mountain in Fielder's photo. Note the town's single moving vehicle on a beautiful summer day — strong evidence that Silverton remains a sleepy, scenic souvenir of Colorado's mining era. In the background sits 13,370-foot-high Sultan Mountain, a multisummited, avalanche-scarred massif 3 miles southwest of Silverton.

JF Jackson shot this old photograph of Silverton when it was a tiny town. Many additions to the infrastructure occurred before and after the financial panic over and subsequent crash of the price of silver, as Tom Noel explains. Silverton is certainly no boomtown today, but just look at its size, then and now.

Standing due north of town, Eric and I couldn't get quite high enough on the ridge in order to perfectly duplicate Jackson's scene — aspen trees blocked our view. Evidence of how many more aspens thrive today exists on the hillside above U.S. Highway 550, seen south of the town in my photograph. Most of the light-green color represents aspens. Very few seem to populate Jackson's same hillside. Nevertheless, Eric and I achieved the correct latitude by considering the angle of the city streets as we moved left and right. Some buildings on Main Street exist in both photographs. Study the other Silverton duo (see Photo Pair 115) for proof.

115

SILVERTON

Main St., 1883

p. 180

3256. MAIN ST. SILVERTON.   DETROIT PHOTOGRAPHIC CO

TN These streetscapes look south with Sultan Mountain in the background. Some of the 1883 frame and masonry buildings survive in Fielder's update, most notably the mansard-roofed Grand Imperial Hotel, the three-story structure with prominent chimneys at the distant end of Main (Greene) Street.

In Fielder's right foreground, note the handsome two-story sandstone edifice with a rooftop entry parapet of the same stone. Louis Wyman built it in 1902 at 1371 Greene St. Wyman arrived in San Juan County in 1885 with 15 burros. By 1900, he owned the county's largest freighting firm, with 45 employees and more than 100 pack animals. Every month, he bought 19 boxcars of hay and grain, and delivered some 1,500 tons of ore to the Denver & Rio Grande depot. To celebrate his burro-borne empire, he built this two-story corner building of local sandstone from the Wyman Quarry on Mineral Creek. The corner entry rises to a parapet framing a bas-relief of a burro — a pet whose portrait Wyman carved himself. After serving as offices, a general store, and a lodge hall, the edifice had become a parking garage before Donald Stott restored it as the Wyman Hotel & Inn in the early 1990s. Don reports, "It's unbelievably well-built, with 3-by-12-foot beams and solid, 24-inch-thick stone walls. Skylights flood the second story with light and stand up to the 21 feet of snow we get each winter in Silverton."

This antique commercial district, which has seen little new construction since 1910, includes several livery stables. Miners from throughout the San Juan Mountains sampled Silverton's recreational amenities, including some 40 saloons, gambling halls, dance halls, and brothels. Of the notorious red-light district on Blair Street, a block to the west, some of the former bordello buildings survive, most notably the Welcome Saloon (1883, 1909) at 1161 Blair St. and the Shady Lady Bar (circa 1900) at 1154 Blair St. "Brides of the multitude" from Blair Street sometimes toured outlying mining towns if business was slow, riding up to boardinghouses in tram buckets.

 Can you count at least three buildings that endure today? They served as the best clues with which to align Sultan Mountain in the background. Notice the mule team in Jackson's scene preparing to deliver supplies to any one of the dozens of nearby mining operations. Can you find today's equivalent "mule team"? It includes the NEWS4 vehicle in town to film one of 52 episodes about this project that ran every Thursday night on Denver television.

This is the only paved street in Silverton today, leaving most of the town's thoroughfares much as they were in the 19th century. What happened in Jackson's day when streets got muddy, either from precipitation or from freezing and thawing? Where did the dirt go from muddy boots? Was there an entire workforce dedicated to sweeping dried mud from building floors? Was there any special device used to rid boots of mud before entering a building?

116

CHATTANOOGA

circa 1891

p. 181

TN Chattanooga lies 7.5 miles north of Silverton and 3 miles south of Red Mountain Pass on the "Million Dollar Highway," U.S. Highway 550. Born during an 1878 silver rush, the camp on Mineral Creek sprouted into a community on the first-available level ground at the southern foot of Red Mountain Pass. By 1883, the town had a post office; Frank Carol, the first postmaster, named it for his hometown in Tennessee. In 1890, 51 residents called Chattanooga home. The Silver Crash of 1893 was followed by the 1894 closing of the Chattanooga Post Office. Yet the 1900 census taker reported 55 people still living there. By 1910, no official residents remained.

However, Ruth Rathmell, in her 1976 book, *Of Record and Reminiscence — Ouray and Silverton*, reported that Chattanooga had a longtime lone resident in Lee Tinsley. "He was always hospitable," she recalled, "and volunteered to make coffee for all comers. His method was to keep adding fresh coffee and water to the old grounds, and to boil that up. He only started with an entirely new lot when the pot became so full of grounds that it would hold no more. The process left a good deal to be desired, but it was hot, and the warmth of his cabin was always a boon."

The sole surviving structure captured in Fielder's shot might be Tinsley's coffeehouse. The cemetery is one of the few other lingering traces of Chattanooga, although a mile above town the Silver Ledge Mine head-frame remains fairly intact.

 Chattanooga still appears on contemporary maps, but there's not much there— only a house and an outbuilding. On the way to Red Mountain Pass north of Silverton, this scene unfolds next to U.S. Highway 550. Because none of the buildings in Jackson's view remain today, Eric and I employed ridges in the distance as perspective clues. We must have come within feet of Jackson's location. Notice the difference in tree cover from then to now. How many towns have we visited thus far that no longer exist?

117

ANIMAS RIVER

*Cañon of the
Rio Las Animas,
1887*

pp. 182–183

TN Jackson's famous 1887 shot is well matched by Fielder, who even persuaded the train crew to light the locomotive headlight. The Denver & Rio Grande Railroad constructed this serpentine line up the Animas River from Durango to Silverton in 1882. The D&RG chief engineer, appropriately named Thomas Wigglesworth, came to appreciate the Spanish pioneers who christened the river below this precipitous route "El Rio de las Animas de los Perditos," the River of Lost Souls.

Today's cliff-hugging Durango & Silverton Narrow Gauge Railroad is not a restoration, but a never-abandoned anachronism in use since 1882, the year Wigglesworth oversaw construction of the 54 miles of track from Durango to Silverton. Wigglesworth achieved a maximum grade of 2.5 percent (a 2.5-foot elevation gain in 100 feet of track). He also used an all-steel track, instead of the iron track that the D&RG had previously employed. Narrow shelves were cut into the rock 400 feet above the Animas River gorge for this cliffhanger of a railroad.

After abandoning the San Juan Extension from Alamosa to Durango in 1970, D&RG continued service between Durango and Silverton until 1981, when Charles E. Bradshaw, Jr., bought the line, upgraded it, and renamed it the Durango & Silverton Narrow Gauge Railroad. The line bears the designations of both a National Historic Landmark and a National Historic Civil Engineering Landmark.

JF This photograph and one other that Jackson made along this famous train route titillated our senses from the moment we saw them in the archives. What fun it would be to ride the train through the most spectacular of gorges, the Animas River Canyon adjacent to Colorado's Weminuche Wilderness. And how much more fun would it be to have the railroad company cater to our needs, finding the locations and stopping the train long enough for us to complete our photographic maneuvers? As it turned out, we got into big trouble!

Yes, the Durango & Silverton Narrow Gauge Railroad company was ultimately glad to provide utility cars and drivers to get us to both locations within the canyon. The engineers would even stop the train at each location in the midst of the busy tourist season so that I could make sharp images. What they did not count on was my fastidiousness for trying to situate the train in the exact spots in the landscape as in Jackson's scenes.

For this particular view, shot from a location well known to the crew (other photographers besides Jackson had taken this picture before I did), I set up my camera prior to the train's arrival. When it approached, I asked the engineer to back up and go forward a few feet more than once to achieve perfection. Between making this image and another not included in the book, we delayed the entire day's train schedule by a half-hour, a fact that had the stationmaster upset with us. What you cannot see in my photograph are the graphic hand signals being flashed at me by the tourists hanging out the windows, a bit perturbed that their sightseeing trip had been interrupted for so long!

118

DURANGO

circa 1893

pp. 184–185

TN Animas River irrigation ditches made possible the greening of Durango, the most dramatic change evident in this duo. One of the few visible surviving landmarks, albeit enlarged, is the Strater Hotel on Main Avenue in the left center of both photos. Durango, established in 1881 by the Denver & Rio Grande Railroad, emerged as the seat of La Plata County and the metropolis of southwestern Colorado. Railroad whistles, smoke, and steam are still alive and well in Durango — but instead of carrying miners, ore, and supplies to Silverton, today's train carries tourists. The Durango & Silverton Narrow Gauge Railroad, as the D&RG here is now called, rates as one of the most popular narrow-gauge steam excursions in the world, drawing rail enthusiasts from across the globe.

These views looking west from what is presently the site of Fort Lewis College show some of the coal-rich foothills of the La Plata Mountains, which attracted the D&RG to the site. As the grid plan shows, Durango was well conceived by William J. Palmer and his D&RG colleagues, former territorial governor Alexander C. Hunt and Dr. William A. Bell. The presence of parks, the Third Avenue Parkway, and tree-shaded streets dates to the original town plan. Palmer, Hunt, and Bell named Durango after the city in Mexico that they hoped their railroad would someday reach. In the Colorado town, the railroad controlled the land, a smelter site, and nearby coal fields. By 1890, horse-drawn trolleys clanged up and down Main Avenue. The "sagebrush metropolis," cheered *The Durango Record*'s feisty editor Caroline Romney, "is really attaining metropolitan proportions."

The railroad, which draws some 200,000 passengers a year, has kept Main Avenue the center of activity in Durango, eclipsing even the new, dun-colored Durango Mall south of town. Durango's suburbs now sprawl northward for 11 miles along U.S. Highway 550 to Hermosa, westward along U.S. Highway 160 toward Hesperus, and eastward to Bayfield along U.S. Highway 160. Despite fast growth in recent decades to a population of more than 14,000 residents, Durango remains what Will Rogers called it in the 1930s: "a beautiful little town, out of the way, and proud of it."

JF Obviously, landscaping eventually caught on in Durango. Who would have guessed that the valley floor was barren in 1893?

    Eric and I quickly discerned that Jackson had stood atop the conspicuous mesa east of town — now home to Fort Lewis College — in order to make this image. Once on top, we only had to drive back and forth on the street that skirts the mesa's western edge until we arrived at the correct longitude. Ridges in the distance seem to align perfectly with their 1893 versions, but Eric and I never found a building to use as a clue. Can you locate a single building that exists in both scenes besides the Strater Hotel?

119

OURAY

Toll Road, circa 1885

p. 186

TN Today's U.S. Highway 550 follows the toll road blasted and carved out of sheer rock cliffs in the 1880s by Otto "The Pathfinder of the San Juans" Mears. His Ouray and San Juan Toll Road connected Ouray with Silverton. The Uncompahgre River below awaits anything tumbling off the highway. The serpentine, two-lane roller coaster of a road between Ouray and Durango is known as the "Million Dollar Highway." Take your pick of theories regarding the origin of the highway's priceless name: 1) the valuable ore used for filling the roadbed, 2) the cost of building each mile of this cliff-hugging highway, or 3) what people will pay to avoid Colorado's scariest, most dangerous, paved, all-year highway.

JF W. H. Jackson made numerous photographs along this fabled route connecting the mining towns of Ouray and Silverton. The Million Dollar Highway still has no guardrails in most places, and tickles the tummies of many a tourist. Eric and I had much fun driving back and forth along this most beautiful of highways for a couple of days while tracking down each of the Jackson locations we chose to duplicate.

This site presented no more of a challenge to find than the others, except for the fact that this precipitous spot had required quite a bit of excavation for road improvements between then and now. Therefore, utilizing the cliffs above and below the highway as perspective clues proved problematic. Ultimately, the peaks in the distance and the rock cliffs on the left in the photograph served as the hints that determined Jackson's location. How well did I duplicate the moment as represented by vehicles, then and now?

120

OURAY

Toll Gate at Bear Creek Falls,
circa 1885

p. 187

TN   Otto Mears spent a fortune building the Ouray and San Juan Toll Road from Silverton over Red Mountain Pass to Ouray. He hoped to pay for it with this toll gate at Bear Creek Falls. Mears, a shrewd businessman of Russian origin, situated the toll gate at a place where it was impossible to drive around it. Today, a pullout allows motorists to stop and marvel at the landscape — or recover from car sickness.

On November 28, 1884, David F. Day, editor of the *Ouray Solid Muldoon*, rhapsodized about the Bear Creek Falls stretch of toll road: "In point of scenic grandeur the road is unequalled on the continent. Leaving the mountain-clad village of Ouray, it ascends by serpentine and easy grade to a level with bluffs above town, where it winds in a southerly direction around cliffs, through wooded parks, and over bridges spanning wild and romantic gulches to Bear Creek Falls; here the route passes over the head of the roaring cataract, 253 feet above the boiling cataract below, and entering the quartzite bluffs, coils round them upon a bed of solid rock from 600 to 800 feet above the river, for a distance of two miles, when the Uncompahgre River is crossed. At this point is afforded one of the grandest views in all the land. A few hundred yards below the waters of the Uncompahgre and Red Mountain creek join and go roaring down a box canyon…with precipitous bluffs of red sandstone…and bright quartzite capped with mountains, crags, and peaks of gray trachyte, reaching from their quartzite base below into the land of perpetual snow."

For eight years, Mears operated the Ouray and San Juan Toll Road. When he sold it to Ouray County, travelers were grateful because the county allowed free use. Mears had charged an exorbitant $5 for a team and wagon and $1 apiece for saddle animals.

―――― ―――― ――――

JF Shopkeeper and businessman Otto Mears built this toll booth, at which point folks traveling between Ouray and Silverton paid a fee. Today, the location from which Jackson photographed is a Million Dollar Highway pullout, where modern tourists can enjoy a fine view of Bear Creek Falls. This spot proved to be a convenient place to make the repeat photograph. Unfortunately, Jackson's contrasty film emulsions overexposed the ridge in the distance, precluding the use of its details as perspective clues. And the toll booth has disappeared! Nevertheless, I think I came very close to standing in Jackson's footsteps.

121

RED MOUNTAIN PASS

*Yankee Girl Mine,
Red Mountain, 1886*

p. 188

TN Only the corrugated metal shaft house of the Yankee Girl Mine survives in Fielder's follow-up shot. The town of Red Mountain has largely vanished. A recent owner has threatened to demolish the few historic survivors, including the Yankee Girl, in order to market the historic locale as homesites.

Colorado's lack of effective land use and preservation laws makes possible such a fate for one of Colorado's most photographed and beloved relics of the silvery 1870s. Founded in 1883, Red Mountain occupied three townsites of that name about a mile apart. The town originated with silver strikes at the base of the mountains known by that name — three pyramidal peaks with bright slopes of oxidized iron. Ouray's *Solid Muldoon* reported on March 9, 1883: "Five weeks ago the site where Red Mt. now stands was woodland covered with heavy spruce timber. Today, hotels, printing offices, groceries, meat markets, a telephone office, saloons, and dance houses are up and booming." By 1913 the town gave up its ghost — and its post office — but it has been immortalized in David Lavender's historical novel *Red Mountain*. Following decades of fire and ice, little remains except the dilapidated shaft houses of the two largest mines: the National Belle and the Yankee Girl.

Along U.S. Highway 550, the giant, century-old Idarado Mine — complete with company housing, offices, and loading apparatus — is largely intact. The Idarado's tailings, which stretch for miles down the headwaters of the Uncompahgre River, have been reclaimed with the help of a network of concrete spillways and efforts to reforest the huge dumps below the town of Red Mountain.

JF This location exists to the north and east of Red Mountain Pass and can be accessed from a dirt road just north of the pass (at least it was accessible in 1998). Obviously, a railroad that followed today's roadbed once transported ore from the lucrative Yankee Girl Mine. Thank goodness the bed is the same: In relation to the San Juan Mountains in the distance, it allowed Eric and me to pinpoint Jackson's location almost exactly. The view looks north, and today U.S. Highway 550 lies in the valley to the left and below. I do not believe that the solitary building in my photograph exists in Jackson's. What do you think?

122

OURAY

1886

p. 189

TN Sunlight spotlights Cascade Falls in Jackson's photo, but Fielder took his earlier in the day as the 80-foot waterfall on the northeast edge of Ouray still hid in shadow.

Ouray, the seat of Ouray County, is wedged into a natural amphitheater surmounted by peaks soaring 5,000 feet overhead—awesome walls of red, white, gray, and purple rock decorated with waterfalls and mine ruins. Prospectors from Silverton found silver along the Uncompahgre River near its confluence with Oak and Canyon creeks; there, they platted the town of Ouray.

Transportation enabled the county to ship out its products at a profit. The Ouray and San Juan Toll Road, which later became U.S. Highway 550, the so-called Million Dollar Highway, connected Ouray with Silverton. The Denver & Rio Grande Railroad arrived from Montrose later but never got far beyond Ouray. Although set back by the Silver Crash of 1893, the town shifted to gold, relying on the Camp Bird, Revenue, and Virginius mines, as well as other auriferous treasure troves.

A National Register Historic District encompasses 331 structures and most of downtown Ouray between Oak and 5th streets and 3rd and 8th avenues. The brothels, gambling joints, and theaters that once made up a formidable vice district have vanished, as has the brewery, whose stone ruins now serve as a picnic ground. Some of the residences and buildings in Jackson's view survive, most notably the Beaumont Hotel, 501 Main St., with its pyramidal corner tower.

Despite a raucous past, Ouray has become genteel. Well-kept Victorian homes line quiet, tree-shaded dirt streets. The city and several motels have harnessed hot springs to heat their buildings. From the beginning, Ouray avoided becoming just another "git-and-git-out" mining town where riches were there for the taking, but taken out of town. It strove for architectural prominence and permanence by building in brick and stone. "Ouray, though a mining town," as Mae Lacy Baggs put it in *Colorado: The Queen Jewel of the Rockies* (1918), "takes its dignity very seriously."

The town dwindled after its population peaked at almost 3,000 residents around 1900. Some 813 residents live there today but many leave during the winter, when elk and bighorn sheep repossess the town and many businesses post signs announcing, "See you next summer." During the 1990s, Ouray began to aggressively promote winter tourism by keeping the municipal hot springs pool open all year, encouraging cross-country skiing, and marketing itself as the U.S. center for the emerging sport of ice-climbing.

Eric and I knew we must climb high and to the southwest of Ouray in order to begin looking for this location. We felt confident this day, having just "bagged" another overview of the town by secretly climbing onto the back deck of a rental house while no one was home. However, we had no deck above the trees from which to shoot this scene, and ultimately had to move 20 yards to the left of what we guessed to be Jackson's location. Too many trees had grown up in the way since 1886. It's apparent that we stood in the wrong place when you consider that the tree in the middle of my photograph is old enough to have been around in Jackson's day.

Not only did we use the conspicuous waterfall as a perspective clue, but many of the buildings in downtown Ouray in Jackson's photograph remain today, including the Beaumont Hotel. How many buildings can you find common to both images?

123

OURAY

Looking through the Gap,
1886

pp. 190–191

TN The oversized, gravelly bed of the Uncompahgre River shows in both photos, but the Timber Ridge Campground and its vegetation block the modern view of Ouray, with Abrams Mountain looming in the distance. As Fielder's photograph demonstrates, swarms of campers, tour buses, and SUVs have replaced the wagon trains of yesteryear.

Colorado has the nation's highest per capita ownership of SUVs. One in every seven motor vehicles registered in Colorado is one of these gargantuan gas-guzzlers, which dwarf the wagons of Jackson's day, not to mention the sedans of previous tourist armies invading Ouray. After mining played out during the early 20th century, Ouray hoped to reinvent itself as a Swiss-style tourist haven with its large municipal outdoor hot springs and picturesque alpine setting.

To make this photograph, Jackson perched on a hill above the Uncompahgre River just north of Ouray. When Eric and I arrived, the trees that had been clear-cut in the 1880s had grown back, precluding any view from Jackson's spot. We had to stand farther down the hill above today's U.S. Highway 550 in order to get any semblance of an unobstructed view. Can you find the perspective clues that indicate our shift in position? Note the covered wagons — probably delivering settlers to Ouray to find their fortune — in the bottom of Jackson's scene. Notice my modern equivalents of covered wagons!

124

DALLAS DIVIDE

Mt. Sneffles Range,
circa 1901

pp. 192–193

MP   Viewed from Dallas Divide, Mount Sneffels, which Jackson spelled "Sneffles," poses one of Colorado's most recognizable landscapes. The patchwork of red oakbrush and golden aspen framed by rugged, snowy peaks creates a scene of unsurpassed beauty.

The peak, towering above 14,000 feet in elevation, also draws its share of mountaineers. Among them was historian David Lavender, a Telluride lad born in 1910 who spent his early years scampering amongst the colorful cliffs above town. He caught the climbing bug early and was soon bagging the summits of the Wilson and San Miguel ranges in the 1920s and 1930s. He observed, "Proficiency gained, there comes to the climber a mania which goads him to furies of effort, strands him in miserable bivouacs, ruins his feet, his clothes, and his digestion, but lifts his spirit to heights unknown by ordinary mortals — the desire to make a first ascent, to stand where no other creature has ever stood before."

Alas, other inhabitants of the animal kingdom often beat humans to these inspiring summits. A member of the Hayden Survey, Franklin Rhoda, climbed Mount Sneffels in the 1870s and was surprised and disgruntled to find evidence that a grizzly bear had beat him to it: "Claw marks on the rocks on either side of the summit showed that the grizzly had been before us. We gave up all hope of ever beating the bear climbing these mountains."

Mount Sneffels takes its name from a misinterpretation originally perpetrated by Jules Verne. Early surveyors of the peak compared the abyss below its north shoulder to the great hole that Verne described in *Journey to the Center of the Earth*, the so-called Snaefell — a mountain situated in Iceland and the supposed inspiration for Verne. However, Verne changed the spelling to Sneffels in his story, and the same spelling stuck to the peak as well.

JF Replete with every picturesque accouterment from snow-capped, serrated peaks, to glorious aspens and scrub oaks, to ranch settings reminiscent of the West's early days, Dallas Divide is one of my favorite scenic locations in all of America. I had been coming here for 25 years to photograph, so my heart skipped a beat when I found this image in the Jackson archives. And I immediately told Eric when we would rephotograph it — the first week in October. After years of trying to "hit" the color at its peak on Dallas Divide, I had developed a pretty good instinct for when to achieve chromatic success.

Jackson accessed this location from the Rio Grande Southern Railroad, which lay only 100 yards behind him. Today, you arrive via State Highway 62, which connects the town of Ridgway with State Highway 145 to Telluride. A quick hike up the appropriate hill promptly revealed that a ponderosa pine tree was growing *exactly* where I needed to plant the tripod. What a bummer! Can you see the subtle clues indicating that I stood to the left of Jackson's spot by no more than 20 yards?

125

TELLURIDE

Main Street, circa 1887

p. 194

TN   The San Miguel County Courthouse with its three-story central tower and the adjacent two-story brick Sheridan Opera House anchor both photos. The New Sheridan Hotel, completed nine years after Jackson's 1887 photo, is the third prominent edifice in Fielder's photo. Note the banner over Colorado Avenue proclaiming the annual home tour. This and many other festivals have made Telluride the "Festival Capital of Colorado." Celebrations of bluegrass, jazz, film, wine, futurology, and mushrooms have helped turn the town into a popular summer destination. To give the community a break from constant celebration, Telluridians have even inaugurated a Non-Festival Festival.

Born in an 1873 gold strike, Telluride boomed again as a ski resort a century later. The town's Victorian architecture, world-class skiing, and summer festivals have attracted a wealthy, sophisticated population including *Megatrends* author John Naisbitt, who built a "mega-cabin." Oprah Winfrey and other Hollywood celebrities have built new homes or bought old Victorian ones in Telluride, a town often described as the up-and-coming rival of Aspen.

Although Telluride's mines operated until the 1970s, their 20th-century production never matched that of the 19th-century boom. Between the 1920s and 1970s, Telluride stagnated, seeing little new construction. Poverty preserved the town, as did its remote location at the dead end of a country road. The isolation came to an end in 1969, when Joseph T. Zoline, a plastics manufacturer from Beverly Hills, California, announced plans to build the Telluride Ski Resort. Within months, property values jumped 150 percent. Newcomers streamed in, mostly monied transplants from other parts of the country.

Most of Telluride was designated a National Register Historic District in 1961, and a 1974 local preservation ordinance restricted alterations, new construction, and demolition within the historic district. The guidelines of the town's Historic and Architectural Review Commission include a 35-foot height limit, setback requirements, and a ban on raw redwood in favor of painted frame materials. The "typical" Telluride house is a gabled, vernacular frame building with simple ornamentation. Many of these modest houses have been overwhelmed with added towers, bay windows, and decorative shingling—changes that met the new-construction guidelines for size, scale, and material but obscured the original design.

Despite ever-mounting development pressures in a town that now has a population of more than 2,221, Telluride has clung to much of its architectural heritage. The main street, Colorado Avenue, built

extra-wide to accommodate the turnaround of mule trains, continues to serve as the commercial center. The street has retained many original false-front buildings, as seen in the right-hand portion of the photos.

These views looking east on Colorado Avenue capture Telluride's dramatic montane setting. Ajax and Telluride peaks and Ballard and Wasatch mountains in the background guard the Imogene Pass route that links Telluride with Ouray and Silverton — at 13,114 feet, the highest major pass in Colorado. The route is usually open only in July, August, and September; in years of deep, persistent snow, it may never open at all. Such mountainous approaches have led some to call this town "To Hell You Ride."

JF The two prominent buildings in both photographs — the San Miguel County Courthouse on the immediate left and the New Sheridan Hotel next to it — proved to be perfect perspective clues. As had the town of Cañon City, Telluride designated a middle lane on its main street, today's Colorado Avenue, for delivery vehicles — originally, as Tom Noel explains, to allow mule trains to change direction. Eric and I only had to pull up in this lane to the correct location, act official, and set up the camera for the photograph. We never had to ask a sheriff to protect our backsides from traffic. And, surprisingly, no law-enforcement officers ever questioned what we were doing, a relief considering the rude Aspen cop who had blasted his siren when we crossed its Main Street too slowly for his taste. I had expected worse from this similar resort town, Telluride.

Telluride rests in the most scenic location for a town in all of Colorado: It is bounded by wilderness. Although efforts have been made to preserve Telluride's historic architecture, the town and San Miguel County have allowed the resort to develop without proper consideration for the integrity of the natural environment. The building of a mega-hotel, an airport, and trophy homes as far as the eye can see has compromised the bucolic scenery that has attracted people to this place for a century. It's a travesty.

Nevertheless, perhaps the leadership in this valley has finally seen the light. In the summer of 2000, the town rallied to try to prevent the last large section of open space from being developed. As of the writing of this book in April 2001, Telluride had nearly raised the $26 million necessary to purchase this property at the town's entrance and set it aside as permanent open space.

126

OPHIR

1891

p. 195

TN   Ophir bears the name of the biblical gold mines in 1 Kings 9:28: "And they came to Ophir, and fetched from thence gold…and brought it to King Solomon." The town combines two adjacent communities known as Old Ophir and New Ophir. Founded in 1878 at the junction of Waterfall Creek and the Howard Fork of the San Miguel River, Ophir reached a population of 127 in 1900, a time when the Rio Grande Southern Railroad served the town. By 1960, the population had dwindled to zero, but since then Ophir has grown as a working-class suburb of Telluride. Once again on the rise, Ophir tallied 113 residents in the 2000 count. These pictures look south on a townsite frozen in time. Pilot Knob is prominent in the background between U. S. Grant and Vermilion peaks.

Whenever I wish to shortcut the circuitous route to Telluride, I take the Ophir Pass road from Silverton to the town of Ophir, south of Telluride. Technically, it's a slow, four-wheel-drive route, but really it's a fast, two-wheel drive, albeit a rough one. Unfortunately, it's only passable in the summer.

At the bottom of the west side of the pass lies the old mining town of Ophir. Jackson stood north of the town on a mountain slope in order to make this image. Eric and I climbed high to find his spot. Regrettably, aspen trees blocked the correct view, requiring us to make the repeat photograph from slightly to the right of Jackson's place. Notice the change in tree cover on the hillside across the valley.

127

SAN MIGUEL COUNTY

Bridal Veil Falls, circa 1887

p. 196

TN In Fielder's photo, you can see lines of the aerial tramway to the Smuggler-Union Mine's 1907 hydroelectric power plant atop the falls. This National Register Historic structure — accessible by a 1.8-mile hike or four-wheel-drive ride from Pandora Mill at the base of the falls — is an unlikely apparition spectacularly sited atop 365-foot Bridal Veil Falls, the highest in Colorado.

Bulkeley Wells, the manager of the Smuggler-Union Mining Company, supposedly chose the site and worked with architects to design a handsome plant with a stone foundation and steeply gabled and dormered frame, giving it a domestic appearance and echoing the angles of surrounding peaks. Power plants are often eyesores, but this one is most photogenic. Although this waterfall shares its name with four others in Colorado, it is unforgettable once you've seen its glistening, lacy white bridal veil.

JR Bridal Veil Creek plunges over a cliff of resistant Telluride Formation conglomerate and sandstone deposited about 55 to 45 million years ago during the early part of the Eocene epoch. The conglomerate and sandstone are composed of materials eroded from the highlands uplifted during the Laramide orogeny 15 million years or so earlier. The Telluride Formation was deposited on a landscape that had considerable relief, so its thickness varies greatly. Here it measures about 240 feet thick, but a few miles to the west it is as much as 1,000 feet thick.

The conglomerate beds contain abundant pebbles, cobbles, and boulders of older rocks including limestone and siltstone derived from Paleozoic and Mesozoic rocks, as well as quartzite, schist, and granite derived from Precambrian basement rocks; these pebbles, cobbles, and boulders are, in effect, the wreckage of the old Laramide uplifts. Some of the pebbles and cobbles in the conglomerate are clearly visible in the contemporary photograph, but hide behind the tree in the left foreground of the historic photo. At Bridal Veil Falls, the Telluride Formation rests on reddish-brown shale and sandstone of the Triassic Dolores Formation, and is overlain by the Oligocene volcanic rocks that make up much of the great massif of the San Juan Mountains.

JF Eric and I arrived at this well-known place in May, just as the snows had left the Black Bear Pass road that accesses the falls from the town of Telluride. Many large rocks littered the dirt road, waiting to be cleared for tourist season — remnants of a typical Telluride winter during which spectacular avalanches pour over the cliffs east of town.

Eventually, we found our way to the base of the falls, several switchbacks up the road. Though the trees had changed too much since 1887 to use as clues, the top of the cliff over which pour the waters of Bridal Veil Creek helped us find the correct perspective. The constant mist from Colorado's tallest waterfall makes it difficult to take a picture without moisture accumulating on your lens. In my photograph, notice the wires that support the aerial tram used to access the old power plant hidden behind the cliff.

128

SAN MIGUEL COUNTY

Mystic Falls, circa 1893

p. 197

At Mystic Falls, near Ophir, the Lake Fork of the San Miguel River cascades over a cliff more than 120 feet high. The resistant rock that forms the cliff is part of the Jurassic Morrison Formation. The Morrison Formation consists chiefly of soft, red and green shale and mudstone, as well as some sandstone. Generally not very resistant to erosion, it typically forms gentle, rounded slopes. Here, however, a thick sill of igneous rock that was intruded along the layers of the sedimentary rocks has baked the rocks of the Morrison Formation. (The base of this igneous sheet lies above the top of the falls and is not visible in the photographs.) The heat from the molten igneous rock that formed the sheet converted the soft sedimentary rocks below it into a dense, hard rock called hornfels—which is extremely resistant to erosion and makes up the prominent cliffs around the falls.

The Morrison Formation was deposited about 150 million years ago by sluggish streams meandering across a broad alluvial plain that covered the eroded roots of the Ancestral Rocky Mountains. The sheet of igneous rock that baked the Morrison Formation here was injected about 25 million years ago, well after the end of the Laramide orogeny. The widespread emplacement of igneous rocks of this age led to the development of the rich gold-silver veins that attracted prospectors and miners to the San Juan Mountains in the late 19th and early 20th centuries.

Between these two images, the main differences in the appearance of the waterfall probably derive from the change in the stream's flow between the time of Jackson's visit and Fielder's return trip. The angle of the view differs slightly, suggesting that the photographers might have stood on opposite sides of the stream, however some of the details and fractures in the cliff are identifiable from image to image. The rocks in the foreground of Jackson's photograph now missing from Fielder's, though large, could have been swept downstream by torrential floods. Humans also could have intervened with the help of dynamite.

JF No one in Telluride or anywhere else could tell me anything about the existence of Mystic Falls. Apparently, the name is archaic. Jackson's photograph number (he cataloged all of his images with numbers) for this one fell, however, in the same sequence as other images made in the Telluride area. Eric and I needed only to explore every tributary of the San Miguel River in order to find this scene! Suffice it to say that many cliffs and creeks in the Telluride basin could combine to make such a waterfall.

On the second day of our search, we knocked on the door of a home nestled at the base of a canyon along Forest Road 625. Just north of this place, the Lake Fork of the San Miguel River joins the South Fork of the San Miguel River; it's a little way downstream from the town of Ophir, near the old town of Ames, if you go to look for the waterfall. With permission from the homeowner, we hiked up the creek in a downpour. Eventually, we heard a roar, and around the next bend in the creek appeared this waterfall.

However, I still have a problem with my version of the scene. I *think* it's the same place, but except for the general lay of the land, I cannot find a single rock feature that matches any in Jackson's photograph. I did not even locate the large rocks between which, in the historic photo, a Jackson companion had wedged himself. Could a catastrophic flood have washed away all of the physical characteristics manifest in Jackson's scene? Is there a twin canyon hiding somewhere in the basin? After discussing this possibility with Jack Reed, who believes this is the correct waterfall, I suppose I should put my doubts to rest.

OPHIR

Loop, 1896

p. 198

With a magnifying glass, look for the cuts and fills, as well as remnants of the bridgework and retaining walls, of the Rio Grande Southern Railroad. RGS Bridge 51-1, constructed between 1910 and 1912 at Ophir, is still standing. For 60 years, this narrow-gauge line catered to San Juan Mountain coal, gold, and silver mining centers, in addition to logging operations. Year-round, this baby railroad also carried passengers and mail.

Built between Ridgway and Durango, the RGS served many small communities along the western flank of the San Juans: Dallas Divide, Placerville, Sawpit, Telluride, Ames, Ophir, Rico, Dolores, Mancos, and Hesperus. The line opened in 1890 and was not abandoned until 1952.

Fighting off abandonment, the impoverished RGS installed a Pierce-Arrow gas-powered automobile engine inside a custom-made locomotive. Dubbed the "Galloping Goose," this contraption had a horn that sounded like a goose, seemed to waddle down the track, and, as it often overheated, usually had the engine-cooling side panels opened. As the goose waddled down the track, these panels flapped like wings. Of six surviving geese, specimens may be found in Telluride, Dolores, and the Colorado Railroad Museum in Golden.

Jackson's panoramic scene is the composite of three photographs. He stood along the tracks of the Rio Grande Southern Railroad on its way over Lizard Head Pass from Telluride to the town of Dolores. Today's State Highway 145, for the most part, follows this route. I also made three images. However, aspen trees prevented me from placing my tripod in Jackson's exact location. Can you find the clues that prove this fact? Obviously, Jackson made his images during winter.

130

LIZARD HEAD PASS

Trout Lake Outlet, 1895

p. 199

TN Both Trout Lake and Lizard Head Pass were stops on the Rio Grande Southern Railroad, a "toy" narrow-gauge line, during its operations between 1890 and 1952. Trout Lake, located on a fork of the San Miguel River about 15 miles south of Telluride, lies along State Highway 145, visible in the left mid-ground of Fielder's photo. The pyramidal-roofed log structure in the lake is the inlet to the penstock for the water wheel that drives the generator at the nearby Ames power plant. Once a popular, busy rail stop for camera clickers, Trout Lake is now a sleepy backwater. Vermilion Peak in the background shows some of its color in the Fielder shot, but blazes brighter in summer under the glow of sunsets and sunrises.

 Trout Lake, a very scenic place just below the top of Lizard Head Pass, always makes a beautiful photograph. Eric and I hoped that the barn Jackson photographed would still exist, but assumed it a stretch to think that cows would still live there. Neither remained, but the ridge trick worked its magic once again. However, this side of the lake had changed a great deal, precluding our ability to find Jackson's exact location. Pleased to have almost duplicated Jackson's snowpack, we moved on around the corner to rephotograph Lizard Head proper (see Photo Pair 131).

131

LIZARD HEAD PASS

1895

pp. 200–201

JR Volcanic rocks compose the spectacular spine of Lizard Head, but, contrary to popular belief (and the claims of some guidebooks), it is not a neck of intrusive igneous rock that marks the throat of a volcano. It is actually an erosional remnant of the great pile of Eocene and Oligocene (30- to 35-million-year-old) volcanic rocks that makes up much of the San Juan Mountains to the east.

The dark cliffs that form the parapet around the base of the spire are outcrops of sandstone and breccia containing abundant fragments of dark volcanic rocks that streams or mudflows carried from some nearby volcano, now long destroyed by erosion. The white band that encircles the base of the spire is a thick layer of consolidated volcanic ash containing fragments of volcanic rocks and abundant volcanic mineral crystals. The dark cliffs that make up most of the spire are a series of at least five flows of dark lava that together measure about 250 feet thick. The tip of the spire is of consolidated volcanic ash, much like that around the base.

The volcanic rocks at Lizard Head rest on Telluride Conglomerate, the same rock that forms the cliffs at Bridal Veil Falls (see Photo Pair 127). The rounded slopes in the foreground are underlain by Mancos Shale deposited between about 100 and 80 million years ago, when this part of Colorado lay beneath the shallow seaway that occupied much of central North America. The low ridges in the mid-ground are chiefly granitic rock that intruded both the Mancos Shale and the overlying volcanic rocks about 25 million years ago. The extremely unstable volcanic rocks that form Lizard Head's encircling cliffs make it one of the most difficult and dangerous rock climbs in Colorado.

The road in the foreground of the contemporary picture is State Highway 145. It follows the bed of the railroad shown in Jackson's picture. The scar a few yards beyond the highway in the contemporary image marks the former route of the highway, which followed the wagon road seen in the 1895 photo.

 Eric and I first arrived at this location in May when the snowpack was similar to that in Jackson's scene. Unfortunately, the clouds manifest in the photograph of nearby Trout Lake (see Photo Pair 130) had descended just far enough to conceal the Lizard Head. Too many other photographic duties filled our schedule that week, so we could not wait out the weather front. We decided to return in the fall.

Around the middle of October, we quickly found Jackson's location above State Highway 145 and made this repeat photograph on a glorious fall morning. Can you find the perspective clues that prove we stood in the correct spot?

132

RICO

*and the Enterprise Group
of Mines, 1893*

p. 202

TN Born with a silver spoon in its mouth, Rico has been malnourished since the Silver Crash of 1893. Prospectors began poking around in the late 1860s, but did not make significant silver strikes until 1879. The Enterprise group of mines pockmarking the hillside in Jackson's 1893 photo created a silver bonanza that spurred Otto Mears' Rio Grande Southern Railroad to build a narrow-gauge line over Lizard Head Pass to Rico. In 1890, Rico's population peaked at around 1,200.

The town's long decline after the Silver Crash enabled prosperous farmers at the west end of Dolores County to spearhead a vote to move the county seat to Dove Creek in 1941. The old county courthouse, a handsome, red brick building trimmed in red sandstone, is now the Rico Town Hall. In 1953, the discovery of iron pyrite, used to make sulfuric acid, led to construction of the Ramco sulfuric acid plant near Rico. Toxic fumes and waste from the plant killed aspen trees and polluted the upper Dolores River before the plant closed in 1962. Today, Rico is liveliest in summer, when tourists stop to gawk at this ghostly mining town that had a 2000 census tally of 205 residents. The coke ovens 1 mile south of town on State Highway 145 serve as reminders of Rico's richer days.

In Rico, the Enterprise Bar & Grille commemorates the now-defunct Enterprise mines. Located on the main street (Glasgow Avenue/State Highway 145), this imposing, 1892 two-story commercial edifice speaks eloquently of the area's skilled stonemasons and fine building stone. The sandstone front flaunts Romanesque Revival detail, with an arcaded second story and a bracketed and pedimented cornice.

 The old mining town of Rico has become somewhat famous lately as an "alternative" to Telluride if you want to hang out in this region of the state. It's not much of an alternative—there's hardly anywhere to stay or live—but it does possess a couple of interesting bar/restaurants, including the Rico Theater and Café. In Jackson's day, the mines seen in the background of his photograph fueled a more vibrant atmosphere in Rico.

Eric and I happened to arrive in June during some awful weather, and ended up staying for a couple of days. The weather was bad enough to prevent any photography, so we returned in the fall to make this image. Finding the location required some tricky four-wheel driving on some old, seldom-traveled mining roads through aspen forests that ultimately wouldn't allow us to photograph from the correct spot. We ended up about 50 yards to the right of where Jackson must have stood, and a little bit lower on the mountain. Which perspective clues do you notice that underscore this fact?

133

DOLORES

1893

p. 203

TN Stagecoaches have given way to cars and trucks in downtown Dolores, although the town retains many of its antique buildings and its small-town ambiance.

Founded in 1878, the community was named for El Río de Nuestra Señora de los Dolores (the River of Our Lady of Sorrows), the Dolores River, which flows through the town. The Rio Grande Southern Railroad served this hamlet, and some 19th-century railroad-era structures survive in various states of disuse. Architecturally, this town's wonders range from the Château-style Del Rio Hotel to the pressed-metal facade of the Hollywood Saloon, which resembles a Western movie set.

The reconstructed Rio Grande Southern Depot, 420 Railroad Ave., houses a museum. Richard Dorman, a Santa Fe architect, faithfully reincarnated the classic Queen Anne–style depot lost to a fire. The steep-pitched upper story contains the stationmaster's quarters, with freight and passenger services below. The new depot makes a fine nest for Galloping Goose No. 5, one of the famed flock of hybrid rail/motor vehicles. Goose No. 5 had a 1925 Pierce-Arrow engine inside a customized Wayne bus.

Railroad tourists often stayed at the Rio Grande Southern Hotel, the three-story, dormered building in the Fielder photo, at 101 S. 5th St. This hotel consists of a two-story original frame structure with a smaller-frame rear addition. It was stuccoed to comply with a new ordinance instituted after a 1913 fire claimed the hotel's icehouse and stables, along with other downtown buildings.

JF None of the buildings in Jackson's photograph of Dolores exist today. The ridge in the distance served as my only perspective clue. Unfortunately, it takes two to tango, that is, two or more points to align with one another to reveal the historic photographer's location.

In cases like this, I used proportion to ascertain the best possible place from which to photograph. I determined what portion of the width of the Jackson photograph the ridge occupied, then went to the place in the street where the slope of the ridge was the same as its angle in the Jackson photograph. Finally, I made certain that specific rocks on the cliff matched the appearance and position of those in the old photograph. With this task completed, Eric and I headed to the nearest bar for lunch and relaxation.

Colorado 1870 - 2000 Revisited

Western Deserts Locations

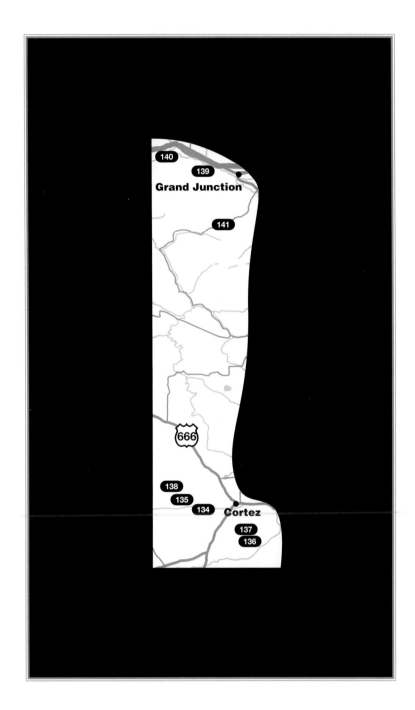

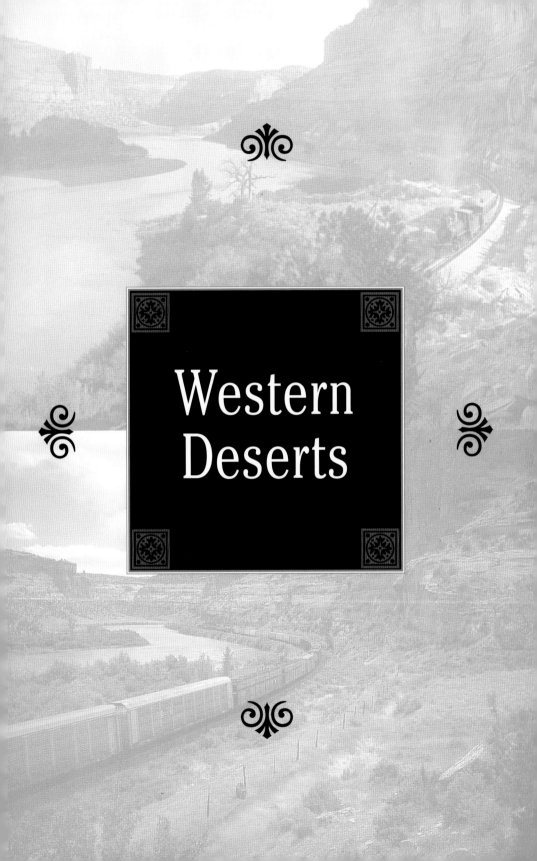

Western Deserts

134

CORTEZ

*Ancient Ruins at the
Head of the McElmo,
1875*

p. 208

TN On the horizon in these photos, Sleeping Ute Mountain, a humanlike reclining figure with his arms folded across his chest, guards the ancient ruins that make McElmo Canyon one of America's greatest archaeological treasures. The Utes, like the Anasazi before them, depended on this mountain near Cortez in southwestern Colorado to protect them from invaders. Alas, for the Utes, this giant went to sleep just a few miles west of Towaoc, allowing the Spaniards to enter Colorado. Subsequently, Plains Indians and pale-faced prospectors also encroached upon Ute domain. But according to Ute legend, the Sleeping Ute will someday wake up — and drive away all non-Utes. Another legend contends that the Sleeping Ute grew angry with the Utes and gathered all the rain clouds into his pockets. Then he lay down on his back, folded his arms across his chest, and went to sleep. When rain clouds finally do descend from Sleeping Ute Mountain, the Utes say they are slipping out of his pockets.

The Sleeping Ute also failed to protect the many Anasazi ruins, burial sites, and other priceless artifacts from pot-hunters and illegal collectors. Not until 2000 did President William J. Clinton designate Canyon of the Ancients National Monument to protect McElmo Canyon's scattered archaeological sites.

Other McElmo Canyon sites had been included in the adjacent Hovenweep (Ute for "deserted valley") National Monument, established in 1923 to oversee widely scattered Anasazi structures in Colorado and Utah. These include square, round, and oval masonry structures reminiscent of medieval European fortifications. Openings in the Hovenweep towers, however, may have been used for astronomical observation rather than for defensive purposes.

 Not only was Jackson one of the first photographers of ancient Anasazi-civilization ruins in Colorado, he was also one of the first Euro-Americans to visit some of them. In 1874 and 1875, he took a break from photographing San Juan Mountains mining towns and hired a guide to take him down the Mancos River and McElmo Creek. Many ruins dot both of these drainages near present-day Cortez.

With the help of local archaeologists, Eric and I found this location a few miles to the east of Cortez. Notice the vestiges of Anasazi towers in 1875 — nothing remains today. Erosion is responsible for some of the loss, but so, too, is the fact that people removed many of the stones to build their own dwellings. Considering that archaeology was not a viable science until the turn of the last century, that no value was placed on such antiquities in Jackson's day, it's not surprising what happened.

135

CORTEZ

Battle Rock,
McElmo Canyon,
1875

p. 209

EP   Battle Rock — or Castle Rock, as it is known today — was the home of 75 to 150 Anasazi people for a scant 20 years. Occupied in the 1260s, the site was abandoned before 1290 and probably was not disturbed again until Jackson visited and photographed it during the Hayden Survey's 1875 reconnaissance of the Four Corners region. What remained of the now-vanished pueblo in Jackson's day is visible in the right-hand portion of his photograph.

Ute Indian tradition holds that Battle Rock was the scene of a violent skirmish. Archaeological excavations and study by the University of Colorado in 1968, and by the Crow Canyon Archaeological Center from 1990 to 1994, identified remains of 41 people — many of whom met their deaths either in a battle or when the pueblo's roof caught fire, caved in, and crushed them. But we may never know just what happened there or why.

The history of Colorado since the gold-rush days spans only one-fifth of the time that has elapsed since Castle Rock's mysterious end — and less than one-thousandth of the time since humans first arrived in the area.

Local archaeologists helped us track down Battle Rock. Now called Castle Rock, this formation lies 12 miles west of U.S. Highway 666 on the north side of County Road G. Though the Anasazi ruins in the right-hand portion of Jackson's photograph have vanished, we did rephotograph other ruins in the area. Some of the piñon and juniper trees in Jackson's scene are the same ones as in my photograph — 123 years later! Can you find the person standing in Jackson's photograph, and Eric Bellamy at the same spot in my photograph?

136

UTE MOUNTAIN
UTE TRIBAL PARK

Two-Story House,
Mancos Canyon, 1893

pp. 210–211

TN   The 125,000-acre Ute Mountain Ute Tribal Park, with headquarters at the junction of U.S. Highways 160 and 666 southwest of Cortez, features many archaic Anasazi and historic ruins first excavated in 1913 by Earl Morris. Visitors must be accompanied by Ute guides, and tours may be arranged through the Ute Mountain Ute Tribal Park. Tourists are allowed to crawl around on the Ute Park ruins, as the Utes take a considerably less cautious approach to ancient ruins than do rangers in the adjacent Mesa Verde National Park.

The Utes — a mountain tribe that has resided here for hundreds, perhaps thousands, of years — have lived in Colorado longer than any other group. They are physically shorter, darker, and stockier than the Plains Indians and also differ from the Plains tribes in that they belong to the Shoshonean linguistic family centered in Utah and the Great Basin. They might have descended from such prehistoric cultures as the Fremont people, who occupied Colorado 10,000 years ago. Seven different Ute bands — the Capote, Grand River, Mouache, Uncompahgre, Uintah, Yampa, and Weminuche — occupied central and western Colorado and eastern Utah.

After the U.S. Army built Fort Garland in the San Luis Valley in the 1850s, the U.S. began to fight with and make treaties with the Utes. During the 1860s, the tribe agreed to a reservation consisting of the western third of Colorado. After whites found silver and gold on that reservation, the Utes signed the 1873 Brunot Agreement, opening up the San Juan Mountains to prospectors. In 1879, a band of Utes killed White River Indian agent Nathan Meeker and several agency employees. The band also ambushed Major Thomas Tipton Thornburgh on his way to rescue Meeker, killing the major and 13 of his men. After that episode, Euro-Americans demanded that the Utes go. Serious repercussions were avoided partly through the peacekeeping efforts of Chief Ouray.

Although the Uintah, Uncompahgre, Grand River, and Yampa bands of northwest Colorado were moved to the Uintah Reservation in northeastern Utah, the Weminuche, Capote, and Mouache bands remain on the Southern Ute and Ute Mountain reservations in the southwestern corner of Colorado. Today, the Ute Mountain Utes welcome visitors to their reservation, where they maintain a casino, museum, and trading post, and operate guided tours of the Ute Mountain Ute Tribal Park.

The other half of the cliff dwellings around Mesa Verde that are not part of Mesa Verde National Park exist within the Ute Mountain Ute Tribal Park. Visitation by nontribal members is prohibited without a guide, whom you can hire in Towaoc at tribal headquarters. I had been to Two-Story House once before and eagerly anticipated a return trip. Anasazi cliff dwellings are wonderful places to visit, even if you have only the least bit of appreciation for ancient cultures. Antiquities such as potsherds and corn cobs pepper the ground in many of these places, lending a haunting air to the mystery surrounding the disappearance of the Anasazi culture around the late 1200s.

Accessing this ruin requires a steep 30-minute hike up from the Mancos River. Can you find some of the perspective clues I employed in order to stand where Jackson did? What's missing from the end of the cliff in the right-hand portion of my photograph? Is the Ute guide in my photograph the same one as in Jackson's? Hint: Life is slow in this part of the state.

137

MESA VERDE

Cliff Palace, 1893

pp. 212–213

TN Jackson's 1893 photograph, one of the first to be taken of Cliff Palace, shows the ruins before Mesa Verde National Park's 1906 creation. The National Park Service has subsequently stabilized and, in some cases, reconstructed these American Indian ruins. Close comparison of these photos helps to answer the often-asked question about how much of Mesa Verde is authentic Anasazi work and how much has been reconstructed.

Cliff Palace, built around A.D. 1200 and abandoned in the 1270s, includes 217 rooms and 23 kivas that accommodated an estimated 500 residents. Measuring 80 feet high, 80 feet deep, and 200 feet long, it ranks as North America's largest cliff dwelling. Fourteen connected storage rooms built into the roof of the cave kept food and other materials cool, dry, and out of the reach of children, dogs, domesticated turkeys, and rodents. To access such remote parts of the cliff dwellings, residents used log ladders, as well as toeholds and handholds carved into the rock. Also notable are murals in zigzag motifs and vigas extending through the masonry walls. Inside Cliff Palace, small chinking stones are fitted into the mortar in the hammered sandstone masonry, which also retains traces of the original pinkish-brown plaster painted with geometric wall designs.

Mesa Verde is Spanish for "green table," as the mesa is wetter and greener than the surrounding lowlands. Here, the Anasazi began cultivating corn and a few other plants about 2,000 years ago. Their stable agricultural economy enabled them to develop one of the world's more advanced civilizations in terms of population density, architecture, and technology. Their achievements are commemorated in this national park, the first park in the world dedicated to preserving the culture of prehistoric peoples. In 1978, the United Nations Educational, Scientific, and Cultural Organization designated the pre-Puebloan cities preserved at Mesa Verde as the first World Heritage Site in the U.S. This is North America's best-preserved collection of American Indian pit houses, pueblos, and cliff dwellings. The park's museum showcases artifacts ranging from baskets and distinctive black-on-white pottery to grinding stones and miniature ears of corn.

The Anasazi constructed irrigation ditches and dams to water their corn, squash, and beans. Despite their water-conscious building and culture, the drought of A.D. 1275–1300 probably forced many of the pre-Puebloans to evacuate their cliff cities. Controversial recent archaeological discoveries suggest the presence of ritualistic cannibalism among these peoples signify that perhaps desperation and/or terrorism preceded their abandonment of southwestern Colorado. They moved to, among other places, the Rio Grande Valley to build the pueblos still occupied by their descendants. Recent lightning-caused fires in the park, especially the July 2000 burns, closed it for several weeks but revealed new archaeological sites, of which Cliff Palace remains the masterpiece.

JF W. H. Jackson made a number of photographs of Cliff Palace, today inside Mesa Verde National Park. He photographed it from practically every angle. With the assistance of the National Park Service, Eric and I rephotographed every image that we found, including this one taken from the right side of the ruin.

Notice the abundance of perspective clues, but observe also how much has changed. When the National Park Service acquired this area, kivas like those in the foreground were excavated and restored, and walls were fortified to facilitate interpretation and arrest erosion of the ruins. Both Jackson and I made our images before 10 a.m. in order to photograph in the shade. Direct light after that hour makes the contrast of highlight and shadow too great for the film to manage: Highlights become washed out, and details in shadows are lost.

138

UTE MOUNTAIN

Cliffs near the Cave Dwellings,
1874

p. 214

JF   The ridges of Sleeping Ute Mountain in the background of this photograph gave away Jackson's location, not far north of Castle Rock, formerly called Battle Rock (see Photo Pair 135). Eric and I ended up on top of a sandstone bluff — if not exactly in Jackson's footsteps, then only inches away. An abundance of ridges and rock formations made perfect perspective clues, but the best ones were the juniper tree and piñon pine on the lower right side of both photographs. Though most of the other trees are probably the same, too, these two trees especially stand out: They had not grown in 124 years! Such is life in the desert.

What's most remarkable is the fact that these two trees are still healthy. Is there a lesson here for another Earth-dwelling life-form, us humans? Six billion of us threaten the integrity of biodiversity and all life on this planet, including our own lives. Each year, we lose 3 percent of what's left of our rainforests on this planet to clear-cutting for agriculture. Do the math! These fertile places harbor most of the undiscovered life-forms on Earth. The great biologist E. O. Wilson estimates that there exist 10 to 100 million species of life on our planet, beyond the 1.6 million we've already found, that haven't yet been discovered.

The notions that human populations must grow in order to remain healthy; that we must increase our company sales volumes from year to year; that we must add more people to our cities to remain economically viable; that we atrophy unless we grow, are sinking our planetary ship. We cannot continue consuming and destroying natural resources at unsustainable rates if biodiversity is to prevail. Consider the process of eutrophication as an example of the cause-and-effect relationship we have with our natural environment: We fertilize our lawns to keep them green; the excess runs off from our lawns into lakes, where it promotes algae growth; the proliferation of algae, in turn, robs the lakes of oxygen and denies fish and other aquatic creatures the ability to breathe. Wasteful consumption and human overpopulation have caused this and many other natural calamities, in effect eutrophying the entire planet — robbing it of its life.

Can we humans survive by limiting population growth? By making more profit through efficiency, not necessarily through boosting sales? By using our resources in sustainable ways? I know one thing: In the long run, cockroaches and coyotes will outlive us if we don't become more efficient like the piñons and junipers in the desert. Now back to history and geology!

139

COLORADO NATIONAL MONUMENT

Pipe Organ Spires, 1882

p. 215

JR   Reddish-orange, Jurassic Wingate Sandstone eroded to form the spectacularly sculpted spires of the Pipe Organ in Colorado National Monument. The tallest spire — capped by a thin, resistant slab of Kayenta Sandstone also of Jurassic age — towers more than 300 feet high. The gentle slopes below the Wingate cliffs are outcrops of reddish mudstone in the Triassic Chinle Formation. Finally, the dark rocks in the foreground make up part of the Precambrian basement. Here, they consist mainly of schist that contains abundant thin dikes and stringers of pegmatite (coarse granite). Metamorphism of sedimentary rocks formed the schist about 1.7 billion years ago. The Chinle Formation was deposited about 220 million years ago. Thus, the contact between the basement rocks and the Chinle Formation represents a break in geologic history of almost 1.5 billion years, about a third of the age of the Earth.

At one time, several thousand feet of Paleozoic sedimentary rock blanketed the Precambrian basement in this area. During the rise of the Ancestral Rocky Mountains about 300 million years ago, an uplift developed in about the present position of the Uncompahgre Plateau. During and shortly after the rise of this arch, erosion stripped away these older sedimentary strata, leaving the basement rocks exposed at the surface. It was on this surface that the Triassic and Jurassic rocks that form the Pipe Organ were deposited.

The Chinle Formation was apparently deposited on a densely vegetated floodplain or mudflat with shallow ponds and meandering streams. The Wingate Sandstone is composed of windblown sand that formed a large series of dunes much like those in the modern Sahara Desert. The sandstone of the Kayenta Formation was deposited along braided, northwest-flowing rivers that probably resembled the modern Platte River in Nebraska and northeastern Colorado.

The erosion that sculpted the spires took place during the last 5 million years or so, during uplift of the entire southern Rocky Mountain and Colorado Plateau region. No appreciable changes are apparent between Jackson's and Fielder's photos except for the vegetation. This continuity might seem strange in an area of geologically rapid erosion, but, in searching for differences, keep in mind that the interval during which the spires took shape might have lasted 50,000 times longer than the interval between the photographs.

My loyal assistant, Eric Bellamy, is a talented technical rock climber. He's as good on slippery sandstone as he is on granite. He took one look at Jackson's photograph of these formations in what is today Colorado National Monument and was able to tell me where we needed to go. Apparently, when Jackson made his photograph, he was standing in front of Independence Monument, a well-known spire that Eric had climbed more than once.

On a hot June day, we made the 4-mile hike up Ute Canyon to try to find this photographic location. We soon homed in on the general area, and a little while later, the black rocks in the foreground. In 90-degree heat, we quickly headed back to the car before precious film began to melt!

140

COLORADO RIVER

*Cañon of the Grand
in Utah, circa 1891*

pp. 216–217

MP   The Colorado River west of Grand Junction cuts a dramatic sandstone gorge through 20 miles of Ruby and Horsethief canyons. Over eons, forces of water and wind carved a labyrinth of tributary canyons on the river's south bank. Collectively called the Black Ridge Canyons, these tributaries contain innumerable spires and pinnacles, the second-greatest concentration of natural arches in the Southwest, perennial streams with plunge pools and cottonwoods, and a huge 300-foot cavern cut by a stream meander in Mee Canyon.

The Wingate Formation forms the massive sandstone walls of these canyons. These walls exhibit the cross-bedded patterns of overlapping sand dunes frozen in place by geologic processes from a time 200 million years ago. In the distance, the mouth of Mee Canyon beckons. A short walk soon reveals towering pinnacles pierced through by windows and arches. A trickle of water nourishes cottonwoods scattered widely along the canyon's sandy floor.

The Black Ridge Canyons Wilderness Area comprises the largest desert wilderness in Colorado — more than 75,000 acres south of the Colorado River permanently protected from development by legislation passed in 2000. The Colorado River corridor lies just outside the wilderness area, but it, too, is protected from mining operations, the creation of gravel pits, and inundation by new dams.

I took one look at this image and knew instantly that Jackson had erred in identifying this area as part of Utah. I had rafted and floated this stretch of the Colorado River several times. You put in on the river at Loma, just west of Grand Junction, and take out at Westwater, Utah. This is Ruby Canyon in Colorado; Utah is 6 miles downriver. Enough of the one-upmanship. I knew from the day that I found this photo in the archives that, other than riding the Amtrak train (which wouldn't drop me off, anyway), I'd only be able to reach this place easily by floating down the river.

In May 1998, I happened to be giving a speech in Grand Junction when I bumped into old friend and fellow environmentalist Norm Mullen. Norm had planned to float this stretch of the river during the following two days, so I asked if I could bum a ride on his raft. What I did not know when I made my request was that he was taking the trip with his girlfriend from Tennessee, whom he had not seen in eight months. Norm was too polite to say no, and I was too desperate to back out, so I joined them on their journey (I got along really well with his girlfriend).

The location proved a cinch to find, and the Union Pacific freight train was kind enough to pass by, allowing me to duplicate Jackson's Denver & Rio Grande train. Notice that the tracks have moved, and that the river has moved, too. Can you explain the shifting of the river? Hint: Think dams and water diversion for irrigation.

141

UNAWEEP CAÑON

circa 1890

p. 218

JR Unaweep Canyon is a deep gorge nearly 25 miles long that cuts completely through the Uncompahgre Plateau between Whitewater on the Gunnison River and Gateway on the Dolores River. At its highest point, near where the photographers took these pictures, the canyon floor lies almost 2,500 feet above the levels of the Dolores and Gunnison rivers. The steep-walled inner gorge of the canyon is 500 to 1,200 feet deep and is carved in Precambrian basement rocks, chiefly granite and schist. The gentler upper walls of the canyon are Triassic and Jurassic sedimentary rocks of the Chinle, Wingate, and Kayenta Formations, which rest on the basement rocks. These rocks cap the mesa in the center skyline of these images.

Two small streams drain the canyon: East Creek, which flows into the Gunnison, and West Creek, which flows into the Dolores. Hayden Survey geologists who visited the area in 1875 recognized that these small streams could not possibly have carved such a large canyon, concluding that either the Gunnison or Colorado rivers must have been responsible. They theorized that the Uncompahgre Plateau's geologically recent uplift diverted the river around the northern end of the uplift, leaving the canyon high and dry.

Later researchers have suggested that some 5 million years or so ago, the streams flowed across a blanket of younger rocks that completely buried the Uncompahgre uplift, which had originally formed 60 or 70 million years earlier during the Laramide orogeny. These geologists believe that the Gunnison joined the Colorado near the eastern end of the present canyon, and that the combined rivers flowed southwest across the buried uplift. As this river cut downward, it eventually encountered the hard Precambrian basement rocks and began to carve the inner gorge of the canyon. However, a tributary of the Colorado that flowed in much softer rocks around the northern end of the uplift was able to deepen its channel and cut headward until it eventually diverted the entire flow of the river into its present course through Grand Junction. Soon thereafter, tributaries of the Colorado cut headward to divert the Gunnison into its present course and Unaweep Canyon was abandoned, probably 3 to 2 million years ago.

Originally, theorists assumed that the canyon's flat floor was underlain by a shallow layer of bedrock. But geophysical surveys indicate that the valley floor is underlain by as much as 1,300 feet of debris washed down from the canyon walls since the canyon's abandonment, and that the original cross-section of the canyon was V-shaped, like the Black Canyon of the Gunnison. However, the probable further uplift

of the Uncompahgre Plateau by 1,000 feet or so since the canyon's abandonment likely accounts for the bulk of the difference in depth.

The water in the foreground of the contemporary photo is a stock pond created by a small dam on West Creek.

<hr />

JF These photographs feature the only Jackson location that I found anywhere in the region south of Grand Junction and west of today's U.S. Highway 50. For many years, I've enjoyed the drive along State Highway 141 between the towns of Whitewater (not really a town) and Gateway. In fact, it's a popular route to Dolores River country, my favorite rafting destination on the planet. Unaweep Canyon, a geologic marvel, boasts scenery unique throughout all of Colorado.

I knew that the drive west on State Highway 141 would eventually reveal Jackson's location. I did not know that one of two new lakes in the valley would have covered up his spot. I made my photograph from the edge of the lake. Can you find the primary perspective clue that proves I stood about 50 yards back from his location?

Bibliography

and Suggested Reading

WILLIAM HENRY JACKSON

Fielder, John, et al. *Colorado 1870–2000*. Englewood, Colo.: Westcliffe Publishers, 1999.

Gundy, Lloyd W., ed. *William Henry Jackson: An Intimate Portrait, the Elwood P. Bonney Journal*. Denver: Colorado Historical Society, 2000.

Hafen, LeRoy R., and Ann Hafen, eds. *The Diaries of William Henry Jackson, Frontier Photographer*. Far West and the Rockies Historical Series, Volume X. Glendale, Calif.: Arthur H. Clark Co., 1959.

Hales, Peter Bacon. *William Henry Jackson and the Transformation of the American Landscape*. Philadelphia: Temple University Press, 1988.

Harrell, Thomas H. *William Henry Jackson: An Annotated Bibliography, 1862–1995*. Nevada City, Calif.: Carl Mautz Publishing, 1995.

Jackson, Clarence S. *Pageant of the Pioneers: The Veritable Art of William H. Jackson*. Minden, Neb.: Harold Warp Pioneer Village, 1958.

———. *Picture-Maker of the Old West, William H. Jackson*. New York: Scribners, 1947.

Jackson, Clarence S., and Lawrence W. Marshall. *Quest of the Snowy Cross*. Denver: University of Denver Press, 1952.

Jackson, William Henry. *Time Exposure: The Autobiography of William Henry Jackson*. New York: G.P. Putnam's Sons, 1940. Tucson: Patrice Press, 1994.

Jackson, William Henry, and Howard R. Driggs. *The Pioneer Photographer: Rocky Mountain Adventures with a Camera*. Yonkers-on-Hudson, N.Y.: World Book Co., 1929.

Jackson, William Henry, and Stanley Wood. *Among the Rockies: Pictures of Magnificent Scenes in the Rocky Mountains, the Master-works of the World's Greatest Photographic Artist*. Denver: Great Divide Pub. Co., 1895.

Jones, William C., and Elizabeth B. Jones. *William Henry Jackson's Colorado*. Golden, Colo.: Colorado Railroad Museum, 1992.

Mangan, Terry William. *Jackson's Colorado Negatives*. Denver: Colorado Historical Society, 1974.

Newhall, Beaumont, and Diana E. Edkins. *William H. Jackson*. Ft. Worth, Texas: Amon Carter Museum of Western Art, 1974.

Thode, Jackson C., ed. *Rocky Mountain Railroad: Steam and Steel Across the Great Divide*. Silverton, Colo.: Sundance Publications, Ltd., 1976.

GENERAL WORKS

Abbott, Carl, Stephen J. Leonard, and David McComb. *Colorado: A History of the Centennial State*. Boulder, Colo.: University Press of Colorado, 1994.

Benson, Maxine. *1001 Colorado Place Names*. Lawrence, Kan.: University Press of Kansas, 1994.

Caughey, Bruce, and Dean Winstanley. *The Colorado Guide: Landscapes, Cityscapes, Escapes*. Golden, Colo.: Fulcrum Publishing, 1989.

Colorado: A Guide to the Highest State. New York: Hastings House, 1941.

Colorado Atlas & Gazetteer, 4th ed. Yarmouth, Maine: DeLorme, Inc., 1998.

Danilov, Victor J. *Colorado Museums and Historic Sites: A Colorado Guide Book*. Boulder, Colo.: University Press of Colorado, 2000.

Fielder, John, T. A. Barron, and Enos Mills. *Rocky Mountain National Park: A 100 Year Perspective*. Englewood, Colo.: Westcliffe Publishers, 1995.

Gehres, Eleanor M., Sandra Dallas, Maxine Benson, and Stanley Cuba, eds. *The Colorado Book*. Golden, Colo.: Fulcrum Publishing, 1993.

Hafen, LeRoy R., ed. *Colorado and Its People*. New York: Lewis Historical Pub. Co., 1948.

Mangan, Terry William. *Colorado on Glass: Colorado's First Half Century as Seen by the Camera*. Denver: Sundance Publications, Ltd., 1975.

Noel, Thomas J. *Buildings of Colorado*. New York: Oxford University Press, 1997.

———. *Colorado: A Liquid History & Tavern Guide to the Highest State*. Golden, Colo.: Fulcrum Publishing, 1999.

Noel, Thomas J., Paul F. Mahoney, and Richard E. Stevens. *Historical Atlas of Colorado*. Norman, Okla.: University of Oklahoma Press, 1993.

Wolle, Muriel S. *Stampede to Timberline: The Ghost Towns and Mining Camps of Colorado*. Chicago: Sage Books, 1974.

Index